T0330022

WORK, LABOUR AND CLEANING

The Social Contexts of Outsourcing Housework

Lotika Singha

BRISTOL
UNIVERSITY
PRESS

First published in Great Britain in 2019 by

Bristol University Press
University of Bristol
1-9 Old Park Hill
Bristol
BS2 8BB
UK
t: +44 (0)117 954 5940
www.bristoluniversitypress.co.uk

North America office:
Policy Press
c/o The University of Chicago Press
1427 East 60th Street
Chicago, IL 60637, USA
t: +1 773 702 7700
f: +1 773-702-9756
sales@press.uchicago.edu
www.press.uchicago.edu

© Bristol University Press 2019

British Library Cataloguing in Publication Data
A catalogue record for this book is available from the British Library

Library of Congress Cataloging-in-Publication Data
A catalog record for this book has been requested

ISBN 978-1-5292-0146-8 hardcover
ISBN 978-1-5292-0148-2 ePub
ISBN 978-1-5292-0147-5 ePdf

Cover design by blu inc
Front cover image: mar-fre/Alamy
Printed and bound in Great Britain by CPI Group (UK) Ltd, Croydon, CR0 4YY
Bristol University Press uses environmentally responsible print partners

To all the respondents who participated
in the research informing this book.

Contents

List of Figures and Tables

Figures

Tables

About the Author

Lotika Singha completed her doctoral research in women's studies from the University of York, UK. Her main research interest is the sociology of reproduction of social injustices through mundane everyday practices that straddle both the private and public spheres across cultures, in particular the British and Indian contexts. Lotika has published in the journal *Families, Relationships and Societies* and *Discover Society*, an online magazine of social research and commentary, and policy analysis. Lotika's previous research, related to her earlier career in orthodontics, was published in the *American Journal of Orthodontics and Dentofacial Orthopedics* and the *Indian Journal of Orthodontics*.

Acknowledgements

I am grateful to Stevi Jackson and Sue Scott for believing in me and to Victoria Pittman at Bristol University Press for giving me the opportunity to publish as part of the Press's Gender and Sociology series and for guiding the book's development. I thank all the reviewers of the earlier versions of the research analysis, the book proposal and the drafts of the book for their constructive criticisms, which greatly improved the finer details of my argument.

I also thank all the people involved in taking the book from draft stage to publication, in particular, Shannon Kneis, Ruth Wallace, Vaarunika Dharmapala and the marketing team at Bristol University Press, Yvonne Percival for her meticulous copy-editing, and Marie Doherty for typesetting and the artwork.

I am grateful to the UK's Economics and Social Research Council for funding the research presented in this book [grant number ES/J500215/1].

I will remain forever indebted to all my respondents, whose willingness to participate, to give generously of their time and share their experiences, made the book happen. I am also grateful for the many, often unexpected, nuggets of information that came my way on the various occasions when I talked about my work to relatives, friends and chance acquaintances whose lives touched mine ever so briefly. And to Rajeev and Karan for participating in the changes to our domestic practices based on my learnings through this work. The journey continues.

Series Editors' Preface

This book is the first in a series that aims to bring original sociological thinking to bear on contemporary gender relations, divisions and issues of concern to feminists. We hope the series will challenge received wisdom, offer new insights and expand the scope of sociological knowledge both theoretically and substantively.

In tackling the issue of paid domestic cleaning, Lotika Singha raises questions that trouble the common feminist view that this work is particularly demeaning and degrading to those who do it and that to pay another woman to clean one's home is against feminist principles. She does not deny the material inequalities that (usually) exist between those who clean and those who use their services, nor the injustices experienced by cleaners, but instead asks why this relationship should be so abhorrent to feminist sensibilities. In investigating this issue, she takes seriously the accounts of women who do paid domestic cleaning, as well as those who use their services, in order to develop an analysis that enables us to view this work and the relationships and contexts within which it is carried out rather differently. She questions the definition of cleaning as unskilled manual labour, arguing that cleaning well involves skill, experience and organisation. She also tackles some of the double standards in play in the moral judgements made about cleaning. If it is politically unacceptable to expect others to clean up after us, why is this issue seen as far more problematic in the home than in the workplace or the street? If it is because it is our 'personal' mess, why do we not care so much when our waste leaves the house? In addressing such questions, understandings of cleanliness, dirt and dirty work are subjected to scrutiny.

Previous research emphasising the exploitative and degrading characteristics of paid cleaning has focused on those most vulnerable to exploitation and abuse: migrant women working full-time for a single employer, and often living-in; this research has attended to racialised relationships between employers and employees. In such situations, injustices abound – a result of state policies that govern such employment as well as the conduct of employers. The research underpinning this book does not involve transnational migrants but situations in which those who clean and those they clean for are of the same nationality and, in the main, the same ethnicity. The cleaners interviewed in the UK were mostly White British women who undertook work for several households. Those in India were often internal migrants, some living out and some living semi-independently in dwellings provided by a household they worked for. Based on interviews with both service-users and service-providers, Singha argues that it is not the work itself, or the fact that private domestic work is commodified, that is the problem, but the conditions and social relations within which it is undertaken. While the book draws on data from two very different contexts to elucidate this argument it is not intended as a comparative study, but rather one that raises questions about the different forms outsourced domestic cleaning can take. In particular, it shows that the much wider social gulf between Indian cleaners and their service-users, in terms of class and caste, compared to the parallel relationship in the UK, makes the work of cleaning very different.

The use of the terms 'service-users' and 'service-providers' underlines the fact that women who outsource cleaning do not, in the UK, generally employ cleaners; rather they contract service-providers for a fixed amount of time or for specific tasks. The British women who do this work do not see themselves as employees (unless they work for an agency) but as self-employed or even as running their own business. For some, it is just a job; many, however, do not see themselves as simply doing meaningless menial work but as providing a valuable service, as having considerable autonomy in organising their work and as having the ability, once they have a good range of clients, to walk out on those who do not appreciate them, make their job difficult or expect too much. The Indian women working as cleaners, on the other hand, are poor and largely uneducated. They do not enjoy the same autonomy and are reduced to the status of menial workers.

At the heart of the analysis is a distinction between cleaning as *work* and cleaning as *labour*. When cleaning is done as *labour* – as was mostly the case in India – it is drudgery; there is little autonomy for the worker, little or no respect for her time and skills and the work is largely non-negotiable. When cleaning is recognised as *work*, the worker has the right to negotiate what she will and will not do, and on what terms; she can organise the work autonomously and exercises mental skills and aesthetic judgment in doing so. For those who clean under such conditions it becomes a job that is in many respects more rewarding, as well as better paid, than others that might be available.

These conditions are more likely to be realised when the service-provider works on her own account rather than for an agency. Being a self-employed woman who cleans does have disadvantages, but these are no different from other forms of self-employment. The analysis Singha offers does not deny the injustices, both material and cultural, associated with paid cleaning work – and it is often the cultural injustices, as she points out, that are experienced as degrading, undermining and hurtful. Such injustices, however, are not exceptional; they abound in many forms of employment. Under current socio-economic conditions, the alternatives to cleaning might be considerably less attractive. If the assumption that it is morally and politically reprehensible to outsource cleaning were to prevent some women from doing so, it would deprive other women of a means of earning their living or making extra money – and sometimes achieving a degree of upward mobility through running a small business.

If we take seriously the accounts of the women who are trying to do domestic cleaning as *work* (as opposed to as *labour*) we should pause to consider whether viewing this work as necessarily demeaning displays a lack empathy or solidarity with those who clean, rather than the opposite.

Professor Stevi Jackson
Professor Sue Scott
May 2019

Introduction

Two observations spurred the research that informs this book: the invisibility of domestic workers, which in my personal experience was exemplified in India, and a feminist/class-related or moral disproval of outsourcing domestic work, in particular housecleaning, among some British people. The feminist perspective argues that outsourcing housework contributes to the stalling of the domestic gender revolution and conflicts with the notion of universal sisterhood. I have known British feminists who outsourced cleaning, as I myself have done, or who had been cleaners previously. Some academic feminists who were outsourcing cleaning felt guilty about it, while others were reticent. It was clearly a contested topic for conversation, even though I often heard harried female colleagues exclaiming 'I need a wife!' The disjuncture between theory and these real lives concerned me.

From my diasporic location, investigating the conditions of paid domestic work in two cultural contexts seemed a way to resolve some of the persisting gaps in its theorisation, guided by two research questions:

- In the UK and India, how do White British and Indian women who provide cleaning services and White British and Indian academic women who use these services (and have an interest in feminism/gender sensitisation), respectively, conceptualise cleaning work?
- How does paid-for domestic cleaning fit into current understandings of work and 'paid' work?

The experiences and meanings of work shared so generously by the domestic workers I met as part of the research process in both India and the UK, alongside service-users' experiences of outsourcing, not only changed my perceptions of the occupation, but also confirmed that the conditions of work are crucial to how it is experienced. This introductory chapter provides my interpretations of the key terms and the italicisation that I have used in the book and an overview of its structure. But first, who is 'I'?

The 'I' in this book

I was born in – and lived in – India for 28 years. For the past 25 years, I have lived in the UK. In my diasporic space I am constantly reminded that we are not born with but into a 'culture'. My diasporic identity and experiences may not mirror those of other diasporic researchers, because of differences in positionalities in diasporic and non-diasporic spaces, for example being a first- or later-generation diasporic person (Henry, 2007).

My father, a civil servant, had a working-class background and my mother was a housewife. Besides four children, my father's income also supported three siblings and his mother for several years. Thus, money was tight. Our middle-class status derived primarily from my father's occupation, as part of which we were 'entitled' to domestic help (see Chapter 3). My parents also privately employed one woman. As an adult, I have twice used live-out housecleaning services: for the first two years of my married life in India, and for eight years in the UK. In the remaining time, my husband and I have shared cleaning as part of our wider sharing/division of domestic matters.

Some other researchers in the field also provide their personal connection to their research. Romero's (2002) mother was a cleaner and Romero also did the work in her younger days, as did Meagher (1997). Anderson (2000) drew on friends and family for childcare. When Constable arrived in Hong Kong to research paid domestic work, she discovered that the apartment rent included the services of a live-out domestic worker. She wrote that 'given the topic of my research, I felt uncomfortable at the idea that I had – even indirectly – hired a domestic worker' (Constable, 2007:xiv). Lan (2006) expressed similar sentiments when living in an American colleague's apartment while writing up her research. Mattila (2011) used cleaning services in Finland and in India, where she conducted her research (also Dickey, 2000a). Mattila defended her researcher identity by mentioning working previously as an au pair and dish-washer. I have not done housework for a living. But the cultural devaluation of service work, and the living and working conditions of those who provide these services concern me, as they concerned all the researchers cited here.

Drawing on Haraway's (1988, cited in Bhavani, 1993:96–97) principles of accountability, partiality and positioning, Bhavnani (1993) stipulated that feminist objectivity hinges on avoiding 'reinscription' of common stereotypical understandings about a researched group; unpacking macro- as well as micro-level power differentials in the research process; and engaging clearly with 'difference' in the process and the product. In other words, any analysis of 'culture' and 'cultural difference' should be mindful of historical specificity to avoid 'set[ting] up sharp [false] binaries between "Western" and various "Non-western" cultures' and making 'essentialist' generalisations (Narayan, 1998:101), and should aim instead to build 'cross-cultural solidarity' (Reinharz, 1992:123). No doubt I embarked on my research with some preconceived notions. But in the field my ontological understandings were challenged by my findings and the argument I present in this book emerged from the data, as did my decisions regarding the terms used.

Terminology

In this book, I use the term 'black' specifically to refer to people of African and/or Caribbean origin. Race/ethnicity is used following the UK Office for National Statistics (ONS, 2015a) categorisation of 'ethnicity', a system that may not be followed in other countries. The ethnic category 'White British' is used in accordance with the ONS (2015a) ethnic categorisation and includes self-identification as White British/English/Welsh/Scottish/ Northern Irish. The terms 'race', 'ethnicity' and 'caste' are used bearing in mind that these are social constructions and not ahistorical social categories. Similarly, 'gender' and 'class' are not givens. The terms 'middle-class' and 'working-class' are not used as fixed social groupings but as social positions structured by 'occupation, market situation, property ownership and education' and shaped by ideas, attitudes and values (Gunn and Bell, 2002: 220). 'Caste' is used as defined by Ambedkar, that is, as an 'enclosed' form of class 'maintained through ... unnatural means' of endogamy and related practices (1916/1979/2004: 144). However, to avoid affecting readability, I have not used quote marks around every mention of all these terms.

The employment category 'self-employed' is used as defined by the ONS: 'self-employed (or "own account") workers: who neither buy labour nor sell their labour to others' (2010:10). In the context of India, the term 'informal economy' comprises 'all the activity generating work and employment that is not registered and administered by public regulation' and which includes the majority of paid work (National Commission for Enterprises in the Unorganised Sector (NCEUS), 2008:12). In the reviewed literature, I use the terms 'employer' and 'employee'/'worker' as used by the authors. In Chapter 6, however, I dispute the assumption that these terms are applicable to all employment relations in paid domestic work, and explain why I use the terms 'service-users' and 'service-providers' in my own contribution.

Housework is 'the sum of all physical, mental, emotional and spiritual tasks that are performed for one's own or someone else's household, and that maintain the daily life of those one has responsibility for' (Eichler and Albanese, 2007:248). Still, there is a hierarchy of domestic tasks, in which cleaning is at the bottom and the 'spiritual' and 'emotional' tasks or duties ensuring the moral status of the household are at the top (Gregson and Lowe, 1994a; Roberts, 1997). Paid-for housecleaning is part of paid domestic work, which is broadly defined as remunerated 'work performed in or for a household or households', in which domestic workers are 'individuals who regularly perform domestic work within an employment relationship' (International Labour Organization (ILO), 2011:2). The outsourced housework under scrutiny varies in published research, although it is implicitly understood that the work is 'women's work' (cleaning, cooking, caring), and consequently, it does not include 'male' jobs, for instance plumbing. Researchers may analyse both live-in and live-out conditions of work or one of them. In this book, I use the terms 'outsourced housecleaning' and 'paid domestic work', depending on the work being cited.

The book draws extensively on the feminist research into paid domestic work. Although the term 'feminism' essentially means a commitment to gaining equality for women in all spheres of life, it comprises a range of ideologies, and there can be differences between feminist positions on paid domestic work. To avoid erroneous generalisations, I use feminism(s) and 'some'/'many' to qualify 'feminist' instead of specific labels, except where I am referring to a particular feminist position.

I use the terms 'UK' and 'Indian' to distinguish between the two cultural contexts in this book. However, this does not mean that these social contexts are representative of the whole of the UK or India – a range of working conditions exist in both countries, as documented in other research as well as through anecdotal evidence.

Use of italics

To break the monotony of the text, I often use she/her for the employer or service-user and *she/her* for the employee or service-provider, in the context of the gendered conception of domestic work and my own female respondents. Similarly, since I use first names for all respondents, the pseudonyms used for the service-providers are in italics and those used for the service-users are in roman text. The terms *work* and *labour* are italicised when used in the context of my argument, including in the chapter titles, to avoid confusion with the broader understandings of both terms.

Finally, Hindi words are *not* italicised, but are explained at first mention, as my analysis is about integrating the findings in two cultural contexts.

Use of quotation marks

The book generally follows the Bristol University Press house style with regards to punctuation. That is: (i) run-on quotes from published sources are within single quotation marks and displayed quotes have no quote marks; and (ii) run-on quotes from oral primary data sources are within double quotation marks and displayed quotes are within single quotation marks. For the sake of convenience, the quotes from verbal and non-verbal secondary data sources (internet forums and radio or television programmes) are also treated in the same manner as the quotes from oral primary data sources.

The structure of the book

In sitting rooms, on railway platforms, in a lunch-break during a dance practice … whenever and wherever people ask me about my research, it invariably leads to a conversation about that person's experience, knowledge or ideas around housework and outsourced cleaning. At other times and in similarly unexpected places, attitudes towards cleanliness, dirt and cleaning are also manifest. Thus, all the chapters begin with a vignette that illustrates the ways in which the argument presented is grounded in everyday lived experiences, not only of the research respondents, but also of the wider social environments in which they and I live.

Chapter 1, 'Conceptualising paid domestic work', first lays the foundations of the book, by defining the work that it intends to interrogate and unpacking the angst around it in some quarters of Western society – that is, concerns about this occupation sometimes incorporate a moral dimension. The discussion here chiefly focuses on the feminist literature where such concerns are evident. The second part highlights theoretical contradictions and tensions in the literature and the assumptions underlying them, such as the work as a problem primarily between women. At the outset, however, I acknowledge the invaluable contribution of this research to our understanding of the historically and socially constructed complexities of exploitation and oppression in paid domestic work. The findings are both intellectually compelling and depressing. Still, no research can be exhaustive, and I draw attention to the gaps and silences that impede a richer understanding of paid domestic work. I conclude that prevailing theories of this work are located within a restricted 'gendered conception of the domestic realm' (Bowman and Cole, 2009:160; also Meagher, 2003) and racialised labour relations, and that a more inclusive feminist approach would have an equivalent focus on class and the historical specificities of the social understandings of outsourced domestic work.

Chapter 2, 'Behind the words: introducing the research project and respondents', first elaborates on the research project and then provides descriptive analyses, to situate my samples in the broader social worlds from which they were drawn. This chapter begins to confirm a few previous research observations: that socioeconomic class mediates the role of other axes of inequality in paid domestic work.

Chapter 3, 'Nuances in the politics of demand for outsourced housecleaning', interrogates the 'need' to outsource domestic cleaning, alongside implications for gender equality and relationship quality in the outsourcing household. It argues that 'need' is not directly related to affluence or status enhancement. The analysis of 'who does what in the house' where cleaning is outsourced shows that there is still plenty of housework for service-users to do themselves, particularly tidying up or 'picking up' after others. Sharing of this task could aid in progressing gender equality despite the outsourcing of cleaning. In this, if (middle-class) women do not see cleaning as their work, they will not expect (middle-class) men to undertake it either. The chapter concludes that claims of outsourced cleaning pitting the liberation of one class of women against that of another risk reducing women's emancipation to freedom from housework and naturalising housework as women's work.

Chapter 4, 'The imperfect contours of outsourced domestic work as dirty work', considers the construction of domestic cleaning as dirty work symbolically and the real, physical work of dealing with dirt. Through the lens of outsourced domestic cleaning – how much cleaning is necessary and what can be outsourced – I show that an 'objective' analysis of human experiences of dealing with real physical dirt is not possible without reference to dirt's moral meanings for the researched as well as the researcher. The chapter thus concludes that the dirty work approach offers an incomplete understanding of paid domestic work and that an alternative paradigm is required.

This leads on to Chapter 5, 'Domestic cleaning: *work* or *labour*', where I introduce the central argument of the book through a discussion of how my respondents conceptualised paid-for domestic cleaning in terms of the structure of cleaning work and whether anyone can do cleaning for a living. The chapter proposes that depending on the conditions of work, cleaning can be done as *work*, that is, using mental and manual skills and effort and performed under decent, democratic work conditions, or as *labour*, that is, requiring mainly manual labour, accompanied by exertion of 'natural' emotional/affective labour and performed in undemocratic conditions. Good paid-for cleaning *work* is also not simply a replacement of unpaid housework that can be done by anyone; it entails much learning and continued commitment and does not come 'naturally' to women.

Chapter 6, 'Meanings of domestic cleaning as *work* and *labour*' locates paid-for housecleaning within the wider world of paid and unpaid work. With regard to the UK, this draws on the previous work experiences of the research respondents, and their reasons for preferring self-employment or undeclared work and selectively using established good business practices. In India, there was a lack of work experience in other industries, and the accounts highlight the intersectional impacts of 'men's work', patriarchy and desire for education on the investment by the respondents in their work and its meanings for them. Together, these analyses show that domestic work is not inherently 'dead-end' – the working conditions make a significant difference to how work is perceived and experienced. In all, my respondents' classed understandings of the work in two cultures indicate that the problem with paid domestic labour is not commodification per se, but the way the work itself – and work more generally – has been commodified.

In Chapter 7, 'The occupational relations of domestic cleaning as *work* and *labour*', I show how cultural injustices obstruct service-providers' efforts to do cleaning as *work*. When the work is done as *labour*, the relationship is substantially unequal because of some combination of class, class–caste, gender and socioeconomic (and racial) disparities, and because the work done is considered low status. That is, both the work and worker are stigmatised. The worker often harbours ressentiment[1] (Rollins, 1985). When cleaning is done as *work*, there will be a friendly work relationship that can be located within wider work relationships. Still, participatory parity between the service-user and service-provider can be hampered by service-users' classed actions that inadvertently or intentionally retrench house work as low-value 'women's work', such as feeling guilty about outsourcing housecleaning or assuming that the service-provider needs help in recognising their rights as workers. Such injustices as practised in relation to commodified 'women's work' in the home are part of the wider cultural injustices that pervade paid work more generally.

Finally, in Chapter 8, 'Concluding the book, continuing the journey', I reflect on the situatedness of the knowledge presented in this book and its relevance to the existing literature and the angst around outsourced cleaning. I sum up the implications of my argument for a cross-cultural feminist theory of paid domestic work, and conclude that the unease around paid domestic work and the gaps in the research prevent recognition of the fact that the exploitation in this work is not fixed and stable, but contingent on certain societal assumptions of ourselves, others and work. The issue of concern for a scholar of gender and sociology is not just that some women are doing the demeaning work of/for other women but is also the classed and casteised evolution of the very meanings of work across cultural contexts.

Conceptualising Paid Domestic Work

....

'I find this a really stupid idea for [research].'

'I am a feminist. I employ a cleaner. He is a man. ... We also employ a man [to] cut back the ivy that covers our house. I have no idea why you have chosen this subject ..., it makes no sense to me.'

In the early days of the research that underpins this book, I posed a question on Mumsnet, a popular British online discussion forum (see Chapter 2), giving a brief explanation about my project. The question was: 'Does having a paid domestic cleaner conflict with feminism?'

Twenty-five people contributed to the discussion. Many respondents found my question "hilarious" – feminism was about "allowing women to earn money". Doing cleaning "as a business" was feminist, "doing it for free or favours" was not. They pointed out that there is no angst around men using the services of other men, car mechanics, plumbers, builders and so on. One respondent had felt guilty "because the people I've paid to do my cleaning ... have all been clever and capable women", implying that "there's something wrong with having a cleaning job". Others told me my research methodology reeked of sexism: it was I who was "making this a feminist issue by assuming that everyone on here is female, that it is their cleaning they are outsourcing, that it is a menial job [and] not one to be proud of, and that all cleaners are female". The exercise left me somewhat shaken.[1]

....

Introduction

Outsourcing of domestic work is an enduring feature of society throughout the civilising process[2]: its trajectory in Sweden (Hoerder et al, 2015; Platzer, 2006; Sarti, 2005) illustrates how this occupation persists despite political, socioeconomic and technological upheavals and advancements. The intersecting patterns of gendered, classed, racialised and socio-legal exploitation in the work are broadly similar in most cultural–geographical contexts: paid domestic work is constructed as an extension of unpaid and unskilled housework, it is accorded low status and value, and is often performed informally, and even illegally, by those with the fewest social, educational and economic resources – predominantly female migrant workers as well as citizens working underhand in the grey economy (Cox, 2006; Srinivas, 1995). Workers may live in the households they work for or live elsewhere and work for one or many employers. They are often denied labour rights at both structural and individual levels (ILO, 2016). There is wide agreement that even when only the 'menial' physical aspects of housework or care work are outsourced, the work incorporates housework's 'spiritual' aspects, aspects which become recast as (invisible) affective labour that is integral to the domestic worker's self (Anderson, 2000; Gutiérrez-Rodríguez, 2014; Roberts, 1997).

The first part of this chapter elaborates on one of my starting points for this book. The context is set with a general discussion of contemporary social meanings of work, the feminist construction of housework and historical considerations in paid domestic work, before considering the angst around outsourced housecleaning in some quarters of Western society. My other starting point, the invisibility of domestic workers worldwide, is well documented and is covered in the review of extant research in the second part of this chapter. This review focuses on existing evidence around intersections of class and race in paid domestic work, followed by the notion that paid domestic work today is often linked to contemporary middle-class women's entry into paid work.

Next, I discuss how paid domestic work is theorised as dirty work, and I look at published viewpoints on professionalisation and regulation of paid domestic work. Finally, I consider the meanings of this work for workers and the cultural injustices in paid domestic work as theorised in previous research. The conclusion summarises the overarching issues that emerged in my review and provided the baseline for my approach to researching outsourced cleaning in two cultural contexts.

Evolving contexts of work, housework and paid domestic work

Social developments in meanings of 'work'

In the West, before the concept of the moneyed wage, work included any activity 'directed at satisfying the human need for survival' or rising above it, and was primarily carried out at household level; with the Industrial Revolution, productive work moved out of the household, and 'work' became 'synonymous with [male] employment' (Edgell, 2012:1, 28; Jackson, 1992; Kaluzynska, 1980). Since then, the social and transcendent status of waged work has continued to increase, with a sense of satisfaction beyond remuneration (Edgell, 2012). Today, proper work is 'masculine' work that happens in the public space – it has a progressive career trajectory, and involves 'trading' in the marketplace (Benston, 1969/1980), motivates the worker to do it (and potential workers to acquire skills to do it), and leads to 'self-actualisation' (Oakley, 1974/1977). The 'feminine' work of social reproduction is 'non'-work, that is, work understood as requiring no or few learned skills (Hondagneu-Sotelo, 2001:xiii). In between is a range of 'uninspiring' waged service work, an 'extension' of women's reproductive work performed in the shadows by both men and women, collectively called the 'working poor'. Yet it is this grey work that keeps society's wheels well oiled and moving (Sassen, 2009; Toynbee, 2003). Some service occupations are subject to wider labour laws, but most legal frameworks exclude domestic work (ILO, 2016). At the time of writing, neither the UK nor India[3] feature among the few countries that have ratified the 2013 convention on decent work for domestic workers (ILO, n.d.).

The masculine (productive)/feminine (reproductive) dualism is just one way in which work has been dichotomised. Other binaries include unpaid/paid, high/low-value, dangerous/safe, skilled/unskilled, clean/dirty, and all these have been developed to enable some social groups to garner power through work. This deflects attention from the fact that all work has multiple dimensions, as Ehrenreich noted following her undercover experiences of three entry-level jobs: 'no job, no matter how lowly is truly "unskilled"' (2002/2010:193). The mental–manual dichotomy directs our focus on the end-value of manual work, limiting understandings of the meanings of the work. When workers articulate positive meanings in jobs generally categorised as low-value, low-skilled or dirty, they are often considered as having false-consciousness – the thought that goes into the work is overlooked, it becomes just 'cleaning' or just 'waiting on tables' or just something 'even a monkey' could do (Lucas, 2011:369; Rose, 2004/2014).

The public–private dualism overlooks the fact that reproductive work also happens outwith the home (for example in educational institutions), and the Victorian country house functioned similarly to a modern organisation. The upstairs/downstairs separation of masters and servants in these houses was part of a larger hierarchy that included secretaries, book-keepers, governesses, gardeners and stable-hands (Sambrook, 2005/2009; Sarti, 2005). Domestic staff controlled entry points to the house (Davidoff, 1995), as do security personnel, receptionists and switchboard operators today, and, as in various departments of a modern organisations, domestic service had its own sub-hierarchical structure (BBC Two, 2012; Sambrook, 2005/2009).

The skilled/unskilled dichotomy hides the gendered devaluation of some work: the same work can be classed as skilled or unskilled depending solely on the gender of the worker (Cockburn, 1991). So contemporary housework ('women's work') becomes low-skilled, even though the human 'home' is a product of people's engagement with other people, technology, processes and activities that require knowledge, hard and soft tools, materials and machines (Cockburn, 1997). Many pioneer and second-wave feminists challenged such distinctions, by politicising the personal and making housework visible as work. However, because of the concurrent belief that women's emancipation necessitates participation in 'productive' work, feminist arguments about the value of housework are often ambivalent (Schwartz, 2014, 2015).

Western feminist theorisations of housework

Early theoretical understandings of unpaid housework as part of women's subordination were primarily grounded in the negative attitudes and experiences of housekeeping among privileged white women, particularly those who were housewives in increasingly nuclear households (Delap, 2011a; Johnson and Lloyd, 2004). While seeking to destabilise the industrial capitalist notion of 'work equals employment' (Edgell, 2012:17), some researchers have argued that the ethno/class-centric feminist rejection of the housewife role entrenched the image of housewife-as-cabbage and the dualisms that devalue housework itself (Ahlander and Bahr, 1995; Johnson and Lloyd, 2004). My focus here is on this devaluation and not on housewifery's role in the structural gendered subordination of women (with due regard to race/class/caste as factors shaping different women's experiences (Glenn, 1992)).

The feminist unpacking of housework used both theoretical and empirical approaches. The Marxism-derived 'domestic labour debate', which constructed housework as proper work through an argument about its utilitarian value for capitalism eventually became passé. Its narrow economistic focus overlooked the historical specificity of the sexual division of labour and the moral homemaking dimension of housework: that is, unpaid housework is done within patriarchal relations, and in same-sex households, regardless of marketisation (Ahlander and Bahr, 1995; Curthoys, 1988; Delphy and Leonard, 1992; Jackson, 1992; Kaluzynska, 1980:45).[4]

In contrast, the empirically derived sociology of housework, spearheaded in the UK by Ann Oakley's (1974/1977, 1974/1985) analysis of the domestic practices of a sample of 20 working-class and 20 middle-class London housewives, has gone from strength to strength, documenting again and again the links between housework/housewifery and women's continued public subordination (see, for example, Lachance-Grzela and Bouchard, 2010; Treas and Drobnic, 2010). In terms of the work itself, Oakley (1974/1985) showed how housework was comparable with assembly-line factory work: it was 'inherently' mundane and alienating work, incorporating dulling routines and standards. The interview schedule, however, included leading questions, such as 'Do you find housework monotonous on the whole?' (Oakley, 1974/1985:210), which might have skewed the findings. Oakley's (1974/1977) participants also commented that liking or disliking housework depended on one's mood. The working-class wives were more invested in domesticity and more likely to like housework. Oakley suggested that these women's lower education status and linguistic proficiency limited their justifications to 'common-sense' reasoning and normative gendered discourses. Their 'satisfaction' probably reflected a resigned acceptance of things beyond their control. In the 1980s, in an English market town, however, 15 white 'wife-mothers', of whom just over half were middle-class, did not approach housework as a mindless activity. Instead:

> their choice was not to adopt the modern methods that would lead to … mindlessness. … [They] were aware of the problems of allowing the machine to take over. Having escaped the tyranny of the factory, the women are not going to fall into the trap in the home which their husbands may endure at work … Through beautifying their homes as well as in cooking, the women realise their creativity. (Hand, 1992:149)

Metcalfe's (2013) sample of northern English working-class women ably expressed views on housework. It is plausible that experiences and meanings of housework vary, depending on life-stage and other aspects of social life.

Johnson and Lloyd further argued that feminists needed to deploy the housewife subject position as the Other in the struggle 'to elaborate a speaking position' for 'the feminist intellectual' (2004:2; also Schwartz, 2015), such that today, liking housework seems socially undesirable. When the *Woman's Hour*[5] presenter Jane Garvey said she enjoyed ironing, her tone was apologetic:

> 'I hate to mention this in a way because I know people will squeal with indignation but maybe ... some women like housework ... I'm one of them actually, sometimes I like a bit of ironing ... it's about bringing order to disorder isn't it? You know there's pleasure to be gained ... It's honest graft isn't it?' (BBC Radio 4, 2012)

It is against such problematisation of housework and contemporary understandings about 'work' more generally that paid domestic work has been theorised. Before coming to that, I review recent historical scholarship that disrupts some popular understandings of contemporary developments in paid domestic work.

Historical considerations in paid domestic work

Manual domestic work has historically been – and continues to be – a site of power and status worldwide (Chin, 1998; Delap, 2007, 2011a,b; Ray and Qayum, 2009/2010; Rollins, 1985; Romero, 2002). At the heart of the well-described domestic master–slave or mistress–maid/servant relationship lies the notion of 'difference', in which the slave/maid/servant and their progeny are constructed as culturally and even biologically inferior, based on class/caste and/or race, fit only for lifetime servitude (Ambedkar, 1916/1979/2004; Davidoff, 1995; Ilaiah, 2005/2017; King, 2007; Moosvi, 2004; Rollins, 1985; Srinivas, 1995). However, as part of the social changes following the World Wars (for example establishment of welfare states and a rise in working-class living standards in the West), paid domestic work almost 'disappeared' for a brief period in some Western countries (Gregson and Lowe, 1994a; Lutz, 2011). These broad notions lend themselves to several widely accepted understandings of Western historical trends in paid domestic work:

- in the late 19th/early 20th centuries, there was a sharp drop in supply ('the servant problem') because of the expansion of work opportunities for working-class women (BBC Two, 2012; Cox, 2006);
- after the Second World War, demand also reduced, because women across classes were exhorted to be housewives (van Walsum, 2011);
- from the 1970s onwards, as middle-class women increasingly entered the paid workforce, paid domestic work resurfaced in the West (Ehrenreich and Hochschild, 2003; Gregson and Lowe, 1994a);
- in all this time, (live-in) feudalistic domestic servitude was transforming into (live-out) capitalist-style exploitative domestic services (Glenn, 1992; Romero, 2002);
- employers and employees are two separate categories: employers are (often white) women, well-endowed with social, racial and economic capital, while employees are women from disadvantaged class/racial backgrounds (Anderson, 2000; Cox, 2006; Ehrenreich and Hochschild, 2003; Romero, 2002).

More recent historical analyses of domestic service in the UK and India, however, destabilise the linear 'servitude → service' and 'disappearance → resurgence' trajectories, and the dichotomisation between *her* and her as belonging to two different social worlds.

In the UK, contemporary popular perceptions of domestic service hark back to a sanitised version of the Victorian/Edwardian master–servant relationship dramatised in television series such as *Upstairs, Downstairs* and *Downton Abbey* (see Hinsliff, 2014; Toynbee, 2014). Servanthood existed before this period, but rather than lifetime servitude, servants formed part of 'a socially pervasive and culturally broad movement of young people from their parental homes to live and serve in the homes of others', termed 'lifecycle service'[6] (Cooper, 2005:367). In times of late marriages and high mortality, this arrangement ensured that orphaned youngsters had a home at all times. Households supplied and used domestic labour regardless of differences in material resources (Laslett, 1988, cited in Cooper, 2005:371), and besides wages, servants received education and training. The arrangement was vulnerable to abuse and exploitation, and thus, individual experiences would have varied (Cooper, 2005).

Lifecycle service transformed into lifetime servitude for working-class people around the late 18th century, when class identities and boundaries became more rigid. Display of status, including having domestic servant(s), was crucial to the emerging middle-class identity (BBC Two, 2012; Davidoff, 1995; Hill, 1996). This metamorphosis of class structure occurred alongside increased longevity and wages, industrialisation, financialisation of markets, Britain's expanding trade and colonial status, evangelical influences on ideas of 'right' conduct of family life among the bourgeoisie and political reforms such as selective extension of voting rights (Cooper, 2005; Delap, 2011a; Gunn and Bell, 2002). Many of these middle-class households would have employed a 'maid-of-all-work', one of the most exploited servant positions of that period (Cox, 2006; Delap, 2011a). Hence, 'service → servitude → service' appears a more appropriate representation of the trajectory of domestic service in the UK, where the configuration of 'service' is a product of its times.

The stringent Victorian class boundaries did not reduce servants and employers to monolithic categories. Not all servants lived with their employers or were lifetime servants. Employers included a range of households from small to large, and a servant could also do farm work (Branca, 1975; Hill, 1996:251; also Delap, 2011a; Todd, 2009). In 18th-century London, bricklayers, milliners and plasterers featured among households in the parish of St Martin-in-the-Fields that employed a single servant (Kent, 1989), while domestic service in late 19th-century Lancaster showed 'subtle gradations within a spectrum of shared social, economic, geographical, and educational backgrounds, rather than unbridgeable divides', with the number of servants varying over the life-course (Pooley, 2009:419). In early 20th-century London, alongside printers and gas workers, 29% of households of clerks and commercial travellers employed domestic help (Booth, 1902, cited in Delap, 2011a:80). Status/religious norms created 'need' even in penurious conditions. East London's immigrant Jewish families regularly employed local Gentile char and washerwomen (White, 1980/2003). A comparison of historical Lancastrian and contemporary UK-wide data reveals similarities in the patterns of outsourcing in relation to class (Table 1.1). Furthermore, female mill and factory workers in the 19th century 'created opportunities for others [in their class] to gain an income from home-based activities' (Jackson, 1992:158). During the World Wars, organised crèches and canteens supported working-class mothers doing other work (Hall, 1973/1980); these likely employed other working-class women. I consider the history of gendering of domestic work in more detail in Chapter 5.

The defining factor of domestic service was not the work, but 'the duty of complete and unquestioning obedience to their masters and mistresses, the subsuming of their own background, social identity and personality in that of their employers' (Hill, 1996:252). This 'duty' extended to governesses, apprentices, servants working in husbandry, daily labourers, and so on.

The literature is conflicting as to whether domestic work was the worst possible job. Some reports state that British women left it in droves as

Table 1.1: Historical and contemporary UK data★ on outsourcing of domestic work

	Historical Lancaster census data (Pooley, 2009)		Contemporary UK-wide survey (Jones, 2004)	
	Servant-sending households (1881 data) (%)	Servant-employing households (1891 data) (%)	Income (£)	Working households employing paid help (%)
Professional	<1	31	<70,000	38
Intermediate	13	34	60,000–70,000	28
Skilled white collar	11	22	42,500–60,000	17
Skilled manual	38	7	25,000–42,500	10.5
Semi-skilled	20	2	<25,000	2.5
Unskilled	17	2		
Class not known	<1	3		

★Data are rounded percentages.

Sources: Table 4, Pooley (2009); Table A, Jones (2004).

factory jobs and shopwork became available (BBC Two, 2012; Horn, 2012), leading to 'the servant problem'. Other research shows that shopwork was similarly harsh (Cox and Hobley, 2014) and factory work similarly stigmatised, with some women preferring domestic service (Branca, 1975; Delap, 2011a) or choosing it as the 'lesser of two evils' (Todd, 2009:187). Indeed, unionising British domestic workers at the turn of the 20th century 'saw their grievances as extending beyond the individual mistress–maid relationship to connect with wider experiences of workplace exploitation' (Schwartz, 2014:175). In the US, Magnus (1934a) argued that it was not the work itself that was at the root of the servant problem, since domestic service training courses that were not tied to employment continued to attract applicants.

A common understanding in 20th-century American research is that live-out work was at the helm of the 'servitude → service' transformation of domestic work, partly triggered by modern housing designed for nuclear-type families and better local transport facilities (Dill, 1994; Hondagneu-Sotelo, 2001). It might have been more liberating for women than home-based or family-business work, because it was 'employment outside the family' (Glenn, 1981:362). In the UK, census records list the 'daily' (or the charwoman, the charlady, the char) since the Victorian era (Delap, 2011a). Although live-in domestic service noticeably declined after the Second World War, the 'daily' was present through most of the 20th century, including the angel-housewife years (Delap, 2011a; Gittins, 1993; UK census 1951, 1961, 1971, Census Customer Services,

2014[7]). Mid-20th-century middle-class European women did not always appreciate being 'servant-less':

> The housewife did not appear as a settled identity willingly embraced by women in the 1950s and 1960s, but rather as a problematic subject position into which women from formerly servant-keeping families had been forced ... it was far from being internalized in the subjectivities of privileged and educated women, and was always bolstered in practice by the [unobtrusive] extensive employment of daily domestic workers ... often of migrant status. (Delap, 2011b:202–204)

Elite Western feminists of this time, such as the American Betty Friedan (1963/1983), the Swedish Alva Myrdal (Myrdal and Klein, 1957, cited in Platzer, 2006:212) and Virginia Woolf, Vera Brittain and Katharine Whitehorn in the UK, like many earlier feminists (Delap, 2011a; Todd, 2009), might not have imagined liberated life as one devoid of domestic help.[8] Popular media representations of middle-class households included chars and cooks (see Delap, 2011a:131 for details), for despite post-war improvements in Western working-class living standards, many working-class women continued working in a range of low-wage jobs – including live-out charring and childcare (Delap, 2011a; UK census 1951, 1961, 1971, Census Customer Services, 2014, see endnote 7) – to make ends meet or for a 'bit on the side'.

What was live-out work like then? Charring was mostly poorly paid, casual work. It was physically more demanding than domestic work today, even when using appliances, as early incarnations of vacuum cleaners and washing machines were heavy or cumbersome to use. Many women worked long hours to earn a living wage (Delap, 2011a).

In India, and several other regions, a much longer trajectory of live-in 'servitude' has been transforming to varying degrees of live-out 'service'.[9] The purity–pollution ideology and the associated caste system, slavery as a consequence of war, and market forces intersected to construct servanthood throughout proto-historical and pre-colonial India; socioeconomic class also mattered, as higher-caste servants were known (Moosvi, 2004). Symbolic concerns – as in the UK (Davidoff, 1995) – meant that even low-income households employed servants for 'polluting' tasks (Frøystad, 2003; Moosvi, 2004; Ray and Qayum, 2009/2010). This longstanding condition of servitude, however, was located, as in the UK, within wider social hierarchical relationships. For instance, in gurukuls students lived with their teachers and performed personal 'lifecycle service' for them as part of their education (Bose, 1998).

The colonial period introduced another layer of complexity in the master–servant relationship: that is, Victorian class norms and morals further tightened caste-based occupational segregation (Srinivas, 1995). Consequently, independence from Britain did not transform servitude to service. Instead, lifetime servitude exists alongside lifecycle servitude and lifecycle service, because modern cultural understandings of work continue to be shaped by feudal and ideological imaginaries. In other words, contemporary demand for servants in India is not linked to women's work status (Raghuram, 1999; Ray and Qayum, 2009/2010). While only one fifth of urban women do waged work (Desai et al, 2010), servants are everywhere.[10]

These historical trajectories of paid domestic work in the UK and India show little evidence of a distinct pattern or relation to public–private and racialised ideologies. In pre-Victorian UK, lifecycle service developed in an essentially white society with rural–urban migration and little public–private distinction. It morphed into lifetime servitude in the same population when the public–private divide became established. When live-in servanthood declined, it transitioned to lifecycle service again, delivered largely by white migrants (for example Irish, Austrian), but this time with the public–private division in place. In India, lifetime servitude existed in a hierarchical casteised society prior to the introduction of colonial ideologies of private–public division. Lifetime servitude was also present in slave societies such as the US, but these have transitioned to lifecycle service despite continued racialised discrimination and public–private division (Dill, 1994; Hondagneu-Sotelo, 2001; Rollins, 1985; Romero, 2002). At this point, it is important to reiterate that employers' and intellectual notions of 'servitude' were not always shared by those doing the work. For instance, the first union of 'servants' formed in Britain in the early 1900s was called 'Domestic Workers' Union', because the women did not perceive themselves as servants but as 'workers' (Schwartz, 2014).

More recently, feminist researchers have highlighted the yet again increasing 'proletarisation of paid domestic work' – from symbolic of 'high' status to a 'necessity' across classes – due to outsourcing of domestic labour by an ageing population across classes in a diminishing welfare state (Triandafyllidou and Marchetti, 2015), as well as outsourcing by women working part-time (de Ruijter and van der Lippe, 2007; Tijdens et al, 2003). These latter works draw attention to the ways in which the demand for paid domestic labour, while still significantly linked to middle-class women's participation in the modern capitalist workplace and to status enhancement, also goes beyond these two oft-cited factors.

Another point of importance here is migrant domestic work, which has been exhaustively researched.[11] Both in- and out-country migration from poorer (rural) to prosperous (urban) areas for any/better work or wages, including domestic service, is a remarkably constant feature of history (Fauve-Chamoux, 2004; Hoerder et al, 2015; Sarti, 2005). In 18th- and 19th-century England, women increasingly dominated in-country rural–urban migration (Branca, 1975; Hill, 1996). Many Indian ayahs also came to Britain with returning colonial mistresses (Visram, 1986/2015), and domestic service also pulled northern European women to the US, Canada and Australia (Momsen, 1999). Indeed, in the 19th century, 'aliens', which included white women, were 'over-represented in the domestic service' in some Western countries (Magnus, 1934a; Moya, 2007). Although absolute numbers of migrant domestic workers are greater today and migratory flows have a greater 'geographical spread', Moya argues the 'new immigration wave has not yet surpassed the old in relation to the world's population' (2007:569–570). The particular problems of contemporary migration-related domestic work include:

- its transformation into a 'transnational activity' (Momsen, 1999:14), in which educated, skilled mothers migrate to look after other people's children with the aim of ensuring a better life for their own children left behind, often in the care of other women (the global care chain (Ehrenreich and Hochschild, 2003) or new world domestic order (Hondagneu-Sotelo, 2007));
- undocumented immigration status, which makes the worker more vulnerable to abuse and exploitation (Anderson, 1999; Momsen, 1999).

Other research shows that these concerns are also pertinent to migrants working in other industries such as food processing and construction (Anderson, 2007; Lalani and Metcalf, 2012; Potter and Hamilton, 2014). However, the research on contemporary paid domestic work reveals a moral concern that is particularly directed towards it.

The angst around outsourced housecleaning

> Something strange is taking place in my world. My friends are employing servants ... lower-middle class teachers, NGO types, trade union organisers ... I have to admit that I have a strong reaction to this – a mixture of self-righteous moralism and class rage .... (Foreman, 2014)

Today, paid domestic work is often considered a 'crisis of care' (Glenn, 2000), in which middle-class women's entry into paid labour and failure of middle-class men to share domestic work play a significant role.[12] Thus, many feminists, including academics, outsource housework,[13] and some researchers such as Meagher (1997) and Romero (2002) had previously worked as domestics. A few argue that commodification of domestic work will eventually encourage gender equality (Bergmann, 1998; Hom, 2008/2010). Many others, however, denounce it, because it continues to be shaped by its historical associations with (female) slavery and servitude, the undervalued work of (oppressed) housewives, religious/secular fetishes around dirt and cleanliness, structural exploitation of workers, and the controversial global care chain (Calleman, 2011; Cox, 2006; de Santana Pinho and Silva, 2010; Ehrenreich and Hochschild, 2003; Foreman, 2014; Gregson and Lowe, 1994a). Many other Westerners (and post-communist era Eastern Europeans) today also express discomfort around outsourcing domestic work, particularly cleaning, because it is seen as a 'return' to a classed society (Cox, 2006; *Daily Mail*, 2015; Kordasiewicz, 2015; Mumsnet, 2013a; Williams, 2012). A few researchers have proposed phasing it out (Cox, 2006; Gregson and Lowe, 1994a), and others – some resignedly – suggest regularising it as 'just another job' (Anderson, 2001:25; Hondagneu-Sotelo, 2001; Romero, 2002) or outsourcing it as a social but not as a consumer service (Devetter, 2016).

For some second-wave liberal feminists such as Friedan (1963), outsourcing of housework formed part of the solution to the white middle-class woman's 'problem with no name'. Radical feminists such as Davis (1981/1983) argued that housework itself was oppressive, because it lacked a concrete end product and recommended industrialising it; but others such as Delphy and Leonard (1992) asserted that the oppression was rooted in the patriarchal conditions under which housework was done. Marxist and socialist feminists are more likely to see paid domestic work as appropriation of one woman's labour by another in terms of classed (or racialised) exploitation that ruptures the ideology of sisterhood (Ehrenreich, 2000; Romero, 2002). That is, while 'both women are subject to the imperatives of the market and to sexual domination, their actual experiences reflect their class positions' (Romero, 2002:59; see also Ehrenreich's (1976) exposition of socialist feminism). As part of this exploitation, domestic workers are denied labour rights on the basis that the workplace is the employer's home (Albin, 2012; International Domestic Workers' Network (IDWN), 2011). Contemporary Marxist feminists also argue that the woman-to-woman transfer of work benefits men, because they can continue to conveniently avoid it (Anderson, 2000; Cox, 2006; Ehrenreich and Hochschild, 2003; Romero, 2002). That is, capitalist exploitation in paid domestic work reproduces the dominant patriarchal structural ideologies of gender, class, race (and caste – see Ray and Qayum, 2009/2010).

Cox points out the role of the ideologies of pollution, the 'relationship between dirt, cleaning and status' (2006:6). Removal of dirt is considered low-status work and most societies assign it to particular groups of people, whose status then is further lowered because of the work they do. Anderson (2000, 2001, 2003) argues that what is being bought in domestic work is not 'labour power' but *her* personhood, because caregiving involves the whole person. The worker's self cannot be divorced from *her* work (also Lutz, 2011): the means of *reproduction* (of gender/class/caste/race) become embodied in *her* as she buys the ability to command *her* whole person.

All of these lenses persuasively show that householders across societies consistently refuse to see themselves as employers, conveniently constructing the worker as simply 'help' around the house or as 'part of the family' (Anderson, 2000; Cox, 2006). These tropes render invisible the class/caste and racialised exploitation, the power imbalance in the economic, social, legal, psychological and physical aspects of the worker–employer relationship. Between the lines of thorough objective analyses, however, sometimes there is a subjective disproval of paid domestic work that goes beyond *her* exploitation in Marxist terms and the cultural oppression of women as a whole and as classed/raced beings (Bowman and Cole, 2009; Meagher, 2002, 2003). This censure sits between the notion of housework as real work (as theorised by Marxist and socialist/materialist feminists) and as oppressive 'women's work', and is largely directed towards cleaning, the domestic task of lowest social value (Gregson and Lowe, 1994a). 'The cleaner comes and applies pressure right where it hurts [the feminist employer]: in the contradiction between theory and practice, between ideals and compromises' (Molinier, 2009/2012:289).

Cox (2006) proposes that the only way to establish a fair society is for everyone to clean up after themselves. Persisting ideologies of pollution and work–life imbalance among the richer sections of society and the lack of state provision of affordable high-quality childcare are barriers to creating this post-outsourcing world. Cox rightly observes that we should challenge social attitudes towards dirt. However, the first step to her solution is not convincing. She suggests establishing state-funded affordable high-quality childcare, in which carers are 'fairly rewarded', which would ensure work–life balance for everyone, with enough time for housework. Anderson concurs with this: 'While a couple might have to employ a carer to enable them both to go to work in the productive economy, they do not *have* to employ a cleaner' (Anderson, 2001:27, original emphasis).

The distinction between childcare and cleaning (both aspects of domestic work) is perhaps made by Cox and Anderson because, in theory, publicly delivered childcare removes the problems that beset paid domestic work: nursery nurses are recognised as workers, while nannies might be considered 'helpers'. The crèche at the first women's liberation movement (WLM) conference in the UK in 1970 was run by men (BBC Radio 4, 2010; Kennedy, 2001). But this practice gained little purchase, and today, professional childcaring remains a low-paid, exploitative transfer of care between women (Department for Education, 2011, 2012, 2014; Eurofound, 2006; Rolfe, 2006), with prescriptive duties and responsibilities, and cleaning up after other (often wealthier) people's children (sometimes at an hourly rate lower than that of a live-out cleaner – see Toynbee, 2003).

What, then, could be the starting point for 'ungendering' of domestic and care work? This question informed my approach to understanding the social construction of the relationship between the structure of housecleaning and women's 'innate' caring abilities in the first stages of developing my argument (see Chapter 5).

Anderson (2000:142–143, 2001) correctly points out that some people might outsource domestic work for status enhancement, because a certain ideal of cleanliness is part of status construction (see also Cox, 2006). She further argues that something peculiar happens when domestic work is outsourced: the 'very act of employing a domestic worker weaves [the two women] … into a status relationship' and 'lowers the status of' the housework done by *her* as she fills her time with something better (Anderson, 2003:105–106, 113–114). Anderson's observation is a defining principle of paid work (Weeks, 2011), and outsourcing cooking, gardening and household maintenance can also be about status enhancement of the middle-class man. Another contention is that much outsourced housework, such as dusting of artefacts, is only about maintaining status, as these artefacts are not 'necessary'. Are mobile phones and bank accounts necessary, except in terms of the times we live in? Even if people give up 'unnecessary' artefacts, they can assert status through participation in, for example, 'high' culture. So while Anderson rightly states that employers should be invested in improving the conditions of domestic work to make it just another job, the subjective elaborations preceding her conclusion muddy her argument. The argument presented in this book thus attempts to be mindful that people reproduce class in multiple ways, and in multiple spaces, in the same timeframe (Lawler, 2005) and its implications for domestic work.

Ehrenreich notes that 'liberal-minded employers of maids … all sense that there are ways in which housework is different from other products and services ...' (2003:101), but that 'sense' veers on hypocrisy: 'someone who has no qualms about purchasing rugs woven by child slaves in India or coffee picked by impoverished peasants in Guatemala might still hesitate to tell dinner guests that, surprisingly enough, his or her lovely home doubles as a sweatshop during the day'. Here Ehrenreich also confesses that she had outsourced cleaning once, to get her house ready for a 'short-term tenant'. She might have used an agency that gave its employees full employment rights, but such guarantees do not take away the cultural and monetary exploitation (Foreman, 2014). Ehrenreich does not dwell on these implications of her action for her theoretical position. Rather she moves on to note how several of her colleagues, 'including some who made important contributions to the early feminist analysis of housework' were employing maids (2003:90). So should one-off cleans by an agency and on-and-off outsourcing be theorised differently from having maids and servants all the time? This conundrum informs the analysis of demand in Chapter 3, which forms part of the foundation for my argument presented later in Chapters 5–7 (see also Meagher, 1997).

Ehrenreich also suggests that employers are reluctant to confess, because the work they have outsourced is the work that their employees 'almost certainly never [would] have chosen' for themselves, had the latter been in the position to make a choice. Ehrenreich's articulate descriptions of dirt found on floors are intended to make readers conclude 'this is not the kind of relationship that I want to have with another human being' (2003:91); finally, she notes that outsourcing housecleaning smacks of 'callousness and solipsism', and children learn to see the cleaner as a lesser being and carry that feeling into adulthood (2003:103). When Lutz (2011) engaged in participant observation, she noted in her journal: 'I wonder whether a home help can find it humiliating, having to pick up and fold a little upstart's clothes'. Her findings did not appear to support her musings:

> None of our interviewees described such activity as 'humiliating'. However, there is a widespread view that a child who is not taught to clear things up after himself will never learn to do so later in life and will end up living in ... [a] kind of 'de-ranged' home ... as an adult. (Lutz, 2011:59)

While I concur with Lutz that people should pick up after themselves, no references were provided by both researchers to support the 'widespread' view that if children are not socialised to do certain things in life, they never learn to do them. Research into the domestic practices of middle-class Indian migrants in the UK revealed that most respondents had done little housework as children in India, but they were doing it as adults in the UK (Singha, 2015; also Westwood's (1984) Asian participants). Feminists against outsourcing can also leave mugs unwashed in the university common room or the parish hall kitchen. While I am not denying children's internalisation of discriminatory (domestic) practices, they are not forever bound by them.

The sociological gaze more generally focuses on adverse aspects of manual work, and Meagher has argued that the analytical emphasis on 'negative experiences … as definitive' has heightened unease surrounding paid domestic work (1997:188). While there is no doubt that there are many real concerns in paid domestic work, domestic workers are neither always unreflexive victims nor always vociferous protestors – subjectivities are fashioned and refashioned both in different situations and over the lifecycle (Bujra, 2000; Constable, 2007; Lan, 2006; Lutz, 2011; Saldaña-Tejeda, 2015). The feminist approach developed in Chapters 2–7 is grounded in, and builds on, these and other previous theories reviewed in the next section – theories that have made visible the work that so many take for granted.

Theorising paid domestic work

Both qualitative and quantitative methodologies have been used to study contemporary domestic outsourcing. This section mainly reviews the qualitative research that largely focuses on the micro-politics of paid domestic work and issues regarding migration and migrant workers. Although this book focuses on local and in-country migrant labour markets, several of the concerns around domestic work as performed by an out-country migrant domestic worker are universal concerns. I also consider the related literature that interrogates attempts to professionalise domestic work, the organising and unionising efforts of workers, and its regulation by states and the ILO. The primarily Western quantitative literature focuses on the demand side – the associations between the present-day propensity to outsource work and utilitarian variables such as economic resources and time availability – and is referred to in Chapters 2 and 3.

Domestic work, class and race/ethnicity

The race/gender axis in paid domestic work, rooted in the ideologies and practices of slavery and colonialism, is clearly an issue.[14] Today in the West, how does class impact on this axis? Milkman et al (1998; also Dill, 1994) showed that the common denominator for the likelihood of outsourcing housework in various American regions was the level of socioeconomic disparity. Other, more recent, Western survey-based research, however, shows people are more likely to outsource in those countries that have greater numbers of low-skilled immigrants (Estévez-Abe, 2015).

Accordingly in the UK, a 2015 documentary claimed that the job is "primarily done by the scores of immigrants arriving in the UK", while white (women) cleaners are "rare" (BBC Two, 2015b). The focus of the programme was, however, only London. Anderson's (1993, 2000,[15] 2007) research on macro- and micro-level abuse and exploitation among migrant/undocumented workers, was also based in London. Cox extrapolated from research mainly conducted in the affluent London borough of Hampstead (where a range of ethnicities were represented among cleaners) and adverts in *The Lady*[16] to describe a picture of 'domestic workers living and working in Britain' (2006:9). Several other studies draw on London-based migrant domestic workers/commercial cleaners (for example Cox and Watt, 2002; Wills et al, 2009; Yilmaz and Ledwith, 2017). Focusing on male domestic work, Kilkey et al (2013), despite noting that migrant populations in the UK are concentrated in London and the South-East, make reference to their research in terms of 'the UK'. In Sykes et al's (2014:4) study of commercial cleaning in various UK cities, 63 out of 93 participants were migrants; the authors noted that their sample was representative of the UK, but the supporting statistics cited indicated that migrants made up around 30% of the non-domestic cleaning workforce.

In contrast, Gregson and Lowe's (1994a,b) research – albeit older – in south-west and north-east England (Reading and Newcastle-upon-Tyne, respectively), had identified two domestic labour markets:

- a high-end national-level market, with placements chiefly advertised in *The Lady*; employees moved from the regions to work primarily in London;
- local markets, in which local people worked for local employers.

Their sample, which included both nannies and cleaners, was remarkably homogeneous: the 20 cleaners were White British working-class women with no qualifications and limited work opportunities, and familial caring responsibilities, living in households dependent on benefits, doing cash-in-hand work; the 50 nannies comprised younger white women from lower-middle-class backgrounds with childcare qualifications. The authors stated that migrant domestic workers were evident in London in the 1980s, but in their research sites domestic work showed little association with racialised migration; they concluded that outsourcing of different forms of domestic work was grounded in a 'class-mediated hierarchy in domestic tasks', in which the lowliest work was outsourced to the older working-class woman and childcare to a woman who was closer in status to the middle-class employer (Gregson and Lowe, 1995:155–159).

Also, Cox, in findings presented at a 1997 conference, indicated that 'while migrant labour is readily available to do such work in London, outside of the capital domestic workers are more likely to be "poor English"' (quoted in Anderson, 2000:87). Samples in more recent studies of low-wage/low-skilled work (Hebson et al, 2015; Rubery et al, 2011; Shildrick et al, 2012) and 2011 UK and European-level census data (Figure 1.1) support these older observations. It is possible that snowball sampling and strong group identities among workers could have affected the ratio in the Sykes et al (2014) study. I elaborate further on sampling issues in Chapter 2, where I show that although my own samples clearly are representative of particular social contexts, they are not representative of entire countries.

On the basis of Gregson and Lowe's findings and Cox's paper, Anderson (2000) argued that the UK was probably unusual among the developed countries. However, post-2000 research evidence indicates that the picture is complex elsewhere too. In Sweden, cleaners include retired Swedish women (Rappe and Strannegård, 2004, cited in Bowman and Cole, 2009:176). Morel (2015) notes that in the largest Swedish commercial cleaning agency, 57% of cleaners were Swedish. In the Netherlands, although domestic work has become racialised in the past two decades, away from urban metropoles, indigenous Dutch students, single mothers on welfare and rural housewives might be the main domestic workers (van Walsum, 2011). Some Portuguese commercial agencies reject foreign applicants (Abrantes, 2014a). In Belgium, just under three-quarters of workers are citizens (Morel, 2015). Most domestic workers in Italy are also Italian, live-in workers are more likely to be foreign (Colombo, 2007). In Germany, Lutz's team focused on migrant workers, because 'we have the impression that the numbers of migrants have been growing' (2011:34), but Shire (2015) draws on official statistics to show that 10% of part-time domestic workers in Germany are migrants. Some parts of the US are still 'very' white (Ehrenreich, 2002/2010). In 2007, 39% of recorded Brazilian domestic workers were white (Tomei, 2011). Elite households in Europe and North America seek 'English' butlers and nannies (sometimes from elite backgrounds; Cox, 1999; Hondagneu-Sotelo, 2001). In the 1950s, on arriving in the 'mother' country, Britain's African Caribbean citizens discovered they were not welcome. Alongside other discriminatory practices, people preferred local charwomen for 'fear' of having a

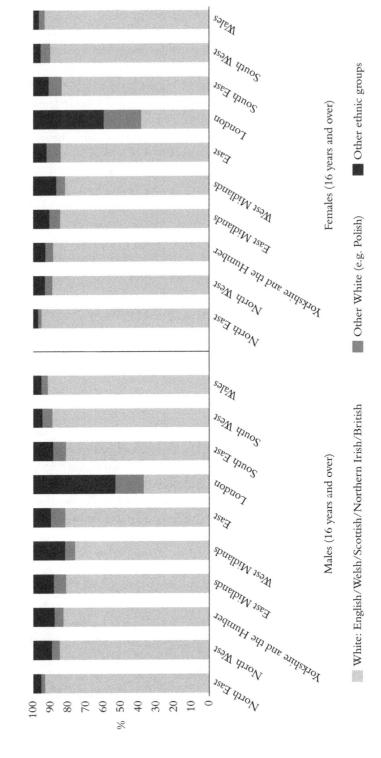

Figure 1.1: (a) People working in low-skilled occupations in England and Wales disaggregated by sex and ethnic group

Males (16 years and over)

Females (16 years and over)

■ White: English/Welsh/Scottish/Northern Irish/British

■ Other White (e.g. Polish)   ■ Other ethnic groups

(b) People working in elementary occupations in several advanced European economies, disaggregated by place of birth and citizenship

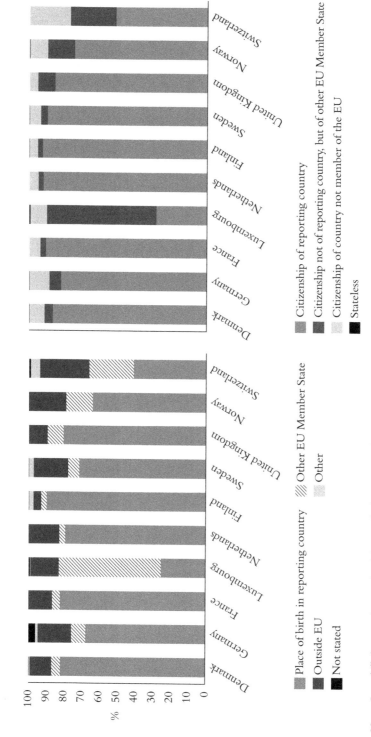

Notes: Low-skilled occupations: caring, leisure and other service, sales and customer service, process, plant and machine operatives, and elementary occupations.

Data sources: (a) ONS, Census 2011, Table DC6213EW – Occupation by ethnic group by sex by age, ONS Crown Copyright Reserved [downloaded from Nomis on 14 June 2016]; (b) Eurostat, Census 2011 Hub (Tables HC29 and HC13) (http://ec.europa.eu/eurostat/web/population-and-housing-census/census-data/2011-census).

non-white person in the house (Delap, 2011b). Similarly today, many contemporary Westerners are reluctant to host au pairs, who in reality are glorified domestic workers, from another culture (Anderson, 2007; Cox, 2015a). At the same time, middle/upper-class migrant households in the West also outsource housework to either local or migrant workers (Hondagneu-Sotelo, 2007; Singha, 2015).

Alongside this research, I looked at the first seven rounds of the academically driven European Social Survey (2002–2014), as this source appears to have been untapped. The majority of domestic cleaners and helpers sampled in Germany and other European countries where research reports an increase in outsourced domestic work (Abrantes, 2014b) stated they did not belong to an ethnic minority group (Table 1.2).

In other world regions, many domestic workers are in-country migrants or migrants from even poorer countries.[17] In Latin America, while more Brazilian domestic workers are black (de Santana Pinho and Silva, 2010; Tomei, 2011), in Ecuador, lighter-skinned employers prefer someone 'like' themselves (De Casanova, 2013). In India, Dickey (2000b:481) argued that while caste played a majority role in determining who did domestic work in India, class reproduction through the occupation was significant in its own right. In all, a greater proportion of ethnic minority women in particular Western countries might do domestic work, but this does not seem to mean that they represent the majority of domestic workers in those countries. The people doing paid domestic work in a particular geographical region in every historical epoch largely appear to belong to the group(s) relegated to the bottom of the social hierarchy in that region and time period.

Regarding the demand side, the statement 'all the employers were German' (Lutz, 2008:44) does not obviously indicate that they were all also white, unless an assumption is made that other citizens could never be service-users. In my home town in the Midlands region of the UK, several middle-class Indians use the services of local service-providers (cleaners, gardeners, handymen, and so on). Upwardly mobile African-Americans and Mexican-Americans, and blue-collar white families in the American south, where domestic labour is 'cheap', also outsource housework (Milkman et al, 1998; Rollins, 1985). Middle-class black Americans may look for service-providers outwith the black community, because of the unfortunate history of domestic servitude in the US (Bates, 2013). While Polish migrants work as cleaning service-providers in the UK, Ukrainian women migrate to Poland for the same purpose (Kindler, 2008). Domestic workers may also employ others to do their housework at various lifestages (Bujra, 2000; Constable, 2007; Hondagneu-Sotelo, 2001; Lan, 2006; Meagher, 2003), and in India, 'upwardly' mobile

Table 1.2: 'Domestic cleaners and helpers' in the European Social Survey disaggregated by ethnic group status

| | Belong to minority ethnic group in country | | | | | | | | | | | | |
| | 2002 | | 2004 | | 2006 | | 2008 | | 2010 | | 2012 | | 2014 | |
	Yes	No	Yes	No	Yes	No	Yes	No	Yes	No	Yes	No	Yes	No
Germany	3	39	3	43	0	45	5	46	0	3	0	16	3	31
Denmark	0	1	0	1	0	1	0	2	0	1	–	–	0	1
Spain	1	106	11	113	0	127	9	108	2	68	6	107	–	–
France	1	44	2	87	5	99	10	96	0	93	5	72	5	139
Netherlands	1	15	–	–	3	42	1	18	–	–	3	43	4	27

Data are weighted absolute numbers.

Source: European Social Survey Rounds 1–7.[18]

23

lower-caste Indians also outsource housework as they try to adopt upper-caste markers of status (Dickey, 2000b; Ray and Qayum, 2009/2010). In several world regions, users and providers may have the same racial/ethnic background, for example in Ecuador (De Casanova, 2013), South Africa (du Preez et al, 2010; King, 2007), the Philippines (Driscoll, 2011) and Zambia (Hansen, 1990).

This suggests that racialisation, a Western construct, neither inheres in paid domestic work (Delap, 2011a) nor is it 'added' to class (Romero, 2002) but that class – and caste – mediates the effect of race. Therefore, in my research, I have focused on class (and caste) alongside gender to add greater depth to the intersection of race with class in the published research, not only in terms of supply but also demand. I now review published research on the latter.

Contemporary middle-class women's outsourcing of domestic work

An association is well documented between middle-class women's presence in the paid workforce and the demand for paid domestic work across societies, regardless of their commitment to gender equality:[19] "'It is part of the whole Stockholm package," one woman explained. "Work a lot, commute, hire under-the-table cleaning help'" (quoted in Bowman and Cole, 2009:168).

In liberal market or welfare states, the modern 'work ethic' does not encourage greater gender parity in household labour as it side-steps work commitment (Collins, 2007). So, white middle-class women's liberation is happening at the cost of the continued oppression of their working-class/migrant counterparts, whose day is spent doing her and *her* housework (Cox, 2006; Ehrenreich and Hochschild, 2003). Indeed, the notion that the dual-career heterosexual nuclear household is more likely to need this service is a springboard for some research into paid domestic work: 'This study is limited to working women [in dual-earner heterosexual households], because decisions on substituting domestic work are primarily theirs ... because non-working women do not face time constraints from their market work' (Tijdens et al, 2003:5).

At the same time, Delap (2011a) has unpacked post-war Western middle-class housewives' dependence on charwomen. A similar situation is also evident among men: contemporary British middle-class men from various ethnic backgrounds outsource their housework (for example gardening and house maintenance) to domestic handymen, to gain parenting or leisure time – time which the handymen then lose out in their turn (Kilkey et al, 2013). Moreover:

- all Western household types outsource housework or host au pairs, and these households might also belong to lower-income groups (Cox, 2015b; Hyland, 2017; Triandafyllidou and Marchetti, 2015);
- status is still a factor in outsourcing (Anderson, 2000, 2001, 2003);
- egalitarian couples might outsource cleaning to gain 'leisure' time (Gregson and Lowe, 1994a);
- increasingly, a range of personal services are being sold and bought on the inter(net)-connected capitalist marketplace, justified through various moral economies: people are outsourcing not just housework but the 'self' (Hochschild, 2012).

These various strands of research into paid domestic work raise some questions. Do time constraints related to work commitments qualify as a valid 'need' to outsource housework? Does outsourcing improve relationship quality, by avoiding confrontations over housework[20]? In Chapter 3, I consider these questions, to show that the factors determining contemporary demand are often complex. Crucially, the nuances in this complexity require attention when thinking of solutions to the problem of paid domestic work. Furthermore, unease about outsourcing domestic cleaning is also based on the premise that cleaning is the lowliest of work (Gregson and Lowe, 1994a).

Domestic work as dirty work

Housework is largely viewed as a chore, as drudgery. These terms are also used in the research analysing 'who does what', particularly in heterosexual households. When housework is outsourced, however, it becomes dirty work.

Wider research challenges historically specific cultural notions about dirt, cleanliness and pollution (Collins, 2007; Cox, 2007/2012a,b, 2011, 2016; Davidoff, 1995; Douglas, 1966/2002), and shows that the link between dirty work, cleanliness and status is not just a female domestic matter. The frontline operatives in sewage or waste-processing units are more likely to be men ('watermen', 'binmen', 'wastemen'; BBC Two, 2014, 2015a; Perry, 1998; Slutskaya et al, 2016), who sometimes process this waste in inhuman conditions (Praxis India/Institute of Participatory Practice, 2014). All constructed areas where higher-status people are found appear more clean and shiny, and are cleaned by Others. Thus, Chapter 4 analyses the transformation of housework from just work to drudgery to dirty work, by examining the intersections between the role of gender in this process and the influences of wider cultural ideologies around dirt.

At the same time, I am cognisant that the paradigm of 'dirty work' as elaborated by other feminist researchers is not only based on cultural meanings but also on the material injustices in domestic work, including in its professionalisation even in progressive democratic liberal societies.

The professionalisation of domestic work

Today, commercial cleaning requires training in safe use of chemicals and handling of heavy equipment, teamwork and efficient use of time. But because of societal assumptions around cleaning as unskilled manual labour, training might be cursorily delivered (Smith, 2009; Sykes et al, 2014). The 'professionalisation' of housework by commercial domestic cleaning agencies across cultures draws on feudal definitions of a good 'servant' in terms of race, personality and behavioural stereotypes, their person rather than their work, embedding rather than reducing gendered and racialised hierarchies in domestic work (Abrantes, 2014a; Anderson, 2000; Constable, 2007; Lan, 2006; Mendez, 1998, Mirchandani et al, 2016). Indeed, feminists have been critical of training, arguing that it is an institutionalised ploy that transfers the soul-destroying hard graft of caring for middle-class homes, children and dependent adults to working-class/racialised women (Romero, 2002; Skeggs, 1997/2002). Furthermore, Anderson (2000, 2001) urges caution in recommending professionalisation: because it can lead to 'specialisation', an 'unskilled' migrant worker doing housework and childcare would then run the risk of earning less for more work than, for instance, a white nanny or cook who could offer a specialist service.

Scrinzi (2010) observed that training offered by French cleaning agencies aimed to denaturalise housework as women's work, by framing it as different from unpaid housework. Migrant women, the main recipients of the training, were expected to put aside their knowledge of their own traditional ways of doing housework, adopt a 'reflexive' approach and learn 'modern' French ways of doing housework. Scrinzi deemed this practice racist, as the 'relational' training incorporated deference and emotional labour, and the migrant workers had to smilingly submit to their employers' cultural notions of housework. Most workers, many of whom had experienced downward mobility on migration, were dismissive of the training. Some migrants thought the training helped them to do the work with more dignity and in a 'more satisfactory way', but Scrinzi did not explore this further. Clearly, there are valid concerns here in terms of the racial/gender axis. However, the research did not appear to consider the class dimension in the migrant sample, and the paper did not mention the reasons why some of the women appreciated the training.

Also, would housework always be done the same way in households sharing the same wider cultural context? In Gregson and Lowe's (1994a) British research, a reflexive element was evident, albeit in a different relational context, where the cleaners had greater autonomy. Bujra, who investigated domestic service in Tanzania, concluded that the notion that women always-already 'know' domestic work because of early socialisation is an assumption, as household skills vary by culture and class, so 'what is learnt at home in one class [or culture] is not always the most useful knowledge for the work place' (2000:74).

Lutz (2011) argued that professionalisation cannot obliterate the 'hierarchical differences' of the private space. But, says Weeks (2011), neither does this happen in the 'formal' workspace. Other feminist researchers have shown that the transformation of domestic work by contemporary independent live-out workers in the West from 'labour power' to 'labour services' includes emphasising competencies and learning to avoid role diffusion, by maintaining boundaries in the workplace (Glenn, 1986; Hondagneu-Sotelo, 2001; Romero, 2002; Salzinger, 1991).

When workers are scolded by employers for unsatisfactory work, the interactions may be interpreted as symbolic acts that 'reinforce employers' higher social status' (Chin, 1998:141). In many instances, no doubt this is the case. But perhaps while everyone can do some cleaning (in the same way that everyone can take photographs), perhaps not everyone can do it well (like taking photographs of the quality that can help to earn a living). Oakley (1974/1985) found a range of cleaning standards among both working- and middle-class women – from being obsessive to being inattentive towards dust and dirt. French agency managers who recognised that paid domestic work is not the same as its unpaid equivalent also noted reduction in service quality when working time was tightly controlled (Bailly et al, 2013). An Australian government report mentions that almost 40% of commercial agency managers surveyed were 'unhappy' with their employees. One in every 2.2 applicants was deemed unsuitable, most commonly because of a lack of obvious interest or technical skills (Department of Employment and Workplace Relations, 2006). Paradoxically, the report concluded that recruitment could be boosted by simply targeting hard-to-place groups such as single mothers, older workers or those with disabilities. More recently, responding to the noticeable fall in the quality of state-subsidised cleaning services in Belgium, Tomei argues: 'training programs for domestic workers are necessary to challenge the entrenched view that domestic work is work that anyone can do and, thus, that workers must be unskilled and not worth much' (2011:204).

In contrast, many workers are dismissive of their work in the first instance. It is 'just' cleaning (Scrinzi, 2010; Smith, 2009), with women more likely to see it as 'an extension of housework' (Bailly et al, 2013; Sykes et al, 2014:33). Persistent questioning by Smith (2009) revealed agency cleaners as knowledgeable about a range of cleaning-related information, such as health and safety issues related to complex cleaning materials and handling of industry vacuum cleaners. The training was frequently devalued, because it was not the training the workers had actively sought (also Sykes et al, 2014). It seems the question is not about whether training per se is a problem, but how the training, and the content of training, is conceptualised.

Another argument why domestic work is not amenable to professionalisation is because it is too 'highly emotionally charged', it incites both 'disgust, shame and pain as well as … pride, sensuality (e.g. the smell of a clean apartment or ironed laundry), delight and satisfaction' (Lutz, 2008:49). Are these emotions absent in other work? Ehrenreich's experience as a cleaner, waitress and retail assistant led her to conclude: 'Each job presents a self-contained social world, with its own personalities, hierarchy, customs, and standards' (2002/2010:194). It appears that ontological and epistemological assumptions about housework require acknowledgement while analysing qualitative data. In Chapters 6 and 7, my analysis of material and cultural injustices in outsourced cleaning is underpinned by this observation.

Concerns around professionalisaton are not just about skills. Researchers, society and domestic worker activists have also considered whether paid domestic work is 'just another job' or whether it is a unique occupation (because anyone can do it).

'Work like no other, work like any other'

The ILO describes paid domestic work as 'work like no other, work like any other' (2010: 12). Some researchers recommend that domestic work should be 'work like any other', because that will 'make the skill level required for domestic work more visible' (Blackett, 2011:14) and 'impose on society the need to reconsider the provision of care and the taken-for-granted role of care workers, economically empower them, and incorporate this historically excluded category into the general political clientele of employees' and their generic labour demands, irrespective of the work they do' (Mundlak and Shamir, 2011:307; see also Neetha and Palriwala, 2011).

But others argue that the nature of the worksite defies regulation, and unionisation is difficult for isolated workers (Bailly et al, 2013; Calleman, 2011:132; Lutz, 2011). Behind the closed doors of home, social inequalities are 'reproduced and challenged on a daily and intimate basis' through 'the most intense, sustained contact with members of the other classes [and races] that most of its participants encounter' (Dickey, 2000a:32). Thus, only when domestic work is shared by all physically able adults in an unpaid capacity will equality be achieved (Calleman, 2011). As briefly mentioned earlier in this chapter, Weeks, who looks at work more widely, argues that what Dickey considers distinct to paid domestic work is fundamental to paid work: 'the work site [that is, any workplace] is where we often experience the most immediate, unambiguous, and tangible relations of power that most of us will encounter on a daily basis' (Weeks, 2011:2). For instance, Potter and Hamilton's (2014) account of exploitation of mushroom-pickers in Ireland raises similar issues to domestic work, including difficulty in organising because of high turnover and isolation of the workforce. Many domestic workers too, from the early 1900s to date, have countered the perception that the home is a distinctive workplace or that their work is not proper work and that their exploitation is different from that of other workers (IDWN, 2011; Schwartz, 2014; Sen and Sengupta, 2016:4). Worldwide, despite isolation and invisibility, these workers have been – and continue to be – involved in collective struggles demanding regulation with admirable successes, for instance the inclusion of domestic work in the ILO agenda on decent work (Pape, 2016).[21]

Domestic work is also considered unique because indirect exploitation of people by households-as-consumers is not comparable: '[organisations] can make use of advanced technology to offshore their tasks to low-wage workers abroad, unnoticed by the domestic customer base, [but] domestic work cannot be exported' (Lutz, 2011:188). On opening up this debate, one would find that the situation is similar for plumbing and other household maintenance work. In the countries to which the West outsources low-wage work, outsourcing of domestic work is even more common (ILO, 2013). Still, many researchers note that domestic work is often work that no-one does out of choice (for example Anderson, 2000; Gregson and Lowe, 1994a; Lutz, 2011) and is a dead-end 'ghetto' occupation (Glenn, 1981; Mattila, 2011). In wider gender and sociological research, however, domestic work is one of many 'ghetto' occupations: 'Ghetto occupations have been classified as those which are female-dominated and of low status, poorly paid, with narrow job content and that offer few prospects for promotion ... clerical work, unskilled factory work, low-grade service work, nursing, cleaning, teaching and caring occupations' (Truss et al, 2013:349–350).

Male-dominated occupations may also be blighted by class injustices and precarious working conditions, such that a range of occupations, regardless of their gendered nature, could be deemed 'poor' work. The characteristics of this poor-quality work appear similar to the feminine 'ghetto' occupations: 'often requiring no or low formal skills or qualifications', such work is associated with 'little room for the expression or development of skills', and it is 'often done under poor terms and conditions of employment (for example lack of training provision, holiday, maternity and sickness entitlement, "zero hour" work contracts and so on)' (Shildrick et al, 2012:24; see also Potter and Hamilton, 2014). At the extreme end of poor work is forced labour, which occurs in several industries besides domestic work (Pai, 2008; Skrivankova, 2014). These working conditions are replicated along a spectrum of worsening conditions across the globe from North to South (for example in India, see Bremen, 2013; Coelho, 2016; Gill, 2009/2012; NCEUS, 2009).

Another part of the domestic work problem is that it can switch from being a job to 'non'-work in a moment, since domestic workers can be hired or fired on a whim (Lutz, 2011). This appears to lead to a risk of naturalising the work of cleaning, because jobs come and go in all fields, with the work taken over by others as necessary in a paid, unpaid or overburdened capacity. In better work conditions, the blow is softened by – often generous – redundancy packages. But, across several industries, informal workers or those in forced labour, work without contract agreements and they are at the mercy of their contractor/ employer (Bremen, 2013; Raju and Bose, 2016). Lutz's analysis seems more revealing of how societies have constructed domestic work to appear different rather than it being inherently different. For instance, in 2010, the pro-socialist Ecuadorian government carried out inspections to ensure that employers of live-in domestic workers were fulfilling their legal obligations and honouring workers' rights (De Casanova, 2013). Indian legislation has also considered home a workplace, because the Sexual Harassment of Women in the Workplace (Prevention, Prohibition and Redressal) Bill includes domestic workers (Sen and Sengupta, 2016). At the same time, ratification of the ILO convention and its recommendation for regulating domestic work was resisted in the UK on the grounds that health and safety legislation or inspection regulations devised for large organisations cannot be applied to a two-person 'special' employment relationship agreed in a private household (Albin and Mantouvalou, 2012:77). Underneath this simple explanation is the reality that it would mean paying more for the service, that is, upper-class notions that service work is not amenable to regulation appear to be part of the exploitation of domestic workers rather than a cause of it. Consequently, one cannot commend highly enough those domestic workers, who, despite the limitations offered by the site and ambivalent legal status of their work, are fighting back alongside other workers in a climate of general weakening of labour protections.

Some domestic workers' organisations have preferred to work separately from other such organisations (Anderson, 2007; Chaney and Garcia Castro, 1989; Varghese, 2006), rooting their grievances in the long and problematic history of servitude and endorsing domestic work as exceptional. In the UK, where historical legal changes led to a shift from domestic workers' enjoying 'sectoral advantage' to suffering 'sectoral disadvantage' in terms of impact of sectoral rules, structures and culture, Albin proposed that a detailed sectoral approach should be the first step to redressal of injustices, because labour law 'has never dealt with' this kind of work (2012:231, 247). But others argue that the 'unique' job approach makes it difficult for workers and the work to lose the subordinating label, risks introducing arbitrary distinctions in waged work, and reduces the ability to deal with socio-legal issues that cross occupational categories (Chigateri, 2007; Hom, 2008/2010; Varghese, 2006).

Unionisation of early 20th-century British domestic workers had roots in the suffragette feminist movement (Schwartz, 2014). The historical trajectory of black Brazilian domestic workers' activism showed that joining forces with wider black and feminist movements and unions was key to making race, class and gender 'empowering' instead of 'disempowering' characteristics (Bernardino-Costa, 2014[22]). At a World Trade Organization conference, the Hong Kong Coalition of Indonesian Migrant Workers Organizations' experience of protesting alongside other marginalised groups, such as Korean peasants and Filipino fishermen, made them aware of the similarities in the issues affecting them and these other groups (Lai, 2007). In the same vein, following their review of the challenges facing regulatory possibilities for domestic workers in India, Neetha and Palriwala concluded that '[t]he complexity of work organization, wage rates, poor working conditions, poverty, illiteracy, caste, migrant status, lack of alternative work, and the exigencies of the life of domestic workers are similar to that of the vast numbers of informal workers' in India, and the 'success of social policy depends on the extent to which [all] these workers' rights are recognized rather than through piecemeal welfare measures' (Neetha and Palriwala, 2011:118; see also NCEUS, 2008, 2009; Raju and Bose, 2016).

Although the research presented in this book is at the micro-level, these broader debates informed my understandings of a more inclusive feminist approach to resolving the issues around regulation and professionalisation at the individual level alongside cultural injustices in everyday practices.

Cultural injustices in paid domestic work

Cultural injustices associated with the distinctiveness of exploitation in domestic work include personalism, paternalism/maternalism, deference and affective labour. Personalism is a characteristic of feudal relationships, where employers are 'concerned with the worker's total person' rather than the quality of their work (Abrantes, 2014a; Anderson, 2007; Glenn, 1986:154). It reproduces racial inequalities, with employers considering skin colour for particular work, for instance, a white au pair but a non-white person live-out cleaner (Anderson, 2007). Other research shows that 'modern' employers routinely seek certain people for certain jobs, using the language of soft skills to mask criteria such as physical appearance and attitudes (Anderson and Ruhs, 2012; Lloyd and Payne, 2009; Warhurst and Nickson, 2009). In the creative industries, 'soft judgements of insiders about whether [freelancers] are trustworthy, reliable and good to work with [are crucial]. Networks and contacts are the main means of gaining employment ...' (Leung et al, 2015:56). Selection interviews in academia, banking, law and so on were historically designed to assess whether the applicant is 'just like us', 'will fit in': even today a white man or Oxbridge candidate may be considered as having greater competence (Archive on 4, 2016; Rivera, 2015).

In sum, personalism remains a key social rule to avert the 'threat to the "natural" order' (Archive on 4, 2016) of racialised or class superiority in every possible space – the workspace, the leisure space, the home. Within this institutionalised injustice, when circumstances permit, domestic workers also assess employers, including on the basis of appearance (Grover, 2017; Lahiri, 2017) and resist unfair treatment despite personalism (Dill, 1994; Hondagneu-Sotelo, 2001). Some do not prefer depersonalisation (Dill, 1994; Lan, 2006; Näre, 2011), because it makes *her* more invisible when working (Molinier, 2009/2012) and encourages stereotyping of workers, reducing *her* ability to negotiate with employers (Mendez, 1998; Tomei, 2011).[23]

Maternalist/paternalist practices in paid domestic work are reported cross-culturally, although researchers have argued about which term is more appropriate in this context (Anderson, 2000; de Santana Pinho and Silva, 2010; Parreñas, 2010, cited in Mattila, 2011:337; Rollins, 1985; Romero, 2002). Such debates risk contradicting feminist efforts to counter reducing women and men to femininity and masculinity, respectively. As King argued, the 'relationship is patterned along paternalistic lines that inverts characteristics of maternalism to enhance the power and image of self in relation to the "other"' (2007:16), that is, both are embodied in the employer, since neither is inherent to her biological makeup.

The critical problem, then, is the pseudo-construction of the worker/servant as infantile[24] and 'part of the family', and their continued dependency on the employer (Anderson, 2000; Srinivas, 1995; Tellis-Nayak, 1983). In this situation, much recompensation is done in kind alongside a low monetary wage, 'gift'-giving (often second-hand), help with children's education and so on. Workers often resent this dependence (and the associated construction of their condition as 'needy' by employers) (Ray and Qayum, 2009/2010). Perusing the wider literature, however, it appears that such dependency is not specific to domestic work. Ehrenreich (2002/2010) and Toynbee (2003) worked undercover in several low-wage jobs in the US and the UK, respectively. Both concluded that they could not live on all those jobs. In the US, the working poor generally live with the constant threat of eviction and hunger, with little chance of owning a home, building a nest egg, having a pension. In the UK, they depend on state benefits, variously known as Family Income Supplement, Working Families Tax Credit and Universal Credit. Indeed, many low-waged workers remain dependants of the state if not of their employers.

At the same time, even though in Western labour relations paternalism is considered unfavourable for development, '[m]ost organizations find themselves operating within this understanding of leadership' (Laub, 2013, n.p.; see also Landry, 2011; Pellegrini et al, 2010). Organisations might mould employees through free courses on 'character' development and so on (Hochschild, 2001). Organisational management discourses adopt the 'language of family values ... to manufacture consent and adjust individuals to preconceived roles' (Weeks, 2011:158; also Dodson and Zincavage, 2007; Hochschild, 2001; Sturges, 2013). These 'values' and welfare provisions, bonuses, Christmas parties and gifts are used to extract more work through '"function creep" – the requirement to do more with less' (Gregg, 2009, cited in Gill, 2010:237; Westwood, 1984) as in paid domestic work. Workers who resist 'can appear ungrateful and disloyal' (Hom, 2008/2010:34; also Hochschild, 2001). My readings indicate that a deeper understanding of the perpetuation of cultural injustices in paid domestic work might require taking these similarities into consideration (see Chapter 7).

Housecleaning can also be degrading due to the implicit demands for deference and servility (Romero, 2002). Gregson and Lowe (1994a) stated that deference in domestic work was context-specific to the US. Still, in their book, they used first names only for the domestic workers, but referred to employers as Mrs So-and-So or 'Ann Bloggs'. They clearly note that their decision was made to avoid confusion and should not be interpreted otherwise. This was useful, as choosing what is usually considered as a show of deference to clarify who is the employer and the employee could be misinterpreted. It is important to read prefaces, introductions, footnotes and endnotes, and appendices before coming to conclusions about others' work. Strategies used by modern organisations to keep low-wage workers 'in their place' (a phrase that regularly appears in titles of articles and books on domestic servants) include cult-like induction programmes and unexpected changes to schedules or work plans: 'In fact often it was often hard to see what the function of management was, other than to exact obeisance', noted Ehrenreich (2002/2010:209–212; see also Hochschild, 2001). Other societies such as India are overtly hierarchical. At the same time, many people are not blind to their oppression and resist it as best they can (Constable, 2007; Dill, 1994; Rollins, 1985; Saldaña-Tejeda, 2015).

Finally, domestic work includes emotional or affective labour, which cannot be captured in a contract. Anderson questioned reducing emotional labour to money, even if it was appropriately remunerated – it would 'bring with it no mutual obligations, no entry into a community, and no real human relations' (2001:31). This aspect however, has been theorised as a particular problem between women:

> Affect, ... not only unfolds context ..., but is also produced in a specific context. Thus, while they [the feelings and emotions associated with doing housework] are expressions of immediate bodily reactions and sensations, which are neither rationalized through language nor situated in a dominant semantic script, they impact people and places, and are situated in a social space, such as a private household ... the affective energies attached to the organization and dynamics of unpaid and paid domestic work in private households evolve within the logic of the feminization of labor. (Gutiérrez-Rodríguez, 2014:47)

Later in the same article, Gutiérrez-Rodríguez acknowledges that all labour 'needs to be conceived in relation to ... feelings, emotions, sensations ... that drive' it (2014:51). Gynocentric conceptualisation of domestic work as a problematic affective terrain traversed only by women risks naturalising affective labour's association with the female domestic worker and its inevitability in the domestic workplace. Feminisation of domestic work is not ahistorical (see Chapter 5), men doing gardening or house-maintenance are also labelled domestic workers (Kilkey et al, 2013), and most work relations have 'instrumental' and 'affective' components (Gill, 2010; Penz et al, 2017). Perhaps it might be that the 'masculine' conceptualisation of paid work on the whole is the problem? The analyses presented in the subsequent chapters were conducted bearing these observations in mind.

Turning the lens from the demand to the supply side also might help. It appears that the single live-in worker is more likely to experience domestic work as 'work like no other',[25] while the live-out worker is more likely to experience it as 'work like any other' – these workers have also had a key role in domestic worker movements, because they are more visible and mobile (Sen and Sengupta, 2016). Workers who have experienced both situations seem to prefer the latter (Dill, 1994; Hondagneu-Sotelo, 2001; Narula, 1999), thus here I mostly draw on accounts of live-out work. In conditions of extreme social inequalities and entrenched caste/race, gender and social/religious norms around purity/pollution, the meanings of the work become intricately bound to experiences of wider cultural injustices. Chigateri (2007) reported how in India Tamilian Dalit[26] women did not want societal inscription of domestic work on their bodies.

The experiences of the variously racialised live-out workers in Western countries are more complex. The autonomy in the work certainly appears to be better than in other low-wage/status regularised jobs – a feature that is deemed important by the workers, as are often the better wages and greater job stability.[27] Dill detected two kinds of attitude among her respondents, 26 black American women who had done domestic work for an average of 37 years. Five women found the experience unpleasant, the work was mundane compared with other work they had done. The remaining women were invested in their work and tried to 'create opportunities for self-satisfaction'. Their ambivalent accounts gave Dill a better 'understanding of the rewards and detractions of the occupation' and she likened their experiences to a generalised experience of work (1994:99). Romero commented that the 'challenge [for her sample of domestic workers] was to find a job outside domestic service' (2002:174); their preference for this degrading work over other dehumanising work was the 'paradox of domestic service' (2002:42).

In Meagher's (2003) Australian study, some workers (that is, migrant and local workers) said they liked cleaning, creating 'order' out of other people's mess, and did not see the work as inherently degrading. Meagher listed five kinds of work orientation in domestic cleaning:

- stop-gap work (for example students, including feminists);
- stepping stone for other work (for example because of learning transferable skills);
- filler work (doing this work as a reasonable source of income, while waiting for an appropriate opportunity for work of choice);

- career (doing this work with the aim of opening a domestic service agency);
- dead-end (doing this work on a permanent basis).

Some workers have expressed a dislike for cleaning toilets (Anderson, 2000; Gutiérrez-Rodríguez, 2014; Meagher, 2003). But others have said that the worst job is cleaning shared housing (for example student accommodation) or just very dirty and messy houses (Gregson and Lowe, 1994a; Meagher, 2003). But workers universally are hurt by their stigmatisation.

Clearly, taking both sides into account acknowledges the agency of the worker, while also recognising its limitations, and this has posed a dilemma for some researchers. My review indicated that this dilemma can aid in reading between the lines of one's own analysis, to ensure that one is presenting respondents' voices at all times. I have attempted to keep it in mind, while writing this book.

Conclusion

Evidence from outwith the core domestic work literature shows that the essential features of paid domestic work are also present in other work. The meanings of domestic work appear to be shaped by several factors:

- the work itself;
- previous work experiences;
- the conditions under which it is done (as a raced, classed, casteised woman or man; citizen or non-citizen; live-out or live-in work);
- relationship with the employer(s);
- what the worker hopes to achieve from the whole experience in terms of their wider life circumstances.

Affect and emotion may be constructed as feminine, but they are intrinsic to all work (Mundlak and Shamir, 2011). Researchers are universally sympathetic to women who do cleaning work – and this is vital within a feminist approach. The gendered theorisation, however, reinforces domestic work as low-value 'women's' work, which then keeps the work in the shadows, instead of what Ehrenreich rightly demands, 'to make the work visible', a project started by second-wave feminists but left incomplete (2000, n.p.). The Mumsnetters responding to my question at the beginning of this chapter may have been a step ahead, because they questioned cleaning as women's work, but cleaning was 'only a bit of cleaning' and, hence, not worth researching. All these ideologies and norms, present across cultures – women's work, work that anyone can do, unique work – appear to undermine domestic workers' efforts to work under a 'contract for service' rather than under a 'contract of service' (Meagher, 2003:149).

The published literature is an invaluable source of information and evidence of many researchers' thoughtful hard work in the growing societal recognition of domestic work as real work. It also shows, though, that subsequent feminist approaches to the continuing conundrum need not only to focus on the work itself, taking into consideration the multiple axes of oppression that continue to operate, but also to seek to situate it within the context of wider work practices, to aid filling the gaps in our knowledge about how this work has evolved as societies have progressed. The next chapter describes the methodology used and the research respondents whose accounts provided the basis for the argument that emerged from the research for this book by attempting one such feminist approach.

Behind the Words: Introducing the Research Project and Respondents

....

In a monthly discussion group comprising mainly White British women over 60 years, we talked about obtaining satisfaction from doing everyday tasks. Those who found them mundane noted that it was often more interesting if you were doing it for someone else. "Perhaps", said one woman, "we should do housework in each other's houses instead of our own!"

....

Introduction

The first part of this chapter provides methodological details of the research underpinning this book, all of which had a bearing on the argument that emerged from it. The descriptive analysis in the second part situates the research respondents in the wider socio–cultural–geographical contexts from which the samples were drawn, providing early evidence regarding the role of class in mediating reproduction of other social inequalities in paid domestic work.

Methodological considerations

The research design

About half the weekly time spent on core housework goes on cleaning (Bianchi et al, 2012), the task that lies at the heart of the 'gendered inequalities that shape responsibilities for domestic chores and childcare' (Gabb and Fink, 2015:111; Grose, 2013). Sharing of this household task then becomes the last bastion of egalitarianism (Davis and Greenstein, 2013). Yet, the practice of outsourcing cleaning endures, and this book focuses on outsourced cleaning in two cultural settings in a particular context of demand and supply: outsourcing of cleaning in contemporary urban households, with cleaning service provision by a local or in-country migrant, live-out service-provider, who works for one or several households.

The separation of the worker's home and workplace has been key for the transformation of domestic work from servitude to service, with the conditions of live-out work deemed more favourable in terms of honouring of workers' rights (Dill, 1994; Gregson and Lowe, 1994a,b; Hondagneu-Sotelo, 2001; Romero, 2002; Salzinger, 1991). It is also increasingly the preferred mode of outsourcing, because it offers the service-provider clearer boundaries between paid work and private life (for example Dill, 1994; Hondagneu-Sotelo, 2001; Raghuram, 1999:216). On the demand side, contemporary middle-class house designs in several world regions do not incorporate living space for a domestic worker. These points led me to conclude that understanding the live-out form of work separately would aid in attending to the gaps in published research outlined in Chapter 1.

Local cultures and geography influence cleaning practices in different social contexts. For example, in dusty tropical locations, whole houses are cleaned daily, whereas in temperate regions, some rooms may be cleaned more often than others. Thus, focusing on a single geographical region risks introducing essentialisms into the analyses (Narayan, 1998). Also, to understand what is happening or not happening in a social space, it is useful to look at similar situations in another social space that appears 'different' on the surface (Douglas, 1986/1987, 2002). When Ray and Qayum tested their 'cultures of servitude' framework developed in Kolkata on two case studies in New York, they found that many of the 'constitutive elements of Kolkata's culture of servitude' were present in New York (2009/2010:27). Given such prior observations and my own experience of using services of local White British and Indian service-providers, it was important to consider the local social context from a cross-cultural perspective for addressing some of the issues highlighted in Chapter 1.

More broadly, on a country level, both the UK and India reflect the current trend in rising social inequalities associated with neoliberal capitalism (Fraser, 2013; Raju and Jatrana, 2016b). But there are differences in the historical trajectories (see Chapter 1), and there is variation in the contemporary structuring of outsourced housecleaning both within and between the two regions (see Chapters 4–7). This book focuses on two particular social contexts in both countries. Geographically, the research was conducted in small- to mid-sized urban areas in the mid- and northern regions of England,[1] and two mid-sized urban areas in the Punjab plain region in north India.[2] Thus, when I refer to respondents as 'the UK respondents' and 'the Indian respondents', I am referring to my research contexts *in particular* and not providing a generalised description of paid domestic work in either country.

The book includes the perspectives of both supply and demand. Feminist and sociological research more generally should interrogate race, difference and diversity in a balanced way (Bhavnani, 1993; Letherby, 2003:56), but with a few exceptions, the excellent research on paid domestic work in the West concentrates on white employers and Other racialised, migrant workers. In other words, over time, race has become a more significant analytical category than class. Yet again and again, in real life in the mid- and northern regions of England, I encountered White British women working as cleaners, including in diasporic Indian households, and some expatriate Indian service-users mentioned how their interactions with these women differed from their interactions with domestic workers "back home".

Given the ethical concerns regarding dyad samples[3] I interviewed independent user/provider samples. Like most other publications on this topic, this book is based on research among women. I made this decision with the intention of interrogating certain assumptions around women and housework that remain unchallenged, rather than affirming the feminisation of domestic work. Also, men – both as domestic workers and as family members of female domestic workers – figure throughout the book, because to understand women's lives and work fully, requires taking into consideration the lives and work of the people they live with (Letherby, 2003:6). Ethical approval was obtained from the relevant university ethics committee.

The broader research project also intended to explore how lived feminism(s) negotiate paid housework. Thus, the service-user groups in both countries were selective samples, limited to senior women academics with an interest in feminism/gender sensitisation,[4] who currently outsourced or had previously outsourced cleaning. However, this criterion does not impact on the findings presented here, as the interviewed service-providers worked for a range of service-users. Also, my pilot samples in both research settings were drawn from the general population. With regard to the supply side, alongside anecdotal evidence, previous Western research (Hondagneu-Sotelo, 2001; Mendez, 1998; Romero, 2002) and internet discussions on cleaning charges (Mumsnet and Netmums, see later) consistently showed that 'independent' service-providers (often called 'private cleaners') had greater autonomy and frequently commanded higher fees than the wages of agency cleaners. Therefore, again, I aimed to recruit 'independent' service-providers over the age of 18 years. Although in India, such workers are considered 'waged' employees (Sen and Sengupta, 2016, see Chapter 6), there are basic similarities in the occupational relationships in the two cultural contexts (multiple clients, fee structuring, lack of engagement of the employer/service-user with regard to social protections, and so on).

The primary method of data collection was semi-structured interviews.[5] These conversations-with-a-purpose allow adapting lines of enquiry depending on respondents' answers, while not losing sight of one's research questions (Bryman, 2008). A questionnaire was also used to capture a detailed snapshot of the division of household labour and material aspects of the user–provider employment relationship (except in the Indian service-provider group – see later). Time-use diaries were not considered appropriate, because first, such record-keeping can be tedious and erratic, and pilot interviews revealed that people sometimes do common household tasks on a fortnightly rather than weekly basis. Second, keeping a time-use diary assumes basic literacy. Most of the Indian service-providers in the sample were illiterate (see later). To minimise social desirability bias (Joinson, 1999; Press and Townsley, 1998), I started the interview with the questionnaire, which helped to break the ice between two strangers who were going to converse about domestic practices. I broke down each broad housework category into components (for example see Figure 3.1), and asked for a proportional estimate of the time the respondent or another person was likely to do a task. Later, I used the questionnaire data for only descriptive analysis or analysing trends, which helped to counter perception bias around time spent on housework by people themselves and others (Crompton and Lyonette, 2008; Lee and Waite, 2005; Press and Townsley, 1998). The accounts given by service-users were corroborated in general terms against those of the service-providers and vice versa.

The book also draws on my pilot interviews and secondary data to situate the main argument in the broader sociology of gender and work. The secondary data comprised:

- UK census data;
- the Labour Force Survey (LFS), the UK's official quarterly employment survey (ONS, 2015b);
- Understanding Society (n.d.), an academically rigorous longitudinal survey of contemporary life in the UK;

- British television documentaries and reality shows, radio programmes and broadsheet reports;
- websites of cleaning agencies/franchises operating in the research contexts;
- British internet forums with discussion threads on paid domestic work.

The relative anonymity provided by the internet allows greater freedom of expression and, thus, 'relatively authentic natural data' (Holtz et al, 2012:56; also Joinson, 1999), although fictional accounts cannot be ruled out (Seale et al, 2010). Two websites in particular – Mumsnet and Netmums – have a wealth of discussion on outsourced housecleaning. Originally aimed at mothers, both websites now have a wider scope and UK-wide membership (with a southern bias). Mumsnet is more representative of 'middle-class values' in line with its demographic: 74% users have above-average incomes; 84% are White (Mumsnet Census, 2009). Netmums has a 'working-class' orientation (Pedersen and Smithson, 2013), with 30–40% of users from lower-income groups (Russell, 2006). Service-users as well as service-providers contribute to the discussions on both sites.

For India, the national report *The Challenge of Employment in India: An Informal Economy Perspective* (NCEUS, 2008, 2009) and the Indian Human Development Survey (Desai et al, 2010) provided robust statistical evidence. I also used Indian media reports, but, to my knowledge, there are no Indian internet forums where both service-users and service-providers participate in discussions about outsourcing housework.

Finally, while a researcher can decide whom to invite to speak, who takes up the invitation is not up to them.

Power in multi-context research

In the 1980s in the UK, Gregson and Lowe (1994a) struggled to find cleaners for their study because they worked alone and were not 'visible'. I did not have difficulty in finding White British cleaning service-providers. But contrary to expectations (Letherby, 2003; Tatano Beck, 2005), women labelled as marginalised are not always willing to talk. Several women ignored my initial attempt to contact them. Others prevaricated, while some refused bluntly: "I'd rather clean for my mother than get interviewed!" Eventually, I interviewed 27 of the 67 women I contacted in various ways. Two women were known to me previously. Five were working for service-users known to me or to colleagues. Here the snowballing stalled and I had to look elsewhere. Two women (one ex-agency worker) responded to my post on a feminist network webpage. I found 16 women by searching Google for domestic cleaners' websites and adverts on Gumtree and Yell.com. Further snowballing led to the last two respondents. Working arrangements varied, from undeclared work to running a quasi-agency (see Chapter 6). I emailed, texted or cold-called to make contact. A few were intrigued by my topic and some respondents were motivated by my offer of a cash gift.

In the Indian research sites, e-communication/texting prospective respondents appeared difficult, as many of the domestic workers I approached were illiterate. Eventually I found 20 workers through an informant or one of their service-users, and nine via snowballing. The higher positive response rate in this group (24 out of 29 contacted women were interviewed) may be due to the culture of reciprocity embedded in many work relationships in India (Thapar-Björkert and Henry, 2004). For example, *Kalpana*[6] bought her cooking-gas cylinder illicitly. Whenever she chanced upon a vendor, she arranged to have a cylinder delivered to a service-user's residence. It is likely that *Kalpana* agreed to talk to me because I approached her through them. But later she herself asked me to talk to her sister, whereas some others approached through service-users could not find time to meet me. One woman I directly approached in a slum refused outright, saying that talking about her life and problems made her tense, and she preferred not to think about it. Elsewhere too, Indian domestic workers have declined to be interviewed, either because they did not want to reveal they were domestics (Raghuram, 1999) or because they were too busy or not interested (Raghuram, 2001; Sen and Sengupta, 2016:45). Deference could have played a part, given the wide social distance between *Kalpana* and me. But deference can be countered by a respondent's level of engagement with the researcher. Some Indian service-provider interviews were shorter, such that these interviews averaged 40 minutes compared with one hour for the rest of the groups. This was in part because I did not use written questionnaires with this group, and also because some women were not as forthcoming as others. It would be easy to interpret this as a manifestation of self-effacement among oppressed Southern women. But some UK service-providers also gave clipped answers. In contrast, both the UK and Indian service-users, who were women invested in feminism/gender sensitisation issues, all gave fairly detailed answers. The Indian women's reticence might have been due to a lower degree of interest in my research compared with me and the service-users. Thus, the mantle of vulnerability in research (Cotterill, 1992) was not always embodied in the respondent from the marginalised social context, but encompassed both my respondents and myself.

The UK service-user sample was drawn from female academics working in the humanities and health and social sciences at universities located in my target areas. Of 82 senior faculty members contacted by email, 62 replied, of whom 24 did not outsource cleaning; 21 of those who did outsource, participated in the research, most commonly because they found the topic interesting. The Indian service-users were also academics in similar positions, and some were located via information provided on institutional websites. I contacted them directly by email or through intermediary contacts, snowballing and cold calls. Since India is among the world regions where outsourcing of housework is more common than in the UK and the West more generally (ILO, 2013), only 38 service-users were contacted in total, half of whom participated in the research; again, many found my topic interesting.

Data collection tools need to take into account the social conditions of intended interviewees. The tasks included in most questionnaire-based studies on housework to date are generally categorised as cleaning, cooking, washing-up, laundry and ironing, childcare and grocery shopping. These are tasks that in the West, since the Industrial Revolution, have been understood widely as 'women's work' in a nuclear-family unit. This broad, ethnocentric categorisation overlooks several variations in households with different living arrangements, class variations and cross-cultural variations in domestic practices, the amount of work a task entails and the frequency and thoroughness with which it is done in each household. For example, ironing was a 'non'-task in a few UK academics' households (one did not even own an iron). Grocery shopping is traditionally outside work in India and often done by men; boiling milk is a major kitchen task, and verandahs, balconies and driveways added to the floor space that required frequent cleaning. Among the service-users and the UK service-providers, men were more likely to do the mechanised work of vacuuming and cleaning of bathrooms and toilets than dusting, which is non-mechanised as well as less strenuous. There could be uncertainty about who 'owned' the housework if the house belonged to only one partner. Living-apart together for part of the week or longer created similar issues. In joint families, different aspects of housework could be owned by different generations. Households may include non-kin, who also might share the housework. Furthermore, because the living and work conditions of the Indian service-providers differed markedly from the other three groups, in which understandings of their work were intricately bound with their broader lives (see also Mattila, 2016; Sen and Sengupta, 2016; and Lutz, 2011, for an out-country migrant worker context), a life-history-style interview schedule was used. Moreover, housework questionnaires are applicable to housework carried out in houses. The Indian service-providers mostly lived in single-room dwellings (Bharati and Tandon Mehrotra, 2008; Sen and Sengupta, 2016; Singh, 2001). In such a context, who cleans the communal toilet would hardly impact on a gender analysis of housework. Many of these dwellings had no windows, so gender differences in who cleans the windows from inside/outside also did not arise. Sometimes the 'cooker' was fabricated of mud and sat just outside the room, in an alleyway. Housework in the slums in the research site also included obtaining water from a communal tap once or twice every day, collecting firewood for the cooking, accompanying children to communal toilets and dealing with cow-dung, while bathroom cleaning became a 'non'-task.

The timing and place of interviews had to be convenient for the respondents. Domestic research interviews are ideally conducted at home, but interruptions by family members or others are likely. Still, both the environment and human interference can add context to respondents' answers. Several interviews were conducted in private offices or public spaces such as cafés with background noise, or sitting on a charpoy[7] in a service-alley, with interruptions from children or neighbours (Dickey, 2000a; Thapar-Björkert, 1999). In interviews conducted over Skype, the sound could fluctuate. Some informants acted as gatekeepers, forming their own ideas of my – the researcher's – positionality (Soni-Sinha, 2008; Sultana, 2007; Thapar-Björkert and Henry, 2004). I ensured inclusion of a range of experiences regardless of the method of contact or place of interview, by increasing my sample number.

Finally, despite preparing for social desirability bias, the information provided in an interview may be 'constructed' in response to specific questions (Kitzinger and Wilkinson, 1996); that is, people, being human, may under-report or exaggerate oppressive experiences or 'good' practices. Respondents' perceptions of the researcher's positionality also influence what is said or not said (Kitzinger and Wilkinson, 1996; Saldaña-Tejeda, 2015; Soni-Sinha, 2008; Tatano Beck, 2005; Thapar-Björkert and Henry, 2004). Despite having advantage of 'intellectual privilege' in the equation of power between the researcher and researched (Letherby, 2003:77), there are many ways in which the latter can humble the former and influence the direction of the research.

Producing situated knowledge

Real-life data are affected by a multitude of factors. Thus, sociological analyses aim to extract interconnecting themes and patterns from empirical data to generate broad concepts and theories about social life (Hodkinson, 2009; Taylor and Bogdan, 1998). There are two principal sociological analytical strategies – analytical induction and grounded theory – which are often used in tandem, because both may be variously interpreted (Bryman, 2008). While essentially following these general understandings, some points regarding the analysis presented here require elaboration for the reader to understand the process behind the theorisation developed in this book.

First, this book does not describe a distinct form of domestic work in a particular cultural context, and it is not based on a single theoretical framework. Several different concepts informed the analysis and they are introduced at pertinent points in the book. The book also does not aim to compare forms of paid domestic work in two different cultures. Instead, it presents a more general understanding of the work that emerged from 'merging' (rather than 'comparing') all the sub-group analyses. This analytical approach is in part a product of my particular diasporic gaze, which I describe as seeing the social through a varifocal lens (see Narayan, 1998).

In part, I was guided by Douglas's (1986/1987:96) anthropology-derived cultural theory analytical framework, through which she showed how simultaneous non-essentialist comparative analysis enhances sociological understandings of the workings of the West's own institutions and culture: 'It is amazing how institutions fall into stable types that we can recognize in different times and circumstances. The fact that we can talk of a bureaucracy of Byzantine complexity ...' (Douglas, 1986/1987:111). In her analysis of perceived risks in different societies, Douglas argues that when:

> a certain kind of society is biased toward stressing the risk of pollution, we are not saying that other kinds of social organization are objective and unbiased but rather that they are biased toward finding different kinds of dangers ... each culture, each set of shared values and supporting social institutions, is biased toward highlighting certain risks and downplaying others. ... [Thus] we mix examples of risk selection among people like ourselves and people such as the Amish and the Hutterites, contemporaries who have a strange appearance to the modern eye. One reason for doing this is that these peoples and their cultures have a pronounced identity, so they can be readily described. (Douglas and Wildavsky, 1983:8, 175)

Cultural essentialism can originate at either end of the pole (Narayan, 1998), because:

> [s]taying within his [sic] own culture, a person is apt to see no culturally standardized forms around him: transgression against the norm is more visible than conformity. The inside experience of culture is an experience of choice and decision, scrutinized and judged by neighbours and press. The local view obscures regularities, but as soon as the local moves abroad, he is forcibly struck by the standardized behaviour of foreigners. The innocent view of [Western] culture is that we don't have it at home; it is only abroad that people are culturally hidebound. A special effort of sophistication is necessary to see our own culture. (Douglas, 2002:25)

Consequently, having lived for almost equal periods in two societies, my location in the space between two cultures offered an advantage. I could test how themes in one cultural context might be reinforced or problematised by another cultural context, to develop a more rigorous analysis by constantly trying to avoid making 'essentialist contrasts between "Western" and "Third World" cultures' (Narayan, 1998:86). In this, I use both English and Hindi terms in both research contexts, as an inclusive global sociology requires cultural intermingling of relevant terms (Qi, 2011:292).

Second, I seemingly use normative hierarchies in my analysis: I introduce the UK respondents first and then the Indian respondents. I first present UK data and then the Indian data. This is because my pre-field ontological position was grounded in my personal experience of outsourcing cleaning in India and the UK, through which I understood that it was the experiences of the White British service-providers that would in the main allow me to test the orthodoxies in both academic and wider social understandings of their work. But, as Douglas (2002) emphasised, I needed to bring in another cultural context – as well as the views of the demand side – to make visible the nuances in work practices of these service-providers. Thus, the Indian data are included where pertinent to reduce the risk of ethnocentrism, in the manner described by Narayan: 'Instead of seeing the centrality of particular values, traditions, or practices to any particular culture as given, we need to trace the historical and political processes by which these values, traditions, or practices have come to be deemed central constitutive components of a particular culture ...' (1998:93).

A simple example would be reasons for outsourcing of cleaning. A physical inability to clean transcends culture, thus, here one does not need to draw on Indian and UK data separately to prove the point. However, addressing gaps in published wisdom about the association between outsourcing cleaning and status and material resources required drawing on data from both cultural contexts, but without setting them up as ahistorical polar opposites (Narayan, 1998).

Third, the book aims to re-present rather than represent the women (Kitzinger and Wilkinson, 1996:13; see also Bhavnani, 1993) whose experiences inform it. Research on paid domestic work often involves a triad: the service-provider, the service-user and the researcher. In the classic feminist tradition (Kitzinger and Wilkinson, 1996) it may be assumed that the service-provider is the Other, given her lower status, and her experiential knowledge should be privileged over the service-user's authorised knowledge (Letherby, 2003). Indeed, the tone of many works in this field is highly critical of service-users (see also Meagher, 1997, 2003). But others have acknowledged that the provider–user power asymmetries are complicated by the shifting positionings of both the service-provider and service-user vis-à-vis multiple axes of oppression (Lan, 2006; Mattila, 2011). As King notes, '[g]iving a forum to only one voice, irrespective of whether that voice is black or white, will inevitably result in an usurping of the space between social reality and representation by the speaker' (2007:ix). In this book, the voices are re-presented 'in the same critical plane' (Morgan, 2009:9), while being mindful that service-providers may know more because they are the doers of the work under scrutiny.

The UK service-users and service-providers and the Indian service-users were interviewed in English, and the Indian service-providers were interviewed in Hindi. Some loss of information during translation is inevitable due to lack of equivalence of some terms between languages (Birbili, 2000; Chun, 1997; Soni-Sinha, 2008). Therefore, only the quoted material was translated (Hondagneu-Sotelo, 2001:xvi), first 'at speed', without regard for grammar or logic, followed by revision (Spivak, 2000:406). Hierarchies within English were also a concern during and after transcription, arising from differences in education, class and country context (Anzaldúa, 1987; Spivak, 2000). The UK service-providers from established middle-class backgrounds had little trace of local accents, while H- and G-dropping was common among working-class service-providers. There were differences in fluency among the Indian service-users. While '[w]e do not speak as we write ... and this should be reflected, where possible, in direct quotes used' (O'Dwyer, 2007:403), an imaginary persona may be created while reading quoted text (Corden and Sainsbury, 2006). That is, re-presentation of linguistic differences could compromise keeping all voices in the same plane (see also Lutz, 2011).

Thus, the quoted material has been lightly edited. This does not reduce the very real socioeconomic hierarchies between the service-users and service-providers, of which the book takes full heed. (The quotes from the Mumsnet and Netmums websites, however, are reproduced verbatim.) All personally identifiable data were anonymised and pseudonyms were given to all respondents: English names for the UK respondents and Indian first names for the Indian respondents. Service-users' names are in roman and service-providers' names are in italics. I also quote or refer to people who were not part of these samples, but who talked to me about their domestic practices during the research period – these data, too, have been anonymised.

Finally, although my contribution comprises situated and partial knowledge (Hondagneu-Sotelo, 2001; Taylor and Bogdan, 1998), it is knowledge that adds to, and I hope will stimulate further thinking in, what is already known about paid domestic work, both in academia and beyond. I will now describe the respondents whose words and silences around their real-life experiences are the building blocks of the argument that follows.

Introducing the respondents

The UK service-providers

Twenty-six UK respondents (aged 20–75 years) self-identified as White British,[8] and one as White Irish (Appendix A, Table A.1). Eight women were working undeclared, 18 were operating as small businesses, and one had worked for a cleaning agency several years ago. For nine of them, this work provided their main income. How representative is this sample of independent workers in the areas from which it was drawn?

Statistical estimates of paid domestic workers are deemed inaccurate due to many methodological challenges (ILO, 2013), such as undeclared workers (Cox, 2006; Gavanas, 2010) and not counting domestic cleaners as a distinct occupational category (Romero, 2002). For instance, in Sweden, between 1960 and 1990, national counts of domestic workers fell from 68,800 to 2 (Milkman et al, 1998: 503), and the 2013 ILO report has no data for Sweden. Recent academic research, in contrast, reveals a thriving in/formal industry in Sweden, with undocumented workers and over 160 companies (Bowman and Cole, 2014:191; Gavanas, 2010). However, some available statistics are useful for examining trends (Abrantes, 2014b; ILO, 2013; Wills et al, 2009), including ethnic profiles (for example Table 1.2).

Between January 2011 and March 2015, among the new wave of employed people entering the LFS, 3,190 were classed as 'domestics and cleaners', of whom 1,300 were likely to have been doing domestic cleaning (those categorised as 'providing independent services to cleaning of buildings' – this descriptor includes homes and public buildings – and those categorised under 'activities of households as employers of domestic personnel'). Of these, 1,034 were women, of whom 690 identified as White British. Regional disaggregation of the data showed that in London the domestics/cleaners were mostly 'Other White' (for example Polish) or non-White British, but in the rest of the UK, they were more likely to be White British (Figure 2.1). A similar situation has been reported in Belgium, where three-quarters of domestic workers in the Brussels region are foreign, but elsewhere in the country a similar proportion are Belgian (Gerard et al, 2012, cited in Pérez and Stallaert, 2016:157).

A third of the female domestics/cleaners were self-employed (n=342), of whom two thirds were White British (n=214). My sample had considerably more younger women (20–39 years; Figure 2.2a) and married/co-habiting women with dependent children (Figure 2.2b) than

Figure 2.1: Numbers of women working as domestics/cleaners in the UK by region

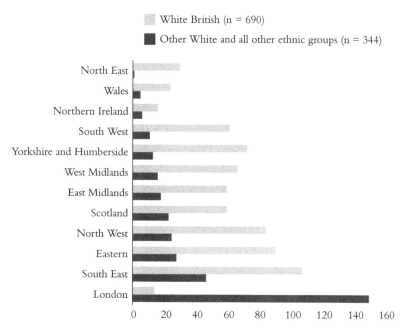

Note: Labour Force Survey wave 1 samples for all quarters from January–March 2011 to January–March 2015, n = 1,034.

Data source: Labour Force Survey, ONS, April 2015.

Figure 2.2: White British female self-employed domestics/cleaners disaggregated by (a) age group and (b) family unit

(a)

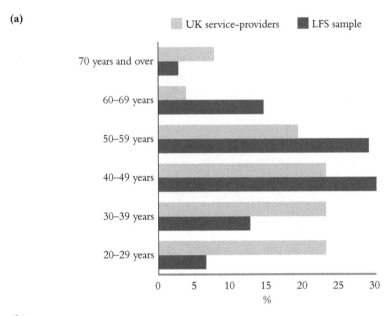

(b)

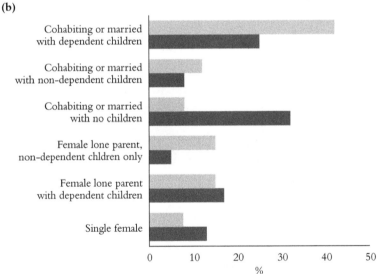

Notes: UK service-providers: n = 26. *Georgia* is excluded from these comparisons, because she was no longer working as a cleaning service-provider. LFS wave 1 samples for all quarters from January–March 2011 to January–March 2015: n = 214.

Data source: Labour Force Survey, ONS, April 2015.

the LFS cohort. The latter had more women in partnerships with no children. Gregson and Lowe's sample (1994a) had even fewer cleaners under 40 years (15%) and a higher proportion aged 61–70 years (30%). The proportion of middle-aged women was similar in the three samples (Figure 2.2a; Gregson and Lowe: 55%). Also, 28% of the LFS women but only 4% of my respondents had no qualifications, and only 14% of the former but 46% of my respondents had Level 3 qualifications[9] (Figure 2.3). Only 15% of Gregson and Lowe's (1994a) sample had left school at 16+ years, the rest having left earlier, and they contacted their participants through their employers. I found most of the younger and 16+ educated women through the internet (as discussed earlier). The LFS sample is selected to be representative of the whole UK population and it uses, for instance, addresses from the Postcode Address File in England (ONS, 2011). Hence, the differences between the samples are most likely due to differences in sampling procedures, since younger workers might have been more likely to use the internet for marketing their services.

Most of my sample were working legally, particular those with Level 3 qualifications (Figure 2.4). The LFS does not collect information on tax

Figure 2.3: Education levels of the UK service-providers and LFS sample of White British self-employed domestics/cleaners

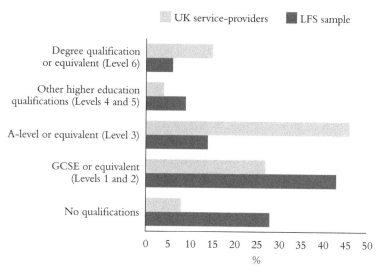

Notes: UK service-providers: n = 26. *Georgia* is excluded from these comparisons, because she was no longer working as a cleaning service-provider. LFS wave 1 samples for all quarters from January–March 2011 to January–March 2015: n = 204 (data not available for the remaining women).

Data source: Labour Force Survey, ONS, April 2015.

Figure 2.4: Education levels of the UK cleaning service-providers

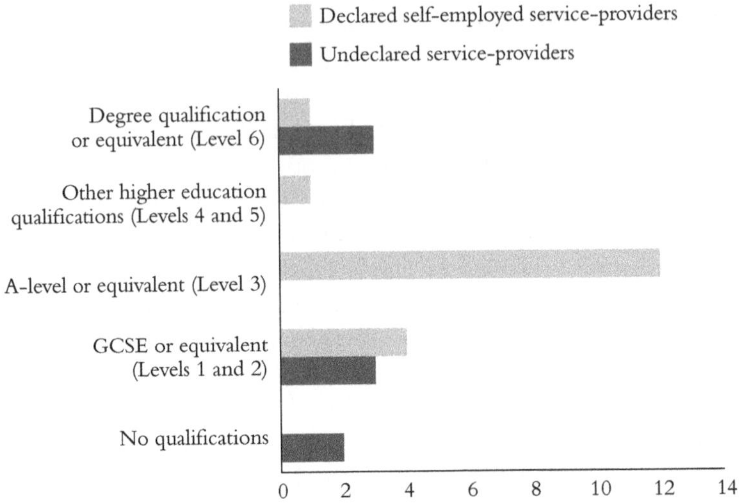

Notes: N = 26. *Georgia* is excluded from this analysis, as she was no longer working as a cleaning service-provider.

returns for the self-employed (S. Milburn, ONS, personal communication, 2015), so the proportion working legally is not known. Assuming that many domestics/cleaners do undeclared work, particularly those with no qualifications (Gregson and Lowe, 1994a), the main exceptional characteristic of my sample is a relatively higher educational level.

The details provided by the service-users of their current service-providers indicated similar characteristics: about half were 40–50 years of age; two were in their thirties and six were over 60 years. All these service-providers except one (whose service-user did not answer this question) were said to be white. The majority were said to be British, one was Irish, and one academic had outsourced to two Irish Travellers running a cleaning business together. A few of these service-providers were in part-time further/higher education. One academic was using a cleaning agency. It is important to note, though, that I did not set out to find UK academics using the services of White British service-providers in particular. Rather, this is what I happened to find. Thus, overall, my limited comparative analysis questions common understandings of the demographics of contemporary UK domestic cleaning service-providers (for example, see BBC Two, 2015b). Two service-users had male service-providers, both of whom were said to be middle-aged White British men. *Zoe's* husband started working with her following redundancy. Similar partnerships were mentioned in internet discussions (Netmums, 2009–2014), while a Portuguese agency committed to gender-balanced employment practices prefers its team of two cleaners to comprise a man and a woman (Abrantes, 2014a).

Some UK academics described their cleaning service-providers as 'exceptional': *she* could hold an intelligent conversation, appeared stylish and capable of finding other work, and declared *her* earnings. For example:

> '[S]he's an interesting person. She has chosen cleaning, because umm, she hates having bosses, she hates working in a corporate environment, she hates the politics of work, the workplace ... when I was having real trouble at work, she was a source of enormous wisdom about these sorts of intolerable situations ... and that's when she told me all about this side of her life ... And she removed herself from it. So she's ... I think, interesting.' (Caitlin)

A service-provider also thought *she* was unusual, because of her middle-class background and education:

> '[I]n my experience of my mum's cleaners, they aren't usually highly educated or intelligent ... and that's my experience. Or they're very young, and they're obviously either didn't do A levels or go to university and they haven't got anything else they would, somebody would employ them to do. ...' (*Evie*)

Yet such 'exceptions' seemed to appear elsewhere too (see Mumsnet, 2013a,b in Appendix B), including in India.

The Indian service-providers

Most of the 24 Indian service-providers were illiterate; three women had studied up to class 5–8 (UK years 6–9). Most women also did not know their exact age, but they had a rough idea of age at marriage and approximate years of marriage,[10] making them between 24 years and 57 years (Appendix A, Table A.2). They identified themselves in terms of their community as determined by the caste system (mostly Dalit communities, for example Balmikis, and the washermen caste). On average they had more children than all the other three groups.[11] Many older children, particularly sons, lived with them. Three women were widowed and one had married again. Most married women were living in nuclear families, although some had lived in patrilocal joint families in their village of origin. Two women had a brother-in-law staying with them, one local woman lived in an extended family (separate rooms for each nuclear family within the same compound), and two women's husbands were living and working in another town. One woman had recently separated from her alcoholic/paedophilic husband with support from a women's organisation and was living with her mother.

Seven women did not live out, nor were they live-in workers. They lived with their families in rented outhouses in the backyards of middle-class properties. While they worked in the main house, their husbands worked elsewhere.[12] Three of these women also worked for other service-users, and some landlords also employed other live-in or live-out workers. I have included these women, as their cumulative experiences sit between those of the live-in and live-out workers, and I have used the term 'part-live-out' to describe their living arrangement vis-à-vis the service-user. Similar arrangements have been reported in other Indian research (Neetha, 2009; Raghuram, 1999; Ray and Qayum, 2009/2010). Since paid domestic work in India is largely carried out within the informal economy, all the women in my sample were informal workers. Seven respondents were currently main breadwinners.

The academics' current service-providers were also said to be approximately 23–60 years old, and mostly from rural north-western India and Nepal. The majority were in their forties and fifties, hence, on average, slightly older than the women I interviewed. Although the academics often outsourced housework to more than one service-provider, and a few had part-live-out workers, cleaning in the main was more commonly outsourced to a live-out worker. Other characteristics, such as age at marriage, number of children and husband's work status were similar to my sample of service-providers. The main difference was that five academics had male domestic helpers, who did all or part of the cleaning work (see also Raghuram, 2001). Furthermore, the profiles of the Indian respondents were largely similar to those of participants in other Indian studies, including that they were mostly married women doing this work 'for their children' (Archarya and Reddy, 2017; Mattila, 2011; Neetha, 2004, 2009; Neetha and Palriwala, 2011; Ray and Qayum, 2009/2010; Sen and Sengupta, 2016; A.N. Singh, 2001; V. Singh, 2007). This is because three-quarters of the contemporary Indian working population is deemed poor and vulnerable. These workers live just above the official poverty line, overwhelmingly belong to the historically marginalised and disadvantaged castes/tribes or are Muslims, are often illiterate or only educated to primary level, often suffer from malnutrition and have seen 'very little expansion of their employment and enhancement in their earning capacity', with no or few job, income or social securities and benefits at their disposal (NCEUS, 2009:iii–iv).

As regards migration history, rural development projects – a marriage between persisting traditional, oppressive feudalistic practices and 'development', the public and private corporatisation of land, in which rivers and other natural resources are implicated in the 'dowry' – have led to the loss of local sources of work for many people, who now form the vast underclass of poor and vulnerable in-country 'footloose' migrants in urban areas (Bremen, 2013; Neetha, 2004; Ray and Qayum, 2009/2010). Thus, in contrast to the transnational patterns of female migration that lie at the centre of the controversies surrounding contemporary paid domestic work in the West, Indian in-country migration often involves whole families. Single women also migrate, such as one service-user's live-in worker. Once in the city and eager to provide their children with a good education, the women either started working immediately or remained housewives until the strain of living on a single low wage or no wage became too much (see also Bharati and Tandon Mehrotra, 2008; Raghuram, 1999; Ray and Qayum, 2009/2010; Sen and Sengupta, 2016).

The UK service-users

One of the 21 UK service-users (age range 37–66 years) identified as European, three as White Australian or White American and the rest as White British (Appendix A, Table A.3). Their professional status ranged from lecturer to emerita status. Three were not working full-time (0.8 or 0.6 FTE[13]). Two adult children were living with their parent(s). Some older academics (over 50 years) had been outsourcing cleaning for nearly three decades. The younger respondents (under 50 years) had been outsourcing for 1–10 years. Five academics had stopped outsourcing 2–7 years ago. A few had recently changed service-providers for various reasons.

Owing to scant demographic details in previous studies, I could not comprehensively compare my sample with other UK research. Gregson and Lowe (1994b, 1995) purposively sampled middle-class (White) British dual-career households with women in professional/managerial occupations. A quarter of my sample had other living arrangements (two lone-women and two single-mother households). Five couple households had no dependent children; and in five couples, one partner travelled a significant distance for work or lived separately for part of the week. Hence, my sample is more in line with the wider picture of contemporary British family units (ONS, 2013). All of Gregson and Lowe's respondents seemingly employed White British cleaners, and in this sense my sample (by chance) largely matched theirs. Anderson (2000) did not provide demographic details of UK employers. Twelve of Cox's (1997, 2000, 2006) sample of 13 Hampstead employers were White British, but many were not doing paid work.

The UK service-providers also reported that their clients were mostly White and with heterogeneous living arrangements, including dual-career nuclear heterosexual families, single-adult households, single-earner couples, retired adults (living alone or in a couple) and stay-at-home-mothers (SAHMs). The occupations of economically active clients ranged from small, independent hairdressing units to medicine. Thus, the described service-user profiles appeared to fit with the employer profile in Jones' (2004) UK survey-based report (see Table 1.1) as well as the profile of outsourcing couple households[14] in waves 2 and 4 of Understanding Society (Figure 2.5), among which the majority of economically inactive people were aged 70 and older. The Mumsnet (2012a, 2014a,f) and Netmums (2012) cleaning discussants[15] included part-time workers and SAHMs. Some of these might be 'ladies who lunch', the most significant group of service-users in Cox's (2006) Hampstead sample,[16] whereas others mentioned making decisions about spending money on outsourced cleaning instead of, for example, takeaways.

The patchy available demographic information about households outsourcing cleaning in other Western contexts also indicates a wide range of household types and socioeconomic status:

Figure 2.5: Occupational category of Understanding Society respondents living in a couple and outsourcing cleaning

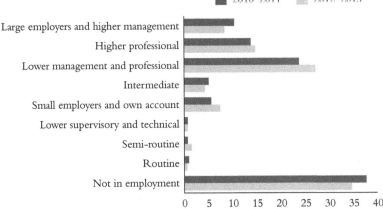

Data source: University of Essex. Institute for Social and Economic Research, NatCen Social Research. (2015). Understanding Society: Waves 1-5, 2009-2014 [data collection]. 7th edn. UK Data Service. SN: 6614, http://dx.doi.org/10.5255/UKDA-SN-6614-7.

- Cornelisse-Vermaat et al (2013): 32% single-adult and 10% single-parent Dutch households outsourced cleaning, compared with 30% of heterosexual couples (see also Aalto and Varjonen, 2007, for Finland);
- Spitze (1999): households with single-adult and same-sex middle-aged and older people in the New York metropolitan area were more likely to outsource routine and occasional domestic work;
- Zick et al (1996): less-affluent Utahan single mothers working more hours were twice as likely to purchase housekeeping services than two-parent households with similar levels of education;
- Tijdens et al (2003): in the Netherlands, almost 25% of Dutch women who were outsourcing were single and 60% had no children at home (see also Barstad (2014) for Norway; and Lutz (2011:34) for Germany);
- de Ruijter and van der Lippe (2007): 39% of dual-earner and 29% of 1.5 dual-earner Dutch couples outsourced domestic work; that is, part-time working women also outsource domestic work.

The Indian service-users

The 19 Indian academics[17] were aged 34–63 years (Appendix A, Table A.4), which closely matched the age range of the UK sample. Two were currently not outsourcing cleaning. All the women queried my use of the term 'ethnicity' in the questionnaire. Thus, one third did not answer the question and the rest identified as Indian nationals or by their regional/religious identity. Similar to the UK sample, their living arrangements varied considerably, reflecting current Indian living arrangements; that is, a mix of traditional, regionally determined kinship-based household types (Uberoi, 1993/2011) as well as the modern Western-type dual-career family-type. Many nuclear families had been (partial[18]) joint families in the past.

All the women had full-time work contracts; one was a lecturer and the rest were professors of varying seniority. Two women had been SAHMs for several years. At the time of the interview, the current service-providers had worked for the academics for about three months to 20 years. All the women, including the two currently not outsourcing, had either started outsourcing domestic work as soon as they had set up an independent household or had helped in the management of the service-providers already employed by their parents or the joint family. Four homes were cleaned by live-in domestic workers. The remaining households had live-out service-providers. Some women changed providers more frequently than the rest, and others had had the same service-provider for a long time.

Owing to purposive sampling, my sample is not similar in one regard to other published samples, that is, the kinds of household that outsource cleaning. However, the Indian service-providers' customer profiles included many single-earner households besides joint, single-adult and dual-earner households, which is in line with previous research showing that household composition in India and several other countries has little bearing on the outsourcing of domestic work.[19] As in the UK sample, socioeconomic circumstances of the Indian respondents also varied. The relationship between affluence and outsourcing is analysed in greater detail in the next chapter.

Conclusion

The demographic analysis in this chapter corresponds with the notion that socioeconomic inequalities mediate the racial/caste inequalities in domestic work (Dickey, 2000b; Milkman et al, 1998). This mediation, however, is complicated, occurring in the intersections between the various axes of inequality, and this point is further explored in Chapter 3.

3

Nuances in the Politics of Demand for Outsourced Housecleaning

....

I met Doreen, a single, middle-aged White British healthcare worker from a working-class background, on my way to interview a service-provider. We talked about my research, and I asked her what she thought about outsourcing cleaning, expecting her to say she had never done it. Instead, she looked at me thoughtfully and said she was not a great cleaner. Some years ago, at her sister's suggestion, she had outsourced cleaning, first to a friend and then to a migrant service-provider. When the service-provider left due to a family emergency, Doreen found out she had been an undocumented worker. This made Doreen reluctant to outsource again. Around this time, her sister became terminally ill. Her sister's husband was working long hours to keep the household going, so they outsourced their housecleaning. When Doreen's sister died, he continued outsourcing cleaning as he juggled childcare with a full-time job. Doreen's elderly parents were helping, but Doreen's mother's eyesight was deteriorating and their own house was showing signs of neglect. Doreen's parents were proud of their working-class roots and, therefore, she said they would not think of outsourcing cleaning. Based on her own experience, Doreen could clearly see a need for it; however, she did not dare to suggest it to her parents.

....

Introduction

A few years ago, Bowman and Cole noted that it was time for researchers to move on from 'being less concerned with the class status and alleged needs of customers' to how its commodification was being structured (2014:199). However, as Doreen's story illustrates, demand or need for outsourcing is not circumscribed to a homogeneous, ahistorical social group. Demand might also shape work conditions, and, hence, requires continual evaluation of how and why people outsource. This chapter presents new perspectives on prevailing understandings of outsourced housecleaning, which then feed into the discussion of the conditions of work in subsequent chapters.

My analysis draws on Ray and Qayum (2009/2010) and Pollert's (1996) theoretical frameworks, both of which slot in with Douglas's (1986/1987) cross-cultural argument that the way people think is constrained by socially created and 'naturalised' institutionalised thinking styles. Ray and Qayum located the labour relations of paid domestic work in Kolkata, India, in the interstices between feudalistic and capitalist work structures. They showed how 'cultures of servitude' in the modern domestic sphere are normalised through 'structures of feeling' – the ways in which present everyday social meanings and values are produced, felt, lived and shaped by past imaginaries (Williams, 1977, 1979, cited in Ray and Qayum, 2009/2010:5). This framework explains why Mattila (2011) took time to understand Jaipuri employers' insouciant attitudes towards employee exploitation when applying a Marxist feminist lens, and it is also applicable to the Western context. 'Structures of feeling' and 'cultures of servitude' were evident in the value systems that hampered the efforts of American live-out ethnic minority workers to modernise the work structure according to capitalist principles (Glenn, 1981; Romero, 2002). As regards gender inequities in paid domestic work, Pollert's historical materialist analysis situates the 'process of gendering *inside* class relations', that is, individual agency manifests as 'compliance, consent or resistance' as it wrestles with institutionalised social processes that are simultaneously classed and gendered (Pollert, 1996:640, 648, original emphasis).

In the West, much quantitative research underpins the mapping of the modern demand for outsourced housecleaning, and I refer to this literature where appropriate. Survey questions, however, may be presumptuous and ambiguous. The UK's Understanding Society (University of Essex, 2015) and the Australian Negotiating the Life Course: Gender, Mobility and Career Trajectories survey (Baxter et al, 2009) ask questions about housework only to couples, erasing experiences of people such as Doreen. The answer choice 'paid worker only' in Understanding Society overlooks that householders outsourcing housework might still be doing some of that work themselves. Also, in the modelling of associations between outsourcing and utilitarian variables – such as resources, time availability and work-hours – the real-life impact of statistically significant but numerically small differences has to be interpreted with caution.

I will now unpack the nuances in contemporary demand for outsourcing housecleaning across two cultural contexts.

Outsourcing housework – affluent symbolism, need or choice

Physical disabilities (Baxter et al, 2009; Spitze, 1999) and learning disabilities might make housecleaning challenging. Pauline outsourced cleaning after a six-year gap, when she hurt her back and could not vacuum. *Zoe* explained:

> 'We do ... some with special needs. Because of that, he doesn't actually work, but he needs a cleaner as he doesn't know how to do it himself. So it's more like a necessity for him.' (*Zoe*)

Doreen's mother's situation highlights the ageing-related decrease in physical ability to do housework. Libby's grandmother had come a 'full circle' – she had done domestic service in her youth and was now outsourcing cleaning. These examples form part of the phenomenon of elderly Westerners' increasing need for paid domestic help (Devetter, 2016) or the 'proletarisation of paid domestic work' (Triandafyllidou and Marchetti, 2015; see Chapter 1) resulting from the 'care-deficit' associated with women's move into paid work, altered household compositions and reductions in socialised welfare provision (Bittman et al, 1999; Hyland, 2017; Lutz, 2008; Triandafyllidou, 2013).

A few of my respondents, who had grown up in the 1950s and 1960s in 'average' middle-class households, said outsourced cleaning had been part of that social demographic:

> 'I didn't grow up in a rich or even well-off household, no, money was tight when I was growing up. But the cleaning lady was just seen as part of, you know, necessity if you like ... I mean obviously if things got very tight, my mum would've cleaned the house herself ...' (Maisie, a freelancer in publishing)

In Kordasiewicz's (2015) Polish study of 37 middle-class employers, of whom only seven were born before 1950, 22 had a family history of employing domestic workers. This indicates that housecleaning was being outsourced in communist/socialist Poland. British historical analyses also show that demand was never circumscribed to particular time periods (see Chapter 1).

Janet's husband paid their cleaning agency because they were replacing his missing labour. Most of the other partnered UK respondents said it was a joint expense. But all respondents said it was affordable, even though incomes varied widely from a single person working part-time to a full-time dual-career household.[1] Many internet posts expressed disbelief that 'ordinary' people could outsource cleaning. Having a cleaner meant being rich, living in 'big' houses (Netmums, 2012); otherwise, "don't see how can a cleaner can be justifiably afforded" (Mumsnet, 2014f).

> 'Who hoovers every day? ... I have a cleaner for an hour a week, she hoovers the entire house and cleans the bathroom. It makes my life so much easier I say balls to what anyone else thinks, I must admit my family were very much like your DH's [dear husband's] when they found out I had a cleaner, a bit of who does she think she is.' (Mumsnet, 2012a)

In Maine, US, when undercover journalist-cleaner Ehrenreich observed that although not all client households appeared affluent, the team leader asserted, 'If we're cleaning their house, they're wealthy' (2002/2010:95). Renee had felt guilty, partly because "there's also the thought that they probably themselves couldn't afford to use a cleaner". But *Jessica* was matter-of-fact when talking about her own outsourcing experience several years ago, when she had been a full-time (low-paid) customer services adviser. *Yvonne*, whose cleaning business had rapidly expanded, was outsourcing her cleaning to a friend, while she cleaned for her customers. Latina service-providers in Los Angeles outsource gardening, housework and childcare to other Latinos (Hondagneu-Sotelo, 2001).

Some service-users dipped in and out of outsourcing, depending on their needs at different life-stages. Harriet, whose childhood had included 'the daily', had outsourced housecleaning when her life had been "work-based". But lately she had reduced her work-hours for a "home-based" life, which included finding pleasure in looking after her house (also Mumsnet, 2012a, 2014a,f; Netmums, 2012; for the Italian context, see Colombo, 2007:221). Naomi had outsourced at three different life-stages, when she had "recognised particular needs ... there were points when I realised that if the house didn't look reasonable when I came home ... it added to my stress levels. So I think the first cleaner I had was in the period after I had my first child...." The frequency of regular outsourcing also varies, as *Zoe* explained again:

'I would say it's probably about 40% are weekly and the rest are what I call fortnightlies, and we do the odd monthly as well. The monthlies tend to be people on a budget who can't afford it every week.' (*Zoe*)

Devetter (2016) distinguished between 'genuine need' of elderly people such as Libby's grandmother and 'need-as-luxury' of time-poor, dual-earner, middle-class households. But *Sophie*, who preferred to work for people 'needing' her services as opposed to those 'wanting' a cleaner, included the latter households in her definition of 'need'. She interpreted 'need-as-luxury' as customers who lounged around while she worked:

Sophie:	I perhaps like somebody who needs you more than wants you … Somebody that needs a cleaner rather than just fancies one because it's a trend! … that's my ideal person that perhaps … couldn't do it themselves …
Lotika:	So when you say they couldn't do it themselves, now that means disability, but what about someone who can't do it because they're busy …
Sophie:	… that probably falls into that same bracket, because they just can't do it because they don't have the time rather than − in the past I've seen people just sitting on the computer shopping while you are [cleaning], you know, those type of people could do it themselves really.

Some service-users themselves talked of outsourced housecleaning as a 'luxury' in the sense of a 'treat', such as meals out, massages, handbags, alcohol, clubbing:

'I kind of wonder … when people go, you know, cause many of my friends at home don't have a cleaner, … cause they haven't got professional, professional jobs, and are like "Ooh you know" − the way I say it, I explain it is it's my luxury … lots of people drink more alcohol than I do, or they buy designer clothes which I don't do, and to me having my cleaner … she is my luxury, I really see her as my luxury, cause … she's a real part of my emotional net, support networks. And just knowing that she comes and, you know, does this amazing job …' (Libby)

Part-time academic Libby was a single mother with young children, who also drew on her family for childcare support.

Choosing the answer 'cannot afford it' in surveys may have deeper meanings (Windebank, 2010). Classed and gendered cultural connotations about women's domestic competence and the legitimacy of commodification, or actually liking cleaning (Baxter et al, 2009; de Ruijter et al, 2003; Jones, 2004; Metcalfe, 2013; Tijdens et al, 2003; van der Lippe et al, 2013; Windebank, 2010), may confound the positive correlation between outsourcing and resources reported elsewhere. Some non-users have said they would outsource if they had enough resources (Mumsnet, 2013a; also Jones, 2004; Milkman et al, 1998; Nelson, 2004).

In India, all my respondents said outsourcing was affordable and outsourced several tasks (for example all cleaning tasks, washing up, handwashing of clothes, ironing, some cooking tasks). Outsourcing also happens as part of a colonial form of status reproduction that is not directly linked to affluence.[2] Public service/state officials are assigned salaried domestics, gardeners and chauffeurs as perks of the job (indiatoday.in, 2014):

> '[the workers] are given officially to us by my [late] father's office ... so ... they get a salary from the sarkar [government] ... you'll have to understand that [some higher officials are] in some ways very spoilt ... because what probably happens is [that] even after they retire they get ... commissions and some re-employment ... so then they have people anyway. I guess they sat together and decided that even after that, [since] you are used to them, might as well [continue] ...' (Ritika)

In sum, the relationship between affluence, symbolism and outsourced cleaning is not straightforward. In South Africa, du Preez et al (2010) proposed that a 'richer/poorer–poorest' matrix more adequately represents the user–provider economic relationship. This matrix is also applicable in India. In the UK, a 'richer/poorer–poorer' matrix is evident, because several factors are implicated in people's decisions regarding outsourcing.

Middle-class heterosexual couples may also outsource housecleaning to avoid confrontations around it.

Outsourcing housecleaning and gender and class inequities

> 'We had a cleaner for years, then had to stop as we were skint, then have just managed to get her in again. We call her "The

Sainted Mary". We LOVE LOVE her. She has saved my sanity and my marriage. … We don't go out very often, and it is the best money I spend each month.' (Mumsnet, 2014a)

Cleaner-as-marriage-saviour is often used as a selling point (for example Alisa, 2008; Ehrenreich, 2002/2010; Marriage Savers Calgary Cleaning Services, 2016; Sherman, 2000; Two Maids and a Mop, 2006). This presentation may appeal to an 'egalitarian' dual-career couple wrestling with: boundaryless work patterns that do not facilitate domestic behaviour changes in middle-class men (Collins, 2007; Cox, 2006; Lyonette and Crompton, 2015; Usdansky, 2011); and cultural norms that still define household management as 'women's' work, in part by characterising men as domestically incompetent (Walters and Whitehouse, 2012). However, as I show here, there are gaps in both the potential bliss for, and the concern around re-entrenchment of gender/race/class inequalities by, such 'egalitarian' households (Anderson, 2000; Chin, 1998; Constable, 2007; Crompton, 2006:198; Devetter, 2016; Ehrenreich and Hochschild, 2003; Gregson and Lowe, 1994a).

Two thirds (n = 11/16) of the partnered UK respondents reflected wider Western trends in their domestic practices – women still do more of the routine housework (Crompton and Lyonette, 2008, 2011; Gatrell, 2004, 2008; Lachance-Grzela and Bouchard, 2010; Lyonette and Crompton, 2015; Treas and Drobnic, 2010). For five women (four were over 50 years), the feminist self walked one step behind on the way home. They accepted their male partners as 'men of their times', took primary responsibility for housework, and outsourced cleaning when they needed help:

'I think it's very difficult to apportion that up equally down the middle … one or the other of you has to be the prime carer. … I do think it's difficult for men and women to share equally the decision-making, the responsibility … I'm not saying that shouldn't happen, … but I think in practice it rarely does … if I see a problem, I look to how it can be solved rather than worrying about, you know, whose problem it is. … I felt that my husband was not more concerned about his career than his children, but that he saw the ability to provide for his family as being brilliant at work. … it's never been a case of that I've felt that I've had the bulk of everything to do because he's lazy and can't be bothered to work.' (Gayle)

The other five women, of whom four were under 50 years, aspired to the ideology of domestic equality, but had not been able to achieve it:

'[B]ut I said the difficulty for me ... is that if I'm going to be doing the cleaning, that's not very feminist either [because] there's not a shared distribution of labour between us. So ... we got a cleaner when we didn't have any children and part of the reason is to take that out of the relationship ... Cause it became an issue, became a kind of resentment and a contentious – why am I doing all this? And you're not doing this, that helped to solve that problem ... If this is going to facilitate a happier marriage, relationship and household then it does seem to be money well spent.' (Beverley)

Are these two examples essentially the same – men's avoidance of housework because of gender privilege? Further analysis precluded a straightforward 'yes' response. Beverley, who admitted to a preoccupation with dirt, had outsourced cleaning to level her relationship. Yet the distribution of household labour remained gendered (Figure 3.1), and when Beverley's husband did housework, he did not do it when and how Beverley wanted it to be done:

'And that's the main thing between us is that he will do things, but it's not in the timeframe, and that's the discussion we always have ... like last night he did all the cleaning up and putting on the dishwasher. He will do things but ... not necessarily to the standard that I have or in the time that I want to do it.' (Beverley)

Beverley said her service-provider did not clean as well as herself, but that was not a problem. It helped Beverley keep her obsession under control. Beverley's willingness to accept lower cleaning standards in a woman but not accept apparent differences between herself and her husband was also a theme in some other households.

Clare and Felicity had been "slovenly" as singletons. Their standards of cleanliness rose in coupledom and were then assumed to be the 'right' standards:

'I was slutty with my house ... I was just like ... "can't be bothered with my precious life to waste it cleaning", that is not that I didn't clean ... I've always kept my kitchen clean, kept my bath, but really in terms of general cleaning, absolutely, like when the floor's about to crawl away ...' (Clare)

Figure 3.1: Division/sharing of household labour (Beverley)

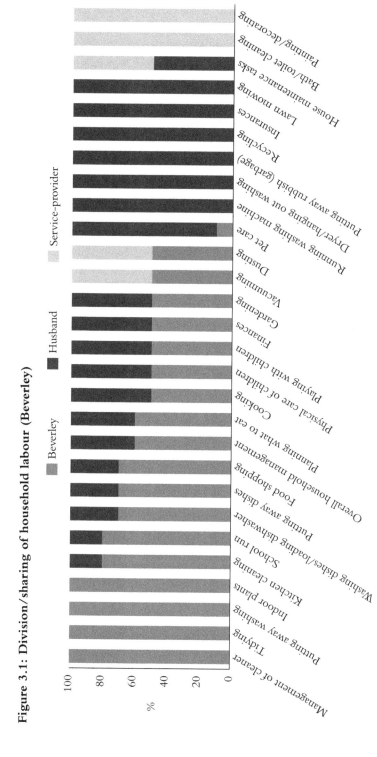

Notes: The bars represent the proportion of time, as reported at the time of data collection by Beverley, that each task was done by Beverley or her husband or a service-provider. In this household, ironing was not done and children were too young to require help with homework.

Conversely, singletons or women released from a heterosexual contract might do less housework (Birch et al, 2009; Craig et al, 2016; de Ruijter et al, 2005) and accept lower housework standards, with reduced import of the physical state of their house for their self-esteem (Nelson, 2004). Felicity's partner still looked after a house that he owned, but in their shared home, she appeared to do more of the work. In the six series of the reality television programme *Obsessive Compulsive Cleaners* (Channel 4, 2016) broadcast before the time of writing, a third of the helpers were men and over half of the people needing help were women. It appears that societal norms around domesticity influence self-reflexivity differently in different household contexts. Rather than 'men can't see dirt', perhaps partnered women are more likely to look for it and partnered men more likely 'don't expect' to see it.

Cooking was not outsourced by any UK service-user, and very few outsourced dishwashing/dishwasher loading or unloading, laundry and ironing. Rubbish disposal, gardening and house maintenance tasks were outsourced more often. In India, some cooking tasks are commonly outsourced by middle-class households (such as chopping vegetables and making dough and chappatis), as are laundry, ironing, gardening and house maintenance tasks. Still, two thirds (n = 7/10) of the partnered Indian academics did more of the non-outsourced housework. Shobha and Ritu's parents-in-law shared some responsibilities. But these service-users mostly expressed little angst around the inequity. As Taruni explained, however much you want your career, "whatever class you may be, you don't want to disturb your family life. You don't want to pay that cost." Lata said:

> '... what I appreciate about his participation is that he's not averse to the idea of helping me out. His perception towards the work is not negative, that he is a male member of the household, that he should not be doing the household work. So given a chance, I mean the right opportunity, he is always ready to help out – not that he actually does it.' (Lata)

Taruni and Lata exemplify the 'new Indian woman', a dual subject attempting to attain individualistic selfhood through a career, while simultaneously participating in traditional middle-class domesticity (Belliappa, 2013; Radhakrishnan, 2009; Shah, 2015; Valk and Srinivasan, 2011). Navita, a singleton who had lived with and cared for her elderly parents, said people constantly assume "you can devote time to these things because you ... don't have a home to run, you don't have a husband and children to look after, and I say I'm not free ... I do more work than anybody else." Kishwar (1991/2005:31) argues that such familial connectedness is a distinguisher of Indian and Western women's emancipation/feminism(s). But when class is taken into account, the East–West kinship-bound versus individualism dichotomy becomes weak. Western working-class women continue to nurture strong kinship and community ties (Metcalfe, 2013).

Moreover, the "right opportunity" for sharing housework, which Lata referred to in the previous quotation, usually arose in the kitchen rather than around cleaning. Shobha explained:

> '[M]y husband, or my father-in-law … they choose to go into the kitchen, that is a question of choice. Similarly with me if I … go into the kitchen it should be a question of choice, that is why I say I sulk when I have to cook. … So when it comes to equality, like when *Asha's* gone home … I make my own breakfast, my husband makes his own breakfast, so it's not that because *Asha's* not there, I'm expected to do the cooking …' (Shobha)

Indian middle-class (and higher-caste) status is still overtly produced by distancing oneself from (polluting) manual work. As Usha, a single businesswoman I met early in my research, commented, men "may not be cleaning, but that's something even you wouldn't do". The rituals of purity implicated in cooking, however, elevate its status (Goyan and Sucher, 2008; Ilaiah, 1995/2004, 2005/2017; Ray and Qayum, 2009/2010; also Verma and Larson, 2001:55). The following extract captures the segmented Indian middle-class/higher-caste domestic socialisation, in which cooking is at the centre and cleaning is at the margins:

Lotika:	Do you think you could have managed without domestic help?
Geetanjali:	I think I could have managed … because I'd been doing both the things. Because this help, it's, it's so unpredictable … as I told you that things are not all that organised here in India, you can have guests who would not like to enter the kitchen or share the burden with you, then it becomes difficult.
Lotika:	And when we talk of this, are we including sweeping and mopping in it? Or are you thinking more of …
Geetanjali:	No, I am thinking more of cooking. Cooking, washing – dusting also – but cleaning I have not thought about so far, no. It's not my domain … if I

> have to do it, probably, ... I don't know how will I
> do it!

Such 'traditional' cultural ideologies could also underpin contemporary 'secular' constructions of middle-classness in the UK (Anderson, 2000; Skeggs, 1997/2002, 2004). Imogen, who had the most shared arrangement of housework, outsourced cleaning because she disliked doing it (even though she had worked as a cleaner in her student days). She did not discuss her decision to outsource with her husband. That is, when she was in a position not to do it, she did not expect her husband to do it either.

Some UK service-users did not see cleaning as 'proper' work. Indeed, disassociation with manual labour is also one of the distinguishing characteristics of British and American 'middle-classness' that developed around Victorian times (Davidoff, 1995; Gunn and Bell, 2002; Hondagneu-Sotelo, 2001). Edwardian middle/upper-class feminists, alongside the men in their social circles, also often considered this work beneath them (Schwartz, 2015). Even later, in Friedan's *The Feminist Mystique*, men did not figure in the 'the problem with no name', with Friedan (1963) advising her compatriots to hire domestic help (see also Rollins, 1985). Friedan's view was subsequently rightly criticised as a narrow, liberal middle-class feminist perspective, and Rollins' account may be dated. However, both remain applicable to some Western middle/upper-class women, such as those in Cox's Hampstead sample, who 'explained that they had always employed help because they had never seen housework as their responsibility' (Cox, 2006:91). Australian women who think that housework does not have to be done by oneself are more likely to outsource than those who believe it is personal work (Baxter et al, 2009). Clearly, a classed view of different household tasks is implicated in the reluctance noted by researchers in middle-class women to address domestic gender politics (for example Walters and Whitehouse, 2012). If a woman does not see a task as her role, she is not going to expect a male partner to do it, regardless of cultural context.[3]

Dividing housecleaning into its sub-tasks reveals more nuances in domestic gender inequities. In the UK, outsourcing hoovering, cleaning of work surfaces, dusting and bathroom/toilet cleaning for four hours at a fixed time every week did not liberate Beverley from cleaning. She still did most of the tidying (see Figure 3.1).[4] Both in the UK and in India, this most frequent (Figure 3.2) and not-outsourced sub-task is more often done by women (Figure 3.3). Ironically, the UK cleaning service-providers said hoovering and dusting was just another job, but 'picking up' after people was demeaning (see also Ehrenreich, 2002/2010; Romero, 2002):

'Well I think … because now people …, they treat you better but they shouldn't expect you to pick stuff … I don't mind, I'll do it … I don't care if it's littered, I'll pick it all up and put it away before I start, no problem, but I don't think people should expect you to do that, because that's like years ago when people were like your servant and they treated people like skivvies … And you had to pick up everything for these people and that's how they treated you, not with respect. Cause if you have respect for someone you don't expect them to come into your house and pick up things that you shouldn't have to do.' (*Davina*)

Also, much other housework was still happening in the time between a cleaning service-provider's visits:

'[W]ell, he's reached professor and I haven't. Just because he can do things differently … he can say no in ways women can't in academia, and I think it's read differently as well … and because he doesn't have the domestic baggage behind him, he doesn't have to think about dinner … [which] gives him an extra hour a day. He doesn't have to think on a weekend about putting his clothes … in the washing machine so he gets extra time there.' (Janet)

These data suggest that outsourcing cleaning need not stall the gender revolution. Men – and children – can share tidying and other cleaning, when the provider does not come, as well as a host of other tasks as described by Janet.

The dishwasher remained a site of tension for Beverley, as her husband did not deal with it when she wanted it done. Orla's 20-year marriage failed despite outsourcing cleaning because, among other issues, her husband felt threatened by her professional success. She was left regretting acceding to his wish to remain childless. Felicity's previous 'egalitarian' relationship ended despite militant efforts to share the housework. She was happier in her present relationship with its fuzzier boundaries around 'who did what' in the house. In India, Seema, who was separated, Rekha, who was divorced, and Meenakshi, who lived apart from her husband for most of the time, also talked about negotiating problematic relationships and behaviours.

In the wider world, in both research sites, celebrity relationship breakdowns provide steady fodder for the media (for example the anguish of the UK television cook Nigella Lawson over the abusive state of her

Figure 3.2: Frequency of each cleaning sub-task in the service-user households

(a) UK service-users

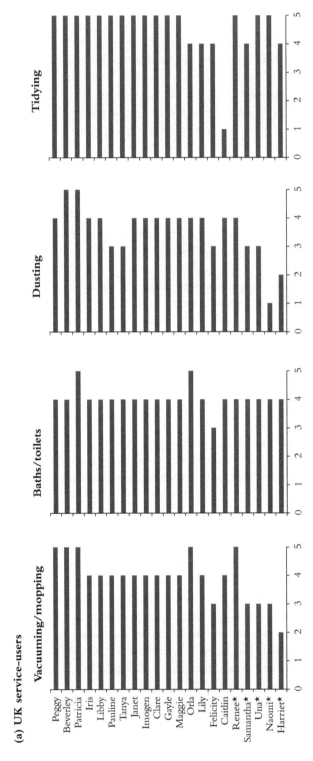

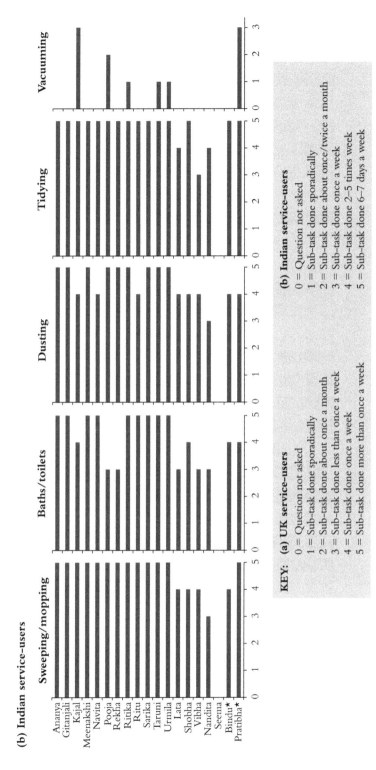

(b) Indian service-users

KEY:

(a) UK service-users
0 = Question not asked
1 = Sub-task done sporadically
2 = Sub-task done about once a month
3 = Sub-task done less than once a week
4 = Sub-task done once a week
5 = Sub-task done more than once a week

(b) Indian service-users
0 = Question not asked
1 = Sub-task done sporadically
2 = Sub-task done about once/twice a month
3 = Sub-task done once a week
4 = Sub-task done 2–5 times week
5 = Sub-task done 6–7 days a week

Notes: The bars represent the frequency of doing the sub-task; ★Not currently outsourcing cleaning.
The scale is not the same in the two parts of the figure, see key for details.

Figure 3.3: Division/sharing of tidying work in the service-user households

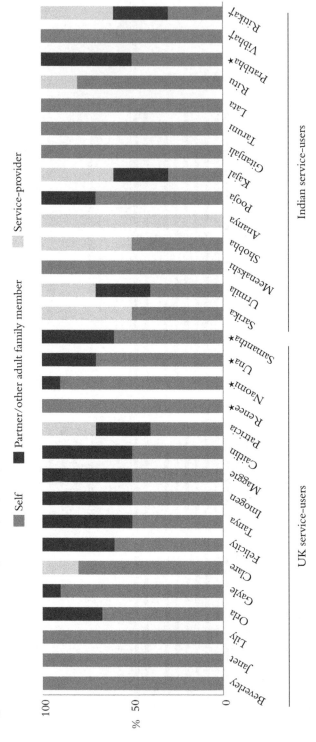

Notes: ★Currently not outsourcing; † Single, but living with a parent.
The bars represent the proportion of time, as reported at the time of data collection by the partnered service-users or those living with a parent, that tidying was done by the respondent or her partner or a service-provider.

marriage while drawing on paid domestic help (BBC News, 2013; Orr, 2013)). It appears that once housework is shared or outsourced, it may lose its significance for relationship quality (Barstad, 2014; Chan and Halpin, 2002; Cooke, 2004; Schober, 2013). In a UK survey asking 'Why do you employ household help', the answer choice 'it stopped arguments' had the lowest response rate (~25%; lack of time: ~75%; would rather do other things: ~80%; it is an affordable 'perk': ~70%; too tired to do it ~45%; a waste of time: ~50%; too big a job: ~30%) (Jones, 2004). In Gabb and Fink's (2015:124–125) study of enduring relationships, sharing housework did not feature per se in people's descriptions of what they liked most about their relationship – support more generally was appreciated.

Still, there are concerns around the gendered and classed inequities in career progression due to time saved by those who outsource domestic work:

> 'A lot of these professional people wouldn't be able to follow their career if it wasn't for the back-up. And the back-up is the cleaning. The cleaning lady, the lady who does. It enables them to carry on with their "good" lives.' (Angie, a cleaner from Lancashire, BBC Radio 4, 2012)

Some UK service-users said outsourcing of childcare was more critical than outsourcing of cleaning in this regard:

> 'many years ago I spoke to a … female professor … and I asked her how did you get to be professor [name], and she said she spent every penny you possibly can on good-quality childcare. And so that's basically what I did. And my spouse and I juggle around a lot as well. Yeah – and we paid. And I was very flexible around childcare, if I thought it wasn't working, then I'd change it. And so I put a lot of effort into paying for childcare that I didn't feel guilty about and the kids were happy to use. [Later] Absolutely, I couldn't have managed without that. In fact when I asked about going part-time, they said no. So even part-time I would have had to rely on childcare but full-time I really had to rely on childcare.' (Imogen)

In fact, the time 'saved' by cleaning could also be used for hands-on childcare, nurturing the relationships involved in this care, or management of elder care. Peggy spent many 'normal' work hours travelling long distances to sort out care-related problems of four elderly relatives.

Outsourcing cleaning could be more about managing many simultaneous demands on one's time:

> 'Sometimes it's not like balance, okay … here it is: it's not about balance, it's about the absolute quantity of stuff that needs to be done, sometimes just too much stuff needs to be done, it's not about too much time with your family, enough time with your family, it's just your family needs loads of attention at the same time … time as your work, it's the absolute amount of energy and number of hours in a day, you see!' (Tanya)

A few of my UK respondents worked part-time (see Chapter 2). Many of my respondents said they would continue outsourcing cleaning even after retirement. As discussed in Chapter 1, couples reporting high levels of sharing of housework may still outsource it for gaining leisure time (Gregson and Lowe, 1994a; Jones, 2004). Even the most family-friendly Scandinavian work model has failed to stem the 'resurgence' of paid domestic work (Bowman and Cole, 2009, 2014; Gavanas, 2010).

For the Indian service-users, outsourcing housework was more crucial for their ability to do paid work. Regarding childcare, only one academic used a crèche. The rest either did not work when the children were young, or drew on family support or domestic help in the house, often though with a family member also present in the house. Besides the persistent domestic gendered expectations, they also said it was the volume of housework and difficulties in dependence on appliances that made outsourcing more inevitable in India. In a geographically dusty region, daily cleaning of the whole house was essential (see also Mattila, 2011).[5] Although appliances (except dishwashers) abounded in my sample, only the washing machine appeared to be used reasonably regularly, but even then, it was rare to depend only on that. This is in part due to erratic electricity supply and timed fresh water supply, and the likelihood of colour bleeding:

> 'In Britain the story is different, everything is automated, everything is at your beck and call. It's not that I'm complaining against my own country, but the thing is, we don't know, the moment you launch your washing machine, we don't know whether the electricity supply is going to be there or not. So that means at times things are timed out, you're not available [when the electricity is there], that's how you need people. And we have plenty of people who are looking for this kind of work. So I don't know who's helping whom. It is embedded

within our system. And had things been different – given a choice, if I'd been staying in UK or in the States or Canada, I've seen my sister-in-law doing all sorts of things …' (Geetanjali)

Several Indian regions are no doubt dustier for geographical reasons and as a result of human interventions. The ritual of daily cleaning of the whole house requires deeper analysis, however, given Ritu's off-the-cuff observation that this was done "because our custom is to do it, even if we don't need it, we do it", and Geetanjali's comment that "[i]t is embedded in our system". Moreover, although mechanisation of housework reduced manual laboriousness of housework in the West, it did not translate into requiring less time, because of the simultaneous market-driven rise in standards of housework (Bose, 1979; Hardyment, 1988; Jackson, 1992). 'Individualised' kitchen cleaning routines are still rooted in wider institutionalised social norms (Martens, 2007/2012). Indeed, Sen and Sengupta (2016) note that the continued dependency on manual labour in India is because it remains cheap due to 'market forces', and the kind of outsourcing practised by my respondents is also practised by housewives (Mattila, 2011; Ray and Qayum, 2009/2010; Verma and Larson, 2001).[6] Clearly, 'structures of feeling' (Ray and Qayum, 2009/2010) around manual labour and cleaning rituals and standards underpin modern justifications.

The 'cultures of servitude', however, are not insurmountable. A few people are resisting societal norms, rethinking utilitarian needs and doing manual housework themselves. Bindu, a single woman, had outsourced cleaning because it was "the done thing". When her service-provider began absenting herself frequently without notice, Bindu realised she could manage on her own, regardless of what her neighbours thought (also one household in Ray and Qayum (2009/2010) and two in Belliappa (2013)). Of 100 middle-class households surveyed by Verma and Larson (2001), 20 had full-time and 62 had part-time domestic help. In several other households in my research, when domestic help was temporarily unavailable or their work was unsatisfactory, a few women (and in rare cases other family members) did the work themselves:

'[I]n the last two days [my maid] had to go, her brother is very sick, he's hospitalised, so I had to get up early. Today I got up at six. Then my husband and I, we cleaned the house. The cooking – that I have to manage at night, beforehand, … I'll cut and keep [the vegetables] in the fridge. So that it takes less time, because cleaning you know takes more time. We've got two dogs as I told you, and they make the house very messy …' (Taruni)

Shobha topped up bathroom cleaning because she thought her service-provider did not pay "enough attention" to these areas. Kajal and Lata's cleaning service-provider did not clean toilets. This is an important point, because toilet cleaning is often considered the most degrading housework based on purity–pollution dogmas (Frøystad, 2003:78; Ray and Qayum, 2009/2011; see also Chapter 4). As in the UK, in India the multiple demands on the women's time also appeared crucial in the persistence of the structures of feeling around outsourcing:

> '... and because teaching the children has come to me. I don't know ... how we made this arrangement, that ultimately [these roles] have fallen upon me ... For example, who's going to lock the house at night, which I think is men's work. That I do ... and now he says that "If I do it sometimes I will forget or sometimes you will think that I have done it and I will think that you have done it", so it's better you do it. So I keep on doing it ...' (Pratibha)

Did the time saved by outsourcing housework help with career progression, or the female service-user's overall liberation from gendered inequities? My respondents gave many examples of gendered workplace issues, such as:

> 'I can't say that I've done badly career-wise, in the sense that I'm a woman ... with a senior post in a good department. But on the other hand there is this thing of going to meetings and blokes are talking, bloke will speak to bloke and it is difficult to get a voice in.' (Maggie)

> 'I do think that there's something of that ... it's one of those slightly hard to describe, intangible things, not that anybody has consciously thought "Oh, she's a woman, we'll pay her less", but I have been less ... aggressive about my own right to increments, promotions and so on, than many male colleagues have been I think.' (Patricia)

> '[T]here was a convocation ... we were a few women who were senators and deans ... the chief guest comes ... all the men are standing there, the women are standing next [to them], [the vice-chancellor] introduces him to all the men and they pass us and they go for lunch. ... I got furious ...' (Taruni)

'Now if I, if I have to negotiate certain things, [I am limited if they] take place beyond formal domain. Because men can very easily, given the cultural, Indian cultural context, they can easily sit together, have drinks, and so projects are negotiated, favours agreed on, things happen that way: I call you, you call me, okay? But I cannot, you know, if I do that, I may be termed as very easily accessible, easy in terms of my character.' (Vibha)

Such issues are replicated and documented extensively cross-culturally and cross-occupationally.[7] Romero (2002) argued that a service-user's workplace exploitation cannot be compared to *her* exploitation, because she can transfer the burden of her sexist exploitation onto *her* but *she* has nowhere to escape. My analysis shows that the service-user's sexist exploitation in the workplace continues similarly to some men's situation: they may have wives to do their housework, but that does not alleviate the discriminations and obstacles to career progression that those men experience in the workplace. Claims of outsourced cleaning pitting the liberation of one class of women against that of another deflects attention from contesting the persisting exploitative features of domesticity, such as 'picking up after others', and risk naturalising housework as women's work and, consequently, reducing women's emancipation to freedom from housework.

Conclusion

Income may be a strong predictor of outsourcing. However, cleaning is outsourced by all kinds of households for a variety of reasons. Moreover, if middle/upper-class women (or men) do not consider some housework as their work, outsourcing it is going to make little difference to classed gender inequities, regardless of cultural context. My findings offer hope, by showing that outsourcing does not mean that householders are totally free from housework, particularly tidying. If all household members were to share at least this work, it would help to reduce gendered and classed inequities. In this, it is important to challenge stereotypes such as 'men can't see the dirt' and women's policing of housework standards and schedules.

Finally, Rivas (2003) argued that the work of paid care is concealed through spatial, linguistic or communication practices, because such work is provided within a framework of 'achieving independent living'. Dependency has to be obscured, as it threatens the hegemonic ideology of individualism. In the same way, reducing middle-class women's emancipation ('independence') to freedom from housework risks obscuring the interdependence that underpins social life. Rather, we need to highlight that 'independent' living requires several workers' input (electricity, water and internet suppliers, rubbish collectors, and so on). The 'housewife' is omnipresent – personified by different people at different times in different spaces. Adding the suffix 'in' to 'dependent' hides the dependence of (in)dependent people and creates a myth about the power of independence acquired through doing 'paid work' outside the home or through outsourcing housework. In the next chapter, I take up Bowman and Cole's (2014) point about considering challenging societal assumptions around service work itself.

The Imperfect Contours of Outsourced Domestic Cleaning as Dirty Work

....

One fine summer evening, when I was writing this chapter, a friend and I were walking by a farm. My friend held her breath to avoid the 'stink', while I thought the smell fitted in with the place and season. But, I see slime as dirt, whereas my husband sees it as just a bit of mucus. But, he sees my hair scattered on the bathroom floor as dirt, and I see it as just hair …

....

Introduction

While an instinctive revulsion to dirt related to a fear of infection or ill-health occurs throughout the animal kingdom, the human biological reaction is shaped by the social, in the form of 'experience and culture' (Curtis, 2007:660; Douglas, 1966/2002). Within that evolving social, 'menial' historically meant 'related to the household' more generally (Albin, 2012:234; Merriam-Webster[1]), but now it commonly connotes drudgery, making the performance of manual housework, particularly cleaning, a site of power. But once outsourced, these 'menial' jobs become 'dirty' work, by being infused with symbolic ideas of polluting matter and constructing those doing the work as people 'out of place', out of the democratic social 'order' (Cox, 2016; Douglas, 1966/2002). Disgust for dirt, then, is in part invoked by anxiety among the privileged of attrition of class boundaries (van Dongen, 2001). However, relying too much on higher-level explanations and theoretical conceptualisations of dirty work risks trivialising the material realities of working with real, physical dirt. Wolkowitz argues:

> What is needed is theory and research that acknowledge that as social phenomenon 'dirtiness' and 'cleanliness' are real social objects and do not exist only within discourse. In particular we need to consider 'dirt' from the point of view of those whose work involves dealing with it. (2007/2012:24)

At the same time, an epistemological assumption that everyone understands dirt and the associated disgust in a similar way needs to be avoided (van der Geest, 2002; also Longhurst, 2000:90). In a 2017 ethnographic study of street cleaning and refuse collection in the UK, the participant-researchers 'squeamishly' put on gloves before setting to work. The workers, however, often did not wear (the cumbersome) protective gear, as it slowed them down:

> While waste and debris frequently took viscerally repugnant forms, such matter was not always seen by workers as inherently 'dirty'. 'Dirtiness' was typically attributed to misplaced or unacceptable waste, as well as to the (orderly or disruptive) manner of its return. Refuse and waste that lay within the boundaries of what could be accepted as normal could be integrated into notions of an essential service and the necessities of work routines, and were rarely a source of disgust. (Hughes et al, 2017:113)

The researchers concluded that there was a material and symbolic 'co-constitution' of dirt. Yet, some material – excrement – surely elicits revulsion? Nurses' handling of patients and bodily waste products and their use of protective gear appears to be influenced by several factors: wider social notions of dirt and the Other; the level of organisational support; specific conventional Western scientific/medical understandings of germs. In the absence of obvious infection, practices might override scientific protocols, for instance faecal incontinence in a (white) child might not be considered dirty or disgusting (Jackson and Griffiths, 2014; van Dongen, 2001). van der Geest (2002) explained that his struggle to defecate in communal toilets during his ethnographic fieldwork in Ghana and to make sense of a Ghanaian night soil-collector's pride in his work was in part due to his internalised contemporary European notions of defecation as a secluded act. Moreover, if in urban areas excrement is dirt, as there is no use for it, in rural areas it is matter in place that enriches the soil in which we grow our food (Cox, 2007/2012b). Urine was used to wash linen in Europe until the industrial period (Cox, 2007/2012a), and urine therapy features in Asian medicinal traditions and in contemporary Western alternative medicine (Christy, 2005; Peschek-Bohmer and Schreiber, n.d.).

Despite the social, geographical and temporal-specific nature of meanings of dirt and dirty work, there are few published descriptions of the physical aspects of outsourced cleaning. This chapter explores how both the service-users and service-providers conceptualised the work of dealing with dirt in the setting of the contemporary urban house, through notions of how often cleaning should be done and how dealing with physical dirt was experienced.

How often should a house be cleaned?

Most UK academics said their house was less clean when they had not outsourced cleaning. For example:

> 'None of us would do the cleaning and then we'd sort of have a day when we would decide we would clean, and we would clean and then the things would get done and we'd go "Ooh, ooh okay!" …' (Tanya)

Also, some rooms were cleaned more often than others:

> 'The kitchen floor I clean every day, … sometimes twice a day, because … it gets really dirty. Even now if you see in the kitchen, you'll see that it's covered in muck. Cause it has dirty shoes, and food and cereal is always all over the floor, bread and so on. So I do that virtually every day. But I have a cleaner who comes once a week and vacuums the rest of the house.' (Peggy)

Pauline's experience of living in co-housing revealed that residents' attitudes to cleaning was an area of tension for the community:

> '[T]here was quite a wide range of views, and it wasn't gendered either, about the level of cleanliness people expected. There was one woman whom I remember said, "Well, I don't bother in my house, so why should I bother about common areas?" […] And then, one of the men was very, very clear that he expected cleaning to be done and done properly …' (Pauline)

The UK cleaning service-providers cleaned more often (Figure 4.1) than the service-users, possibly due to traditional classed ideologies linking respectability with cleanliness, such as polished doorknobs and whitened doorsteps (Hand, 1992; Nicholson, 2015). Still, I encountered variations – *Amelia's* living room had birdfeed strewn over the floor, while *Martha's* was 'squeaky' clean.

Generally, the amount of both unpaid and paid housework done was greater in India (see Figure 3.2), with service-users often arguing that this was because India was a more dusty country. But standards were not set in stone, even though they were often assumed to be: Shobha's service-provider did not work on Sundays, and if she did not come for two to three days at a time, the live-in worker cleaned, but:

> '… it is very rudimentary – sweeping will be done, but no vacuuming, no mopping … because we have a dog, and if he's brought in too much dirt, a particular room will be swept. But so, if I don't factor that in, then it's every day.' (Shobha)

Pratibha had relaxed standards since they had stopped outsourcing:

> '… and I do not actually like the work that they would do, they would do it in a very … and I have to train them again and again and they would go away … So everyday this kind of hassle was … and now I am very free and tension free, and I find that I can go home and do work at my leisure. If I'm busy … we are not very particular about cleanliness or that the sink should not be, the sink should always be clean, we are not very particular. We do it as it comes …' (Pratibha)

The Indian service-providers cleaned their own homes daily, but given that their living spaces were materially different from those of the other groups (see Chapter 2), a comparative analysis is precluded.

In sum, my respondents in both contexts did not ascribe to a universal, ahistorical standard of cleanliness. So, how much cleaning is *absolutely* necessary in contemporary urban life?

In the UK, housekeeping magazines exhorted early and mid-20th century housewives to ensure that homes were always-already orderly for husbands to feel welcomed in the evenings (Gatrell, 2008; Oakley, 1974/1977:228). This cannot be dismissed as women 'playing house'. Although whole-house cleaning is often not done daily, as Tanya said, "you don't want to be depressed when you walk in your front door, because the house is a disaster zone" (see also Hochschild, 2001).

Indeed, many service-users said that their spirits lifted on coming home to an already clean or orderly house on the day the service-provider had been (also Baby Center, 2013; Mumsnet, 2014a,n; Soukup, 2012). Being greeted by 'order' rather than 'disorder' made a difference, indicating that this is not a gendered ideology: whosoever goes 'out' to work would like a wife (also Metcalfe, 2013: 220–222):

> 'Why did we start [outsourcing cleaning]?! … it wasn't so much to create more time, but to create more pleasantness, because what tends to happen is that things just don't get done and umm, and so it was to make them get done, to make things less unpleasant.' (Una)

> '[H]aving a house that feels nice, that really does matter to me, otherwise I get miserable as well … And I think in terms of wellbeing, it really is making an enormous contribution and I mean that quite seriously, not in a kind of patronising, sort of, you know, "Oh your work does matter" [kind of way] I honestly believe, … more so than if I spent that money on an hour with a psychotherapist.' (Felicity)

Unsurprisingly, the UK service-providers often mentioned receiving appreciative thank-you notes or texts.

In India, only Seema, who spent much time travelling, voiced similar sentiments. This did not mean the others did not care. When housework is done daily to the same extent, as Navita said, the service-users were more likely to note what was not done, the matter 'out of place'. If a service-provider did not come, the service-user could experience the heart-sink noted in the UK. *Mohini's* account confirmed the silences in the Indian data. *She* wished that *her* service-user would appreciate what *she* had done, rather than focusing on what *she* had missed:

> 'I have noted that however pleased I am that I have done everything in a tip-top way, that this time ma'am will come back and say, "*Mohini*, you have done a great job". But ma'am will somehow point out some deficiency or the other. Then I get that feeling within me, "I've been working since morning and I'm tired, and now see, ma'am is speaking to me in this way." Yes this hurts a bit. If ma'am would appreciate at that time, how much work I have done it would make me a bit happier. This is how it should be.' (*Mohini*)

Figure 4.1: Frequency of each cleaning sub-task in the UK households

(a) UK service-users

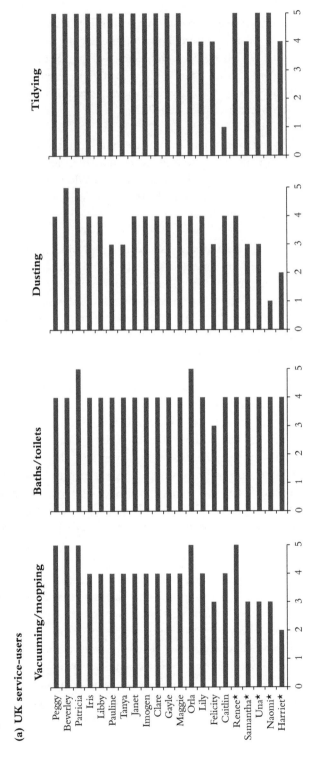

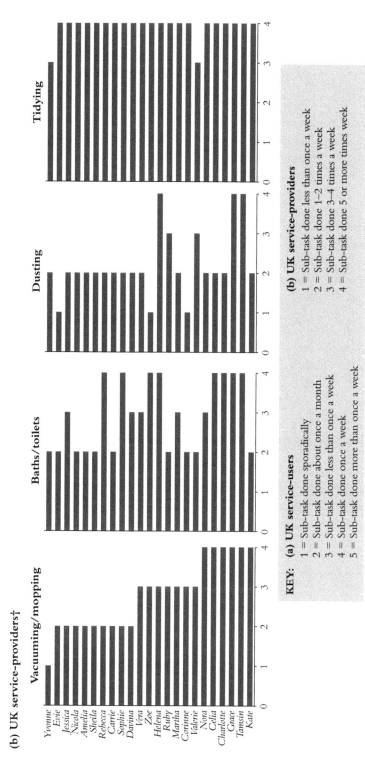

(b) UK service-providers†

Vacuuming/mopping   Baths/toilets   Dusting   Tidying

KEY:

(a) UK service-users

1 = Sub-task done sporadically
2 = Sub-task done about once a month
3 = Sub-task done less than once a week
4 = Sub-task done once a week
5 = Sub-task done more than once a week

(b) UK service-providers

1 = Sub-task done less than once a week
2 = Sub-task done 1–2 times a week
3 = Sub-task done 3–4 times a week
4 = Sub-task done 5 or more times week

Notes: The bars represent the frequency of doing the sub-task. †N = 23 (question not asked to remaining service-providers). *Not currently outsourcing cleaning; see key for details. The scale is not the same in the two parts of the figure.

The desire for order may be grounded in symbolic notions of status and respectability internalised in childhood (Douglas, 1966/2002:50; Elias, 1994/2003).[2] Quentin Crisp's flippant dismissal of housework because '[a]fter the first four years the dirt doesn't get any worse' is well known. Second-wave feminists, too, questioned both symbolic and secular (germ theory) arguments underpinning modern housecleaning practices (Ehrenreich and English, 1978/1988). Western research also suggests that standards of housework more broadly appear to have 'fallen' in contemporary times (Bianchi et al, 2000, 2012; Lader et al, 2006; Sullivan, 2006).

But such challenging of strict traditional Western norms in the 20th century and beyond is still a bounded challenge, because at a structural level, 'the more advanced feeling of what is offensive [had] been on the whole secured. It is relaxation within a framework of an already established standard' (Elias, 1994/2003:119). The success of British reality television programmes such as *Obsessive Compulsive Cleaners* (Channel 4, 2016) bears this out. So, while Western dual-earning couples might be doing less housework, they might despair at the state of their home when entering it after a long day at work (Hochschild, 2001); and Indian households continue to depend on domestic workers for that good feeling day after day.

So, what aspects of cleaning can be – or should not be – outsourced?

Dealing with physical dirt or waste

'I am agonising over getting a cleaner. I can't seem to get my head round it. It feels wrong to me to have someone in my house "picking up after" me. I don't know why but it does.' (Mumsnet, 2013a)

This post was part of a larger discussion started by someone who disproved of her singleton friend's decision to outsource cleaning. The poster noted that "[d]omestic cleaners clean intimate, private parts of our houses, and clean up our bodily mess …", where the "private/intimate" parts were "the bits of the house I have washed in, slept in, thrown my dirty tissues in". A few posts by cleaning service-providers did not agree. One commented: "Er..I don't clean anybody's private intimate areas" (Mumsnet, 2013a).

The service-users in both social contexts construed specific tasks as 'personal' and out of bounds for outsourcing, but there was no consistent pattern. In the UK, bed-making and laundry were outsourced by some, but for others these were personal tasks (see also Kordasiewicz, 2015).

'Umm, the cat's litter tray, so cleaning out the cat's mess, umm, doing things to a dirty loo, anything to do with my, with the bed. The bed that's been slept in, I shouldn't expect the cleaner to make it or change it. Because these are personal, and for the same I wouldn't ever ask her to do washing, clothes, these seem to me to be personal jobs. If you like, I see that she's got a defined role which is to keep the surfaces of the house clean and that's it … there's a fairly inflexible set of, you know, category of things that *Sandra* does, that seems to me, I wouldn't feel at all good about asking her to do any of the more intimate, like "dirty" jobs.' (Maggie)

As cleaning is socially considered the lowest work, are Maggie's justifications meaningless? In India, although laundry was frequently outsourced, many service-users washed underwear and some emptied their bathroom bin themselves. Unease around service-providers seeing or touching undergarments was also occasionally evident in the UK. Indeed, meanings of 'secularly defiled' underwear appear to be underpinned by intersecting perceptions of what counts as physical (personal) dirt and wider cultural beliefs around sexuality. Bindu recalled that when she had outsourced cleaning: "I wouldn't want her to go in my kitchen and bathroom, I think they are very private spaces for me".

The lack of consensus about the 'personal' in housecleaning is evident widely. According to Gregson and Lowe (1994a), housecleaners deal with personal dirt. Meagher defined paid housecleaning as work that 'd[id] not involve personal care' (2003:8), and Romero's (2002:185) cleaners did not do the personal tasks of laundry and childcare. However, in domiciliary job descriptions and other guidance on personal and household services, the former includes body work (for example cleaning up after defecation) and the latter includes ironing (Draycott Nursing, n.d.; European Federation for Services to Individuals, 2013; Gullikstad et al, 2016; Rubery et al, 2011). The UK service-providers who had previously been carers confirmed the distinction: "We don't do personal care now …" (*Nora*). *Amelia's* primary interest, T-shirt printing, required her to work flexible hours in her second job, so she took up housecleaning (see Chapter 6), even though she preferred care work. Cleaning personal dirt had meaning for her, cleaning a house did not:

'Yeah! I don't know why I prefer to do one over the other. I think it may be because the house is material, and a person is obviously physical.' (*Amelia*)

Other service-providers included removal of pet faeces in personal work. Unlike the Filipino worker in Anderson's study (2000, 2003), who found removing dog hair from carpets demeaning, my respondents said this was not a problem. Emptying lined bins was sometimes just another task: "they're all in bin liners and I just pull them up, I don't see a biggie about it" (*Charlotte*). For *Evie*, bathroom bin contents were more "personal" than those of the kitchen bin. Since my data collection, concern around use of plastics has been increasing and this aspect now, however, requires further research. Some UK service-providers offered ironing or laundry work or grocery shopping, but others did not. More generally, in contemporary urban contexts, few people wholly clean up after themselves. Used sanitary products and the water used for washing soiled undergarments and dishes, and the contents of our bins eventually enter the public space. But when 'my' dirt becomes part of the collective dirt and is processed at a distance by a (male), usually employed, worker, it appears to lose its moral connotations. No-one in my interviews talked about this aspect of dirt-processing.

The UK service-users often did 'pre-tidying', that is tidying up before the cleaning service-provider comes. Some UK service-users gave practical reasons:

> 'Yeah! I pre-tidy, so I don't umm, you know, all the kids toys and whatever, I just – that's like a nightmare, cause to me that's what's obstructing her getting on with her job, so I kind of you know, we do have this, you know, "Get it up! it's cause *Robin's* coming tomorrow and she has to hoover", so the kids are kind of getting into that. But yeah, I do kind of like try and, ... try and do stuff so that she can maximise her clean, actual cleaning rather than just messing around, yeah!' (Libby)

Others felt uncomfortable about someone else sorting out this mess. When Renee was on maternity leave, although she had a househusband, she outsourced cleaning because "even with the two of us, we still found that we just couldn't keep the mess under control". However, after two months she stopped outsourcing, because she realised their problem was tidying, rather than cleaning:

> '... but it didn't last for very long. Umm, ... I think the reason was partly that we felt it didn't seem to help that much because the problem we were having wasn't actually so much with the cleaning but it was with tidying. And, I mean, maybe there are people – I don't know – who have cleaners who come in

and actually tidy up their things, d'you know? … We certainly wouldn't have felt able to ask.' (Renee)

The UK service-providers appreciated customers who tidied up before their arrival. Some did not mind tidying away children's toys or washed dishes, or washing dishes, as long as their customers factored in additional time in their fees:

'Why pay a cleaner and do the work yourself? I often used to be told "Oh! the house is in such a mess", yes that's what you employ me for.' (*Nicola*)

'Washing the bedding, sometimes, I've got a couple of clients where I'll strip the bed, put it on to wash, but I just leave it in there really, I'm not there long enough for the wash to end and sort it out. [Later] sometimes there's a bit of crockery lying around, I don't mind washing that up. I've got one client, she's got twin babies, and I'll wash their bottles and put them in the steriliser for her. I'm quite laid-back in my approach really. In that I'll do pretty much anything [in the agreed time] …' (*Jessica*)

Some service-providers said they preferred a house to be somewhat messy, otherwise the outcomes of their work would not be clearly visible:

'I don't think there's a need to clean the house before the cleaner goes, which is what some people tend to do, because I like to go in and, when they come back or when they see it, know I've been.' (*Sophie*)

From their point of view, tidying became a problem when dealing with it demeaned and disempowered them, as in 'picking up after others' (Anderson, 2000, 2001; Lutz, 2011; Pérez and Stallaert, 2016; Rafkin, 1998; Rollins, 1985; Romero, 2002). This was more likely a consequence of the social relationship within which the work was done than the nature of the work itself, as illustrated by the following quotes:

'I've got one lady, she has five hours a week … she's got health problems, so she is there, but she can't do a lot. But she's got a family and you can leave some bin-bags on the table and they'll be exactly in the same position next week. Following week. So nothing is done in between. … But they don't look down on you ... It's just their way of living. You got to accept that people live in different ... I like to be clean, but, you know, some people, it doesn't bother them. They're not dirty, the house is clean, they're just cluttered and that's their way of life.

[Later]

'I've got one customer ... I think she's training to be a doctor but she doesn't speak to us – this is the really untidy house, she just leaves everything ... They'll leave wrappers, and they've had tea last night and things are still all over the place, they're just piled on – I mean it's just like they think the cleaner's coming in today. ... So it is quite, and ... she doesn't really speak to us, she just grunts at you, and you just feel a bit as though she looks down at you really.' (*Tamsin*)

The notion of pre-tidying was absent in the Indian interviews. On the practical level, since cleaning was mostly done daily, 'pre-tidying' may have been subsumed within daily tidying. Also, a live-out service-provider may clean only ground-level surfaces (see Chapter 5), often in a squatting position. Here, they may have to tidy, for instance, footwear left lying around, which was experienced as demeaning.[3] Service-users may be wary of live-out providers touching artefacts because they appear comparatively 'dirty' – an inability to practise modern hygiene rituals due to lack of amenities can be conflated with symbolic dirt (Dickey, 2000b; Frøystad, 2003; Suresh Reddy and Snehalatha, 2011; also in Brazil: de Santana Pinho and Silva, 2010). A caste-based sense of entitlement also prevails (Lahiri, 2017; Ray and Qayum, 2009/2010), and 'clean' part-live-out workers often 'pick up' after service-users.

'Yes, I think some work is [personal work], like when clothes are left lying around, your own things you should put away yourself. Okay, we can do the other work, but ... the clothes are lying somewhere, the shoes are lying elsewhere, and everything needs to be tidied up. I feel that if he did this himself, it would make my work a bit easier.' (*Pallavi*)

But this analysis is not about a primitive-to-modern linear progression, in which the West is significantly ahead, as suggested by Mattila:

If I think of the periods when I myself have hired somebody to clean my house, it has been the quality of cleaning work that has mattered the most. For the employers in Jaipur, … this seemed of little concern. In fact, none of them mentioned it as a criterion when recruiting a new worker … It was more important that the person was clean than that they cleaned properly …. (2011:241–242)

Douglas argued that 'the difference between pollution behaviour in one part of the world and another is only a matter of detail' (1966/2002:43). In the UK, historical notions of the lower orders as 'the great unwashed' underpin contemporary cultural differentiators of class (Skeggs, 1997/2002), and cleaning is still seen as a job fit for particular groups of people based on class, race, gender and (lack of) intelligence (Cox, 2006; Gregson and Lowe, 1994a). *Evie*, a middle-class woman who took up cleaning due to lack of other work alternatives at a particular time in life, clearly felt the stigma:

'[D]espite the fact I earn, well including my caring, I earn £750 a month, I can work the hours I choose, and totally fit around my children's, I can drop them at school, I can pick them up if they're ill, I can be with them, holidays I can be with them, and umm, so really there shouldn't be any stigma at all. I should be able to hold my head high and say this is what I do. But there is constantly that question of a, umm, but surely you must want to be something else, or do something else.' (*Evie*)

While I do not excuse notions of inherent 'dirty-ness', the continued stigma experienced by UK service-providers (see Chapter 7) problematises Mattila's (2011) piecemeal explanation of her practices as rational versus those of her Indian respondents as idiosyncratic. 'Intimate' personal activities – from defecation to sex – also happen in the public in both 'advanced' and 'developing' societies, and here most people rarely clean up after themselves; the work is left to Others (Sykes et al, 2014). A few UK respondents did both commercial and domestic cleaning (Appendix A, Table A.1) and people exhibited similar behaviours and attitudes to them as those documented in the private sphere:

Yvonne: … I don't know if it is just in my head but you find that … some people are dead friendly and everything but you don't get the same sort of, similar sort of respect cause you're just the cleaner there, whereas they're working in the office … Even though that's

	not how it should be, because I've done both, on
	both sides of it, but from the outside coming in as
	the cleaner I don't like it.
Lotika:	Okay, so that feeling is there more in the office than
	in the house?
Yvonne:	Yeah, definitely. Yeah, yeah, cause the office, they're
	there to work and you're there to work but obviously
	they're like a sort of step above even, you know even
	when they're not but … that's how it feels.

Much 'personal' work is also commonly performed outside the home, such as hairdressing. A third of over 1,000 female secretaries reported doing personal work for male bosses, such as booking a back wax, walking the dog, researching for his child's homework, buying gifts for his wife, collecting his parent's ashes from a funeral parlour and sewing trouser seams (Truss et al, 2013; see also Chapter 1).

Toilet cleaning is perhaps the ultimate social equaliser (Ehrenreich, 2002/2010:91; Maushart, 2003). The private domestic toilet first made an appearance as a marker of status; hygiene-related explanations promoting this practice developed much later (Elias, 1994/2003). Some service-users said they took care to leave the toilet 'respectably clean' for the cleaning service-provider. A few UK service-providers had not encountered dirty toilets:

> 'They're always normally clean, to be honest. Yeah! I don't really ever come … I mean I have heard people that I've known, they've said "Oh! God, I went to this house and it was really bad, and it'd been left there", but I've never ever had any problems, most of my clients are quite clean already to be fair.' (*Grace*)

Many said they would rather customers did not leave toilets dirty, and if they were in a position to do so, they dropped such clients. *Sheila* had "learned over the past year to become more, a lot more picky" when potential customers approached her:

> '[W]hen I first started out, I did some really disgusting places. Whereas now I can gauge it a bit better as to … if these are nice people, if they are going to treat me well. If they've got high standards anyway themselves.' (*Sheila*)

The remaining women, often those with children of their own, appreciated customers who did not leave toilets dirty, but said it did not bother them – wearing gloves[4] and armed with bleach, the task was done:

> 'Messy toilets, not literally, just not flushed, but yeah there is, sometimes. Dirty. But all I do is, I check the kitchen and the toilet first anyway when I go in, and if there is scale on the toilet, poo in the toilet, I'll just put some bleach in and I'll leave that, go and do the kitchen and it's disintegrated by that time. I just use a brush to get rid of it. Nothing fazes me really.' (*Jessica*)

None said they 'liked' toilet cleaning though. Why were these literate women willing to clean other people's clean, and even dirty, toilets, when most could have worked in another industry or still did another job (see Chapter 6)? Toilet cleaning was considered as part of housecleaning work:

> 'In my personal experience, I think that if you put yourself down as a cleaner you've got to be prepared to do everything. ... I mean you can't go to a house and say I'm not going to clean the toilets because it's part of the set-up and the job ...' (*Sophie*)

Also, in these women's experience, every job had good and bad aspects and, at the time of the interview, the advantages of independent housecleaning outweighed the returns offered by other jobs.

Toilets are still not universally used in India, and worldwide, a third of us still defecate in the open (World Health Organization, 2012). About half of the Indian service-providers in my research used communal toilets, and one woman had no access to a toilet (except in a service-user's home). This situation is partly related to pollution ideologies, in which caste continues to significantly define occupation in India (NCEUS, 2008, 2009). Particularly pertinent here is that manual scavenging still exists in India, despite legislation banning it, because of persistent caste practices that sanction exploitation of particular groups through dire occupational conditions (Human Rights Watch, 2014). Thus, cleaning service-providers from both higher and lower castes may refuse to clean toilets. This task is still often allocated on the basis of caste to 'toilet cleaners' (the jamadar and jamadarni (male and female cleaners, respectively) (Ray and Qayum, 2009/2010; Sen and Sengupta, 2016). A few of my respondents cleaned their toilets themselves.

When Lata was temporarily living apart from her family, the toilet in her flat was cleaned by a cleaning service-provider. In the family house, a male cleaning service-provider cleaned the bathroom but not the toilet, which Lata's family cleaned themselves. Previously, when living in another city, the toilets had been cleaned by a jamadar contracted for the estate where Lata's family lived. The service-providers in my sample who cleaned toilets were ambivalent about it:

> 'I don't want to learn fancy cooking … you could be stuck the whole day in the client's kitchen. With jhaddhu-pochha,[5] I do my work and I come away, you do your work – I do the sweeping, I do the mopping, I wash the dishes and the clothes if any and I mean then it's done. … Do any work, there is no shame in doing any work. Shame lies in stealing. Whatever your work, do it sincerely and eat three meals a day thanks to your hard work … Our work, this work, now, don't we do this work in our own houses? In the village we take the cow-dung, we carry the cow-dung on our heads, even in the rainy weather, get wood [to cook], we get grass for the cattle, so even in the village all this work is there to do … we are also doing the same here.' (*Sonali*)

The construction of service work as honest, authentic work is common among low-status 'dirty' occupations (Ashforth and Kreiner, 1999; Simpson et al, 2014; Slutskaya et al, 2016). Were the service-providers using ideological justifications to maintain their self-esteem in front of me? Ehrenreich (2002/2010:91), an investigative journalist, found cleaning dirty toilets and removing pubic hair from baths repugnant. But she did this work as an employee of a cleaning agency with Taylorist[6] work practices that deny autonomy and may instil a sense of inauthenticity and heighten feelings of 'core disgust' in the worker (Goerdeler et al, 2015). Rafkin (1998), another university-educated, middle-class white American, whose parents employed a cleaner, worked as an independent service-provider, while establishing herself as a writer. She had no issues with hair in sinks, dirt-rings and soap scum in bathtubs and showers, or toilets as long as they were clean. She disliked nail clippings and never changed beds – she found them 'very personal'.

Interpreting counter-tendencies as false-consciousness rather than a genuine explanation is presumptuous, especially if researchers accept explanations that are in line with their own thinking (for example cleaning is drudgery or dirty work) (Näre, 2011). Based on an investigation of late 19th- and early 20th-century literature and other data sources, Delap argued that the contemporary gaze through which paid domestic work is viewed is itself shaped by 'an attempt to assimilate and make pleasurable or titillating that which disgusts', and, thus, 'to associate service exclusively with disgust would be an impoverished reading' (2011a:237). Bujra, researching domestic work in Tanzania, noted that given her 'own political sense was that it was a demeaning and exploitative occupation', her pre-field research goal had been 'to document rather than to challenge the institution of domestic service'. But while interacting with her respondents, Bujra realised that the occupation 'had many other facets, even for those who were subjected to servitude' (2000:191). Salzinger's research, into the working practices of middle-class Latina domestic workers belonging to the Choices cooperative in Los Angeles, challenged her assumptions about housework as being naturally demeaning work to the extent that she herself began to see outsourced housework as 'clean' rather than 'dirty' work (1991:158).

As *Sonali*'s comment reveals, meanings of current work are also shaped by prior work and life experiences (also Stacey, 2005) and particularly in India, by caste. For many women, the conditions of work were not much worse than the conditions under which they lived and did their own housework (see Chapter 2; also Sen and Sengupta, 2016; A.N. Singh, 2001; V. Singh, 2007). Many Indian women like *Sonali* had migrated from villages where they had done back-breaking agricultural work, often in harsh weather conditions, and handled cow-dung as part of their housework.[7] Perhaps this is why *Kalpana*, a survivor of domestic sexual, other physical and verbal insults, said: "we did it for the people in our own house [who abuse us], so what was the harm in doing it for others?" Cleaning toilets in an urban brick-and-mortar home may not then be perceived in the same way. But some would not do it on caste grounds. *Rashmi*, whose account revealed much exploitation, had had her refusal to clean toilets accepted by her otherwise unreasonable service-users.

A few service-providers said cleaning vomit or blood stains was disgusting. My data confirm previous research showing that across cultures both private and public cleanliness has been symbolically linked to mortal and immortal 'godliness', in which individual cleaning practices at a particular point in time are governed by 'a complex and often contradictory web of scientific and cultural, rational and emotional, physiological and psychological prompts' (Campkin and Cox, 2007/2012:2).

Conclusion: the limitations of theorising outsourced cleaning as dirty work

The biological reasons for body cleaning may deem it essential work (Curtis, 2007), with the sight and smell of human waste evoking a 'natural' reaction of disgust in many people. However, the work of cleaning of contemporary living spaces is socially constructed. Today, some sense of order and/or cleanliness appears desirable to many people for optimal functioning; that is, the outcomes of housework are valued, even if the processes are considered mundane.

How clean and orderly a private living space should be, is governed by a 'complex algebra' (Douglas, 1966/2002:10) of visceral reactions and social historical processes of increasing, yet 'flexible', self-control as a marker of being civilised (Elias, 1994/2003:135), as well as of maintaining social order (Douglas, 1966/2002). Academic attempts to separate the two aspects could result in an analysis influenced by the researcher's own epistemological understanding of dirt. While being mindful of 'false optimism' in workers' accounts, an emphasis on just the material would be reductionist, and 'both components are fundamental to understanding experiences of dirty work' (Hughes et al, 2017:120; also Näre, 2011).

The 'dirty' work in the work of cleaning up dirt in the setting of the contemporary urban house seems more about the undemocratic social relations under which the work is done and which preserves historical hierarchies than about natural human repugnance for physical dirt. One common finding, however, in both cultural contexts, was about workers' attitudes to tidying, picking up after people with a sense of entitlement. This was overwhelmingly experienced as demeaning work, and obviously should be highlighted to service-users and discouraged or challenged. It could still be argued that housework is immanent 'drudgery', and I consider this point in Chapter 5.

5

Domestic Cleaning:
Work or *Labour*

At the Gender, Work and Organization conference GWO2014, I presented a paper based on my early findings. Later, a researcher questioned my choice of White British cleaning service-providers as a basis for theorising paid domestic work.

Introduction

Romero's (2002) excellent delineation of the structuring of unpaid and paid housework showed how outsourced housework was being transformed by modern live-out Chicana[1] cleaners from servitude into a service occupation in the US. In this, she argued that stay-at-home employers' close supervision of cleaners simply manifested their class privilege, as they overlooked the cleaners' housekeeping knowledge, whose paid work experience ranged from five months to 30 years. New workers, however, often underwent induction into the work. So were they all efficient cleaners? Did they all work the same? I started my research with the assumption that all the cleaning service-providers I interviewed were good cleaners. But as I heard the service-users' comments about their service-providers' work, and, more importantly, the service-providers' own descriptions of their work, the following questions arose:

- Are some people better at doing housework than others?
- Do (female) domestic workers inherently 'know' what to do, because they do housework at home?
- How do we know when housework is well done or not well done?

Crucially, I would not have thought of these issues had I ignored the work experiences of the White British cleaners. In the process of addressing them, my argument began to develop: that cleaning can be done as *work* or as *labour*.

The words 'work' and 'labour' are used variously in literature and beyond. In Marxism, labour is understood as the human capacity to do work that produces a product, with work being the activity performed by that labour (Weeks, 2011). Hence, the oft-used term in Marxist feminist literature on domestic work is 'paid domestic labour'. Arendt (1958, cited in Weeks, 2011:14–15, 88) used the terms to distinguish between tasks based on their social valuation and what they entail: reproductive activities are 'labour' and productive activities are 'work', linked by common political activity, 'action'. Weeks (2011) rejected such categorisations, since they essentialise or valorise work or labour, taking it for granted. She uses the terms interchangeably in her argument that the key to social progress lies in doing less work. I use the terms – in *italics* – to show how varying the conditions under which a particular activity is done can change its social meanings: in this case, outsourced housecleaning.

Two aspects of work are key here. First, paid domestic work is often theorised as a matter 'between women'. Historical inquiries show feminisation of the paid context is more likely driven by political-economic-social factors than its cultural framing as 'women's work' (Banerjee, 2015; Bujra, 2000; Moya, 2007; Neetha, 2009; Ray and Qayum, 2009/2010; Sarti, 2005). In late 18th-century Britain and Europe, the servant tax made it more expensive to hire men, who were increasingly absorbed in the expanding day labour and white-collar occupations required by industrialisation. Still, the evolving domestic 'standards' of the emerging middle-classes raised demand. Consequently, women, who were permitted few other occupations and were cheaper to employ, began to dominate domestic service (Hill, 1996; Sambrook, 2005/2009; Sarti, 2005). Similarly but later, in India, focusing on Bengal, Banerjee (2015) showed that increasing industrialisation in the early 20th century transformed the work that poor and vulnerable women had done as part of a caste-based occupational structure into 'men's work', pushing women into domestic service. Another surge of feminisation commenced in the 1980s, consequent to 'development' activities that have adversely affected agriculture-based work opportunities and led to in-country rural–urban migration – the illiterate migrant women are cheaper to employ (Lahiri, 2017; Ray and Qayum, 2009/2010; Sen and Sengupta, 2016; also Bujra, 2000, for Tanzania).

The second aspect relevant here is the manual–mental division of work. Common instrumentally oriented vertical occupational classifications present cleaning as an 'elementary' occupation. These occupations are assumed to involve simply the performance of a series of discrete physical tasks that require minimal mental exertion and little – if any – formal education (ONS, 2010; Rose and Pevalin, 2005:15). Rose's detailed accounts of many low-status manual and service occupations, such as waitressing, revealed 'an intricate interplay of thought and action' (2004/2014:xix; also Coelho, 2016). My analysis of 'thought and action' in cleaning starts with a consideration of whether cleaning is something everyone can do and the dis-continuities between paid and unpaid housework, and culminates in the central argument of this book.

Cleaning fairies versus khichh-khichh

> 'People expect it, they think you're a cleaner, you're a miracle worker with a magic wand, [but] it doesn't work like that.' (*Vera*)

Victorian middle-class domesticity separated 'menial' from mental housework (Roberts, 1997). The former was outsourced to working-class women constructed as ignorant, to be moulded by employers and domestic science courses. These courses 'did not benefit workers but rather cheapened their labor service to labor power' (Romero, 2002:125). In this, *her* ability to do (paid) domestic work is often uncritically accepted, with a few researchers (for example Dill, 1988; Cox, 2006) questioning the assumption that anyone can do this work. In the online forums, however, some people waxed lyrical about their amazing cleaners, while others despaired about their experience of outsourcing:

> 'My lovely cleaner ... does a thorough clean of the kitchen and bathroom. Cleans all hard floors and hoovers throughout. She makes sure all glass is clean and dusts. When she started she cleaned all doors and door framed [sic] etc and kept on top of all that. It's the best £20 I spend!' (Mumsnet, 2014d)

> 'My mum ... has had cleaner after cleaner and has given up. She has found (and I agree) that as their standards are so much lower than hers, it's not worth the money. They tend to clean the surface of things but not thoroughly.' (Mumsnet, 2014a)

A few service-users in my research, too, did not like the work of some service-providers. Petulant privilege? *Vera* described how one service-user mistook stained bathroom sealant for mould and unnecessarily harangued the service-provider:

> '[B]ecause I'm a painter and decorator as well, [I know] what you can't clean and what you need to get decorated … So you've got sealant round the bath, which is chalk. If mould and mildew and stuff gets into it too much, it can't be cleaned … [and they] came back to me saying it's disg[usting], she's done absolutely nothing. So I blasted them a bit to be fair … She's a good nit-gritty cleaner, … and if they hadn't been so arsey … they would've got an explanation about why the bathroom isn't [looking] cleaned because it needs resealing. So you do get some people like that.' (*Vera*)

Vera said "some people" are "like that". Others might have genuine concerns?

> 'If I'm to be honest, sometimes one of the things that frustrates me a bit about having a cleaner is that most of them I feel do a less good job than I would have done myself … particularly the agency ones … so that was another reason for sort of thinking, "Oh well you know we're paying a lot of money for something that …"'(Una)

UK service-users were often reluctant to address niggling issues, wanting to avoid confrontations.[2] Elsewhere, workers may be freely scolded for poor work (India: Rani and Kaul, 1986; Ray and Qayum, 2009/2010; Singh, 2007; Brazil: de Santana Pinho and Silva, 2010). The interaction is effectively captured in the Hindi phrase 'khichh-khichh', the constant quibbling around work apparently half done or not done:

> 'She will sweep what she can see, and what she can't see – under the beds, under the chairs – what is not easily visible, is just left out! When cleaning the washroom, if she feels that nothing is "looking dirty", she will just mop the floor. So when I enter the washroom [and see what she has left out], I point out to her … [Later] Sometimes she comes late and I'm not there. Then I have to point it out the next day. But otherwise the moment I see something … I point it out immediately.' (Ananya)

> '[S]ome people will follow you around, looking over your shoulder, and I don't like that, nor do I like it when people

quibble about work. You tell me what to do, I will do it. But this khichh-khichh, I don't like it.' (*Jyotika*)

In Western literature, khichh-khichh manifests itself as the close supervision or monitoring by a service-user (for example Rollins, 1985; Romero, 2002). Khichh-khichh challenges the notion that outsourced cleaning is a natural extension of women's 'unskilled' unpaid work, and suggests that some of the despair expressed by service-users requires further attention.

The dis–continuities between unpaid and paid–for housecleaning

'... most of the ladies do their own work at home, so they know how to do it.' (Sarika)

Some service-providers said they cleaned customers' houses like their own:

'I don't think most cleaners clean ... my mum's cleaner never seems to bother with things like that, or if you open the door, there's always a triangle behind the doors. I think most of my clients would agree that I clean properly ... I wipe down everything ... my approach to it is that I clean as if it's my own house.' (*Evie*)

'I could have considered other work had I been educated ... That's why I could only do housework ... I don't think there is anything wrong with it, I put my heart and soul into anything I do, I never think it is somebody else's work. I work like I would in my own home.' (*Pallavi*)

But others stressed that their own home was not cleaned in the same way:

'[W]hen I'm at my sister's, I'm always thinking, "Have I done it well enough?" ... I clean thoroughly, I make stuff look nice ... it's like I'm looking at it from the outside and thinking: Is that okay? Have I done that? I clean her kitchen floor every week. My kitchen floor does not get cleaned every week. ... So, you know, being more thorough, being more aware of ... that there is an external observer to my work, whereas here I'm the observer!' (*Carrie*)

'There is no difference as such, but this is there, that their work is done to a somewhat better standard. I do my work a little differently. They ask for a very high standard of cleaning. We also do cleaning in our own home, but in our own way ... So our [paid] work is to clean spotlessly. There should not be even a speck of dirt.' (*Chetna*)

To explain these apparent contradictions, I unpack the construction of cleaning by my respondents in terms of site of work, the time-bind, the work that needs to be done and its outcomes. In this book, the phrase 'time-bind' encapsulates the subconscious intermeshing of 'clock' time and 'social' time (Adams, 1995) by people in the estimation of the time required to do paid-for housework. I explain this further during my elaboration of this point later.

Some live-out cleaning service-providers in both contexts said that their workplace was not in their private sphere: they went out to work. The first visit to a service-user's house can be daunting, and the conditions of work and the work itself can vary. For instance, *Nora* thought her paid work was similar to her housework. But her housework was part of 'doing family' (Morgan, 2011) and doing outsourced cleaning was about providing a paid service within a customer–vendor relationship. Unpaid cleaning may or may not be subject to routines, while paid-for housecleaning is expected to happen at regular times at regular intervals. Both require tangible amounts of time, but its accounting is optional in the unpaid context and crucial in paid work:

'[W]hen you're doing housework you can sit down, have a brew, watch telly for a minute and think, "Oh I'll do that in minute". When you're doing a clean, you've got two hours to get a whole house done. ... So I think you don't realise how much different it is to doing it in your own house, cause you don't ... "Oh! I'll just sit down and watch this, just a minute!"' (*Tamsin*)

'No the thing is, if she going to give you an hour, in the hour she has to clean up the entire house, obviously she's not going to clean it as if it's her own house ... she may avoid the upstairs, or she won't err, mop the stairs or where the bathroom is concerned, she might just kind of mop the floor. They're not going to spend time you know, cleaning the grout or you know, cleaning behind the tap.' (Shobha)

In the numerous internet discussions on the reasonableness of service-providers' quotes, many respondents quickly responded that it was 'just about' the number of bedrooms and bathrooms. Some measured responses said it also depended on the tasks to be done. Very few (often by service-providers themselves) pointed out that the time required also depended on the area, design and state of the house (also Rafkin, 1998).

People can also gradually increase the work expected – *she* might as well wash (more and more) dishes, while cleaning the sink in the same time. *Neena* described working for a pair of sisters, one of whom started to do this and ignored *Neena's* protests. After a few months, *Neena* decided not to work for them and refused to go back when the sisters' neighbour tried to cajole her into it.

When Navita said her service-provider could not 'multi-task', I thought she was asking *her* to do a lot in little time:

> 'She is not able to multi-task. And I realised that one day when my friend was visiting and I said do this, and after five minutes I said can you do this and after another five minutes I said can you do this? [My friend] said you're giving her too many things to do, she's only able to do one thing at a time.' (Navita)

Some UK service-providers negotiated the resultant time-bind, by doing an initial, more expensive, 'deep' clean, followed by regular 'maintenance' cleans. Others used the 'creep and go' method – doing one room thoroughly in rotation with lighter cleaning of other rooms. Oven cleaning is increasingly offered as an 'extra' – a few respondents learned to do this with experience. These data show how the home is considered a locus of social-time as opposed to the clock-time of the workplace (Adams, 1995). Since housework is also less valued as work, the time spent on unpaid housework is imagined to be less than the actual time required:

> '[Y]ou often find, particularly with mothers who are returning to work after maternity leave … they kind of underestimate … how much time they physically spend in running a home. … They'd go, "Oh! a couple of hours twice a week" and I'd look at them and go, "Really? Right, keep a log – even if you're just wiping down the draining board and it took you two minutes, you write that down. Do that for a week … You will be horrified, because putting out the recycling, sweeping the kitchen floor, wiping down the baby's highchair, you think it takes ten seconds? It doesn't – it

takes five minutes. You do that and then get back to me and tell me realistically, how much time you think I need" ... women, particularly, don't realise how much time they spend on domestic tasks.' (*Nicola*)

Some service-users monitor the service-provider by clock-time, while expecting them to work in social-time. They request odd jobs to fill 'spare' time or chastise the service-provider who leaves early despite finishing agreed work (khichh-khichh). Service-providers with sufficient work in both research sites often stopped working for clients who kept an eye on the clock or added work without increasing the fees. There are other service-users like Shobha, whom I quoted earlier, who acknowledge that good and thorough cleaning requires time:

> 'I've got one I go twice a week, on a Monday and a Friday. Both times they want the kitchen doing and on Mondays its upstairs and Fridays its downstairs. ... she doesn't overload it, so it can be done at a nice pace, where you can do a thorough job and don't have to rush to fit it all in.' (*Charlotte*)

Like the time spent on housework, worker competency is also not 'natural'. The UK service-providers lived in houses whose basic design was similar to their service-users' houses, although they might have had, for instance, cheaper floor coverings. Many Indian service-providers' families, however, slept, cooked, ate and lived in a single room. A minority had a kitchenette. The slum tenements had mud walls and floors, a few shelves but often no windows. Built tenements often had rough cement surfaces, whereas service-users' houses could have marble floors and granite kitchen surfaces. Could the service-providers be assumed to 'know' how to clean windows, worktops or cookers, or use cleaning products they could not afford to buy themselves?

Pratibha had given up outsourcing partly because "[m]ost maids come as raw hands and are to be painstakingly taught the nitty-gritty of efficient housekeeping – before they are lured away by the neighbours! I had so many maids leaving at this stage [as] I had become well known for my 'training programmes'." Many service-providers too said they learned on the job (also Lutz, 2011:56; Sen and Sengupta, 2016; Singh, 2007):

> 'Yes, my employer taught me, holding my hand. Sweep like this, mop like this, I mean like this, all the work. So this is how I learnt [how to do it] after I came to this city.' (*Urvashi*)

'The woman who was already working in that house teaches you how to do it: you need to sweep like this, mop like this, wash the clothes like this, do this like that. She tells you whether the verandahs have to be cleaned, what has to be cleaned, how to clean the photographs, she instructs in all these things. [Lotika: Is there a lot of difference between the houses?] Yes there is a difference. Also, in one's own house, people do what they want to do. In others' houses you worry about it – what if something gets left? What if I am blamed for something [like breakage or missing valuables]? You might have to work under fear of something going wrong.' (*Brinda*)

Some UK service-providers talked about a learning curve. *Yvonne* had been subcontracting work to her friends. This arrangement had led to customer complaints and she gradually realised that not everyone cleans in the same way:

'[O]bviously with the level of cleaners that I've seen now that I've got – some of the girls are dead slow and compared to some of them, they're really, d'you know they're really good and everybody loves them … and they make sure that everything is done with an eye to detail. So it isn't just as you can either clean or you can't, there is a bit more to it, when you … know about it, when you're looking for it.' (*Yvonne*)

Male domestic workers often do not do housework in their own homes, because across classes and cultures the unpaid work of cooking, cleaning and childcare is largely women's work. Clearly, regional, cultural and class-based variations in the materiality of domestic spaces, and domestic work itself, affect worker competencies (Bujra, 2000; Flather, 2013).

Service-users can move the goalposts of their own unpaid cleaning when they outsource it. They impose 'specific cleaning methods, and [add] ritual cleaning', because outsourced 'cleaning' is also about class reproduction (Romero, 2002:161; also Anderson, 2000, 2003; Gullikstad et al, 2016):

'And as I say, the people who I don't work for anymore, and it doesn't happen very often, but there are people who still treat you with a complete lack of respect and as if you don't have a brain. I call her "Emma Threecloths", she's, I dread to think how much she is worth, her house is immaculate, but you go in and clean it for two hours … she had a very expensive, umm, one of those halogen hobs and [the] first day I went in, she explained she had a "three cloth way" of cleaning her hob … Well, on the fifth time that she told me [laughing] the way she wanted to clean it, I just wanted to tell her to stick her cloths somewhere … I am cleaning it properly, it doesn't matter, I really object to you being so ridiculous. So I don't work for her any more.' (*Evie*)

'How will they be able to do all the work? If no-one helps them, they will cook themselves and eat. I mean, they will not relax as much as they are doing now. But will they do all this work all day? Like now, they will use three to four dishes, but if she is doing it herself, she will use only one dish. She will manage to do all the work with one dish. Like when I mop, she tells me to change the water in the bucket twice. But if she was doing it, she would do it with one bucketful. All of it. … I do it every day but she would do it every third day.' (*Gauri*)

From the business-minded British service-provider's perspective, however, some kinds of 'extra' work become added-value work (see Chapter 6):

'I think some people don't clean to the standards that I do and you have to have a high standard in this job. Because … even though you go into somebody's house and you know that they never clean their skirting boards, I would still do that. Because it's about impressing people as well, it's about, you know, they are, they can clean their house for free, [but] I want [the work], they are *paying* me to clean their house, it needs to be that little bit extra. … I clean my bath and sink out and I leave water there after I've done it, but in a client's house I would wipe away all the watermarks on the shower screens … even though they wouldn't necessarily. [Then] they walk in and think "Wow. Isn't it lovely", you know, and they like that and I get complimented on that.' (*Jessica*)

At the same time, the standards expected from service-providers in both the British and Indian social contexts varied. This was despite the Indian service-users' point that cleaning was done every day because India was a more dusty country (see Chapters 3 and 4). In the UK, the starting point of paid-for cleaning differed: sometimes the work started with tidying, and at other times it was just about 'topping' up an already clean house. Some service-users did not desire perfection. Naomi stopped outsourcing cleaning to a friend because:

> '… what I needed was somebody to go around, do the kitchen and toilets … And tidy things away and do a bit of dusting. But she got very frustrated by the fact that … our house is a very open house and there are always lots of kids in and out and it needs to be clean but not necessarily meticulously clean.' (Naomi)

Beverley, who was compulsive about cleaning, said outsourcing cleaning to a woman who did not pay the same attention to detail helped her to keep her obsession under control, she was "less worried about it" – and her "mental health seems to be linked to having a cleaner". In India, Navita, a singleton, was "very finicky" and examined "every nook and corner", her "whole concentration is on what is not clean". Nandita, another singleton, however, was "not one of those people who try all the time to see specks of dust in the house. I'm just a minimalist, that is my principle." Other service-users mentioned tolerating substandard work for different reasons,[3] often topping up paid work with unpaid work:

> 'Now she has learnt, but sometimes I still feel that she is not doing it to my satisfaction so I need to tell her. But she is a good, responsible woman. She does it more or less, and if I explain this to her [once] I don't have to explain again. But because I myself am a bit fastidious I feel … it's all right. But on the whole she's okay …' (Rita)

> 'That they don't do, in any case they don't do [housework as well as we do it ourselves]. You have to accept … isn't it, that if it is not like this – you have to think, you have to rationalise it and then [you think] it's okay, it's okay. At times you lose temper also, it's so very human, I cannot say that I do not get upset, and that happens. [And] at times I ignore it also, it's a mix of things.' (Geetanjali).

At the same time, many service-users in both countries and the UK service-providers themselves (including internet posters) did not think everyone could clean well enough to successfully earn a living. *Nora* and *Casey*'s clientele had expanded rapidly, but growing the business, finding subcontractors, was proving difficult despite many enquiries:

> '[W]e set a lady on last week and she just lasted one day. Yeah!
> she came with me, she'd done cleaning before so she was
> experienced. She was a mature lady, so ... I thought that was
> good, not that I'm ageist or anything like that. [But] when
> she came with me, she stood in the bath with her shoes on so
> consequently we had a dirty bath that was clean to start with.
> So you know, she wasn't as experienced as I thought she was
> or she thought herself.' (*Nora*)

That women do not 'naturally' see dust has generally not been researched
sufficiently. The differences in unpaid and paid-for cleaning became more
evident in the initially separate and then merged analyses of the structure
of paid-for cleaning in the two cultural contexts.

Cleaning as *work* versus *labour*

> 'I think it's partly seeing things, it's actually paying attention, ...
> putting a bit of energy into it, not physical energy, but, you
> know, actually seeing what needs doing. Which I'm quite
> likely not to see really. And then when it's done the whole
> place does look nicer. So having a little bit of an aesthetic
> sense really about how you tidy things up and make things
> look nice, that's what *Enid*'s got ... "sprinkle fairy dust" is an
> expression I use ... I don't know what she does!' (Patricia)

When I asked service-users and the UK service-providers whether they
thought that anyone could clean for a living, the responses varied.[4] In line
with common wisdom, some stated it "did not require any sort of skill –
obviously with time you learn these things" (Sarika). A few service-users
acknowledged that paid-for cleaning required skills, although they did
not pinpoint them – like Patricia: "I don't know what she does!" Indeed,
work learnt through socialisation often becomes cast as unskilled (Elson
and Pearson, 1981).

Other comments, however, made me realise that the issue here is not
about skill, which is itself an ambiguous term. Definitions of skills shift
over time and with, for instance, the gender and race of the worker
(Game and Pringle, 1983; Pollert, 1981). Currently, 'skill' has become
an encyclopaedic term with behaviours and attitudes morphing into
'cognitive' skills, which, argue Lloyd and Payne (2009), is a 'skilful' way

of invisibilising 'emotional labour' to avoid its valuation in economic terms alongside 'real' skills. Rather, the issue here was whether paid-for cleaning qualifies as:

- *work* – requiring both manual and mental effort and performed under decent, democratic work conditions;

or as simply

- *labour* – requiring mainly manual labour, accompanied by exertion of 'natural' emotional/affective labour and performed in undemocratic conditions.

In the UK, outsourced cleaning generally meant cleaning all interior surfaces (floors, counters, and so on), bathrooms, toilets, windows and mirrors, high and low dusting, and buffing steel surfaces, finishing with the home looking and feeling pleasant. Floor-level surfaces were vacuumed or mopped, mostly standing and occasionally on hands and knees. External areas such as driveways and garden furniture were excluded. Some respondents did laundry and ironing and occasionally fed the cat, and they often worked to routines that accommodated changes in customers' lives. When customers were away, service-providers could still work, often using this time for less-frequently done tasks, such as cleaning and tidying kitchen cupboards. Mostly, all housework was outsourced to one independent cleaning-provider or quasi-agency (see Chapter 6) that ensured the same service-provider went once a week or fortnightly, and rarely twice-weekly or monthly.[5]

Such a service-provider requires knowledge of cleaning materials and procedures, including cost-efficiency, and which products reduce 'elbow grease' and least affect own health. *Kate* and *Nicola* used eco-friendly products, because they were prone to allergies (see also Smith's (2011) review of health and safety in domestic work). As Salzinger noted after ethnographic observation of the training sessions of a domestic-worker collective, 'it is easy to see how not knowing some of these things could lead to disaster' (1991:147). A few UK respondents referred to online cleaning guides.[6] Many women bought the products they preferred to use, including vacuum cleaners, or asked their service-users to do so. They often used colour-coded gloves and cloths to avoid contact with dirt and contamination. Technical knowledge alone, however, is not enough to be a good cleaning service-provider, as *Carrie* explained:

> '[Y]ou have to be able to *see* what needs to be done, you have to be able to prioritise your time, and you've got to have the motivation.'

Carrie was echoing Maisie's explanation why she had had the same service-provider for 25 years:

> 'What *Clara's* got is the ability to make a room look nice, because you can clean a room and it can be technically clean but it can look terrible. And she's got the ability to clean a room and leave it looking … looking so sparkling, neat and rather wonderful.' (Maisie)

Contemporary urban houses have similar room assignments regardless of architectural design. But individual preferences transform houses into unique homes; conversely, a house looks and feels different when occupied by different people. Thus, good service-providers aim not "just to cart out rubble and go away" (Maggie), but clean in a way that refreshes but does not disturb the individual homeliness of the house. But such 'care' with which work is done is not a natural feminine virtue. It is the mental labour involved in cleaning work, which in part comprises 'responsiveness', the essence of which is captured in the italicised parts of the following quotes:

> '[What makes a good cleaner is] having some knowledge about how to do a thing properly, which they've learnt from somewhere … And, *probably a certain willingness to listen when I say I want more of this and less of that.* Yeah! so there is a, a skill element and a kind of … responsiveness element.' (Iris)

> '[A]nother reason I know that I'm good [at my work], is because I've had cleaners in the past … three cleaning ladies before and even quite a big company, and … *they seemed to sweat*, and, and you know, *they seemed to be doing all this, but* when I went around afterwards, *it wasn't really to my … standard.'* (*Jessica*)

Responsiveness has been reported previously, although it has not been recognised as such. Hondagneu-Sotelo observed that service-providers have to 'exercise creativity in responding to' service-users (2001:157), and Cox (2006:132) mentions service-providers having to 'mind-read' their service-users' wishes. Molinier views it as a non-feature of the work done: housework, 'if it is well done, should not be seen and should not disturb the daily life of whoever is benefiting from it' (2009/2012:293), while Lutz notes:

> domestic workers have to be adaptable … [the work] requires many skills like a talent for management, accuracy, diligence, psychological knowledge, empathy, intuition and patience, endurance, the ability to endure frustrations, discipline, the capacity to put oneself in perspective, self-reflexivity, emotional intelligence and a good memory. (2008:50)

In such theorisation, responsiveness becomes an inherent characteristic of the service-provider, exploited as affective labour (Anderson, 2000; Gutiérrez-Rodríguez, 2014; Lutz, 2008, 2011) and theories contradict each other. For Molinier, 'effective' paid-for cleaning is that which bears the mark of the service-provider and will 'never fully satisfy those it serves': '[t]he care which we bring to a domestic space – even if it is not our own – is *personalised in our own image*' (2009/2012:294–295; original emphasis). For Lutz, the problem is the opposite: '[b]ecause the home is the employer's place of identity performance … there is little space for the employee to deploy their own creativity in the household' (2008:55). Some commercial companies abuse the task of making homes look nice. When Ehrenreich (2002/2010) worked as an undercover cleaner, she was told to only make sure the obvious dirt was removed and things 'looked alright'. I have been on the receiving end of a superficial clean accompanied by a liberal spraying of freshener to give that 'good' feeling.

My findings show that casting responsiveness as a low-status, inherently feminine trait delegitimises the mental *work* that both service-users and service-providers need to do to establish a satisfactory outcome for outsourced domestic cleaning. Lutz also notes 'a learning process on the employer's part' (2011:51). Responsiveness takes time to develop (see also Hondagneu-Sotelo, 2001:170), and is not a mindless one-size-fits-all response on both sides. Responsiveness is also not about service-providers imposing their aesthetic sense, but about restoring the service-user's style (Dill, 1988), so additional mental work is required where the two styles diverge. Lutz (2011) considers this a 'problem' for the service-provider, but I do not agree. Paid-for cleaning should not be about service-providers working in non-autonomous ways to satisfy whims and fancies of service-users with a sense of entitlement. It is about doing specific tasks, but in a creative way that takes into account the singular character of each serviced house. The situation is akin to restoring an old painting. The contemporary artist is not supposed to put their own stamp on the painting, but to recreate the original. This need not suppress their creativity; rather, responsiveness means using one's creative potential to recreate something. In a study that recorded experiences of both men and women in low-paid work (Shildrick et al, 2012), caring was considered one of the more creative jobs.

Regarding affective labour in domestic work, the UK service-providers' accounts of their work history revealed that affect was desirable in any work relationship, or else the worker was reduced to an atomised being (see Chapter 6). Many service-users also talked in terms of affect in relation to their own paid work, and the language of love and passion for the work is often used to play down exploitation (Gill, 2010) in the 'moral commitment' expected in the employment relation of higher-status jobs (Rose and Pevalin, 2005). When cleaning was done as *labour*, *Georgia* (who had been an agency employee) and *Pallavi*, both of whose experience of being a cleaner had been largely negative, explained how service-users' affective labour was important for being "treated like a human being really and not a skivvy":

> '[Y]ou'd want to do more for her because she treated you like a friend ... and she'd chat with you and she'd sometimes work alongside you. So if you were cleaning a room, she'd come in and do some ironing while you were there. And she'd chat with you. She'd treat you like an equal. You know, but these other women, they'd be sat in the garden with their friends ... And they don't ... her house was always clean when you got there. So obviously you start to clean it but she wouldn't leave knickers out and the toilet not flushed and horrible things like that. She would have a bit of respect for you. And she'd say "You don't mind doing the windows do you?" She'd ask you nicely and just say if you don't like, don't want to do that and she was so polite, so lovely. So you do, do more for her.' (*Georgia*)

> 'And now when my son was going abroad, bibiji [ma'am] gave me much support, she talked to me and said it was hard to let go of one's children. She helped me understand this a lot. In such a time when someone talks to you like their own, it makes a lot of difference. ... But with some people you can develop greater affinity. ... Now whenever he calls he asks after bibiji, because she also talked to him. He was also full of trepidation just before he left and she encouraged him a lot. Just saying something is not enough, but taking time to make someone understand – there is so much difference [between service-users].' (*Pallavi*)

A feminist perception of housework, however, would deem this affect as mental labour expended by the service-provider and that is necessary for responsiveness to develop when cleaning is done as *work*. This is supported by other research. For instance, Kessler and colleagues (2015) found that healthcare assistants' management of patient emotions involved expending emotional labour as part of the manual–mental relational labours of care work. Rather than their maternal caring experiences, the healthcare assistants' previous experiences in social care explained their greater ability compared with nurses to manage patient emotions. In other words, emotional intelligence was involved in this care work (BBC Radio 4, 2015) in a two-way process – responsiveness – that produces value for both the carer and the client (Bailly et al, 2013; Rubery et al, 2011; Stacey, 2005).

The caveats appended by the UK service-providers who thought that anyone could do cleaning for a living revealed that responsiveness also depended on attitudes to cleaning on both sides. Among the more established workers in my sample, those who clearly articulated a commitment to the work appeared to be doing better. If you do not enjoy cleaning, said *Martha*:

> 'you're jogging uphill … You have to be quite thorough, and you have to have attention to detail. You can't just clean stainless steel. You have to work at it and buff it up, if you've not got that inclination to do it properly it won't look right, it won't look nice.' (*Martha*)

Valerie stopped using subcontractors who did not pay attention to the finer details:

> 'The toilet is the main thing. Missing cleaning the toilet, not wiping when you do a handbasin. The water runs down … make sure you clean around the bottom, because there's always like little drips down there isn't it? … you get scummy if you're not careful. But I notice things like that. What you have to do, and people don't realise is that if you sit, put the toilet lid down and sit on the toilet and look at the bathroom, you're seeing at the level as the customer … .' (*Valerie*)

Nora straightened her back when she categorically told me that "not everybody can do it. Like I said you've *got* to enjoy it. There's no point coming for a cleaning job really if it's [only] for the pay …."

In Australia, some cleaning managers have observed that employing people with an interest in cleaning for cleaning jobs would improve the quality of work delivered (Smith, 2009). But do such people exist? Given that 'drudgery' is practically its synonym, the vociferous way in which cleaning is disparaged as manual labour (Spitze and Loscocco, 1999), it is "bizarre isn't it!", said *Carrie*, that she liked cleaning. The internet discussions were also peppered with self-remonstrations:

'I am one of those freaks that enjoys cleaning ...' (Netmums, 2012)

'I am interested in doing cleaning or ironing as I enjoy both – am I mad?' (Netmums, 2009–2014)

'I quite like cleaning (I'm a loser).' (Mumsnet, 2014a)

In housework week on *Woman's Hour* (BBC Radio 4, 2012), some Lancashire-based cleaners all said they liked cleaning. Angie was "ashamed" that she had had a "very low opinion of cleaners" when she had been head of claims in a legal company. But now she did not want to stop cleaning, "because I like it ...". 'Contrary to popular imagery', the majority of Dill's (1994:83) sample of 26 black American women working as domestics articulated ambivalence, rather than antipathy, towards their work.

The commonest reason in one study (Windebank, 2010) for not outsourcing housework, even when people could afford to, was that they liked looking after their home. Four more survey-based studies reported ambivalence rather than drudgery as the commonest feeling towards cleaning (Robinson and Milkie, 1998; Stancanelli and Stratton, 2010; Sullivan, 1996; van Berkel and de Graf, 1999). In Oakley's (1974/1985:70) study, similar proportions of working- and middle-class women were 'satisfied' or 'dissatisfied' with housework more generally, but in a Work Foundation survey, those earning less than £25,000 were seven times as likely to enjoy housework as those earning £70,000 or more (Jones, 2004). Does that mean the people with fewer material means are deluded? Or, as my data suggest, perhaps sometimes they can see the picture more clearly.

It follows, then, that responsiveness requires the user to respect the provider as another fully developed worker rather than as just 'the cleaner'. Khichh-khichh and the converse assumption that the service-provider already 'knows' what to do, and 'reluctance' to give clear instructions because of fear of behaving 'hierarchically', can prevent the development of responsiveness (Bailly et al, 2013; Hondagneu-Sotelo, 2001:170; Molinier, 2009/2012:290).

> 'I do tend to ... specially with the ones that ... I didn't know before ... I do sometimes do a bit of a customer service thing on them and ask them if they're happy and if anything needs improving and stuff like that. Just, for my own peace of mind, you know, not that they are going to look around really.' (*Sophie*)

> '[Good customers are the] ones that stand back and let you do it and if they've got something they want you to do in addition or they want you to do differently, they're happy to say.' (*Martha*)

Responsiveness includes trusting that the service-provider will work responsibly in a service-user's absence, rather than thinking they will be 'nosing' around. Key-holding is a huge responsibility and a significant mental aspect of cleaning work. All the UK service-providers held house-keys and a few service-users paid a retention fee when they went away for long periods to service-providers where there was a responsive relationship.

Mental work in cleaning also involves crafting 'an economy of movement', as in waitressing (Rose, 2004/2014). Cleaning service-providers need to think of the best way to move and work through different areas of a house, and manoeuvre around furniture, maximising the efficacy of their physical labour in the least time. Also, while many service-users said their minds would be elsewhere when they did housework, most UK service-providers said they focused on the work at hand to work (and multi-task) in a time-efficient way:

> 'Obviously you'll go in and put all the products in the kitchen or in the bathroom, and you'll bleach the toilet and leave the spray in the bath, and then do the dusting in the bedrooms and obviously do the floors last – but you'll also switch the kettle on as soon as you get there just to boil the water for the mop ...' (*Yvonne*)

They occasionally altered routines, which forced them to remain mentally alert and not miss out areas or things. Mental alertness was also required where tasks were split between visits and for avoiding breakages. *Evie* had "a picture in my head" about how she worked.

Independent service-providers also need to communicate assertively but in a responsive way, for instance issuing discreet warnings about condoms left lying around. *Nora* pointed out that a 'smart'-appearing person was more likely to be treated as a service-provider, rather than as 'the cleaner'. Organisational skills ensure efficient use of time not just while cleaning but also timetabling. *Sheila* scheduled customers who lived near each other on the same day, to avoid wasting time travelling. Internet skills are useful for marketing.[7] Those declaring their earnings required learning about bookkeeping and accounts (or using an accountant). An internet discussion thread (Netmums, 2009–2014), started by a self-employed service-provider for cleaning business-owners to swap knowledge and tips, revealed many aspects to the business of cleaning.

In India, most service-providers worked for all their clients six to seven days a week, and outside areas such as verandahs and driveways could also be cleaned. The work was often fragmented, because of:[8]

- persisting caste-based segregation of occupations (Raghuram, 2001; Ray and Qayum, 2009/2010);
- countering inefficiency from absenteeism (if one worker did not turn up, the other may be asked to do that work) (Sen and Sengupta, 2016);[9]
- managing the volume of (middle-class) housework (cleaning, cooking, laundry) required on a daily basis (Mattila, 2011; see De Casanova (2013) for a similar situation in Ecuador).

Thus, live-out service-providers often only cleaned inside (and outside) ground-level surfaces, without providing what *Vera* called the nitty-gritty "finishing touches", such as plumping the cushions. One provider may do different tasks in different households – from chopping vegetables, kneading dough and making chapattis in one to dusting or kitchen cleaning or washing-up and manual laundry work elsewhere. Bathrooms/toilets were sometimes cleaned by the jamadar/jamadarni (see Chapter 4) or the service-users themselves. Similarly, ironing was outsourced to the dhobi or done by the householders themselves or by the live-in worker. The dhobi is usually a man who irons for a living and often belongs to the caste that has for centuries done laundry work for a living (washing would be done by both men and women).

The materials and tools for the job were provided by the service-user (see also De Casanova (2013) regarding Ecuador). The service-provider was unlikely to test materials/tools as mentioned by the UK service-providers. Cleaning was mainly done in the squatting position, using traditional brooms and hand mops. Many service-users had vacuum cleaners, but these were infrequently used. Then, often the men used this machine rather than outsourcing its use. Almost all Indian homes had no dishwasher (see also Mattila, 2011; Ray and Qayum, 2009/2010).

Responsive cleaning, as described in the UK context, was reified somewhat in the Indian setting (see also Sen and Sengupta, 2016:163):

> '[T]hat girl has qualities that we educated people don't have, the understanding that girl has, how good natured she is. I never have to tell her what work she needs to do, you have not done this or that. … She is mindful of the work she has to do. If I give her clothes to wash but she has decided she will do this other work, she will ask can I wash the clothes tomorrow? She is mindful that today I have to do this work, I didn't do this yesterday, she knows what she has to do – I don't have to tell her what to do. I consider it my luck to have found her. … Usually … there is no interest in the work, they just do a cursory job and leave … I have no worries.' (Vimla, a retired headteacher)

Urvashi spoke with greater interest about a job where she had had 'full responsibility' for the household. More generally, in the fragmented work setting with impoverished living conditions, most Indian service-providers showed little investment in their paid work (see Chapter 6), with little evidence of responsiveness. As has been well established in previous studies, there is often a disjunction between the views of middle-class service-users with a sense of entitlement[10] or even benevolent ones[11] (see Chapter 7), and the service-provider's own view of their lived experience of being a low-wage, low-status worker. So Vimla's comment that "they just do a cursory job and leave", is *her* response to being treated as an invisible non-person, who then "just does the work and shoots off" (*Anjali*). This can breed reversed responsiveness, a palpable tension between the two sides manifested as acts of resistance by the service-providers to maintain their self-esteem. One defence mechanism is absenteeism, which then hampers responsiveness because of a constant undercurrent of anxiety in many service-users (Bharati and Tandon Mehrotra, 2008; Ray and Qayum, 2009/2010; Sen and Sengupta, 2016; Singh, 2007):

> 'The most irritating thing was their unannounced absenteeism. The day I would have an international delegation coming, my husband would have an important assignment, and the kids were to be dropped to their school function, our maid would just decide that is the day she needed to visit her ailing

mother. A cursory glance at the pile of dishes in the sink and the chaotic household was enough for my blood pressure to shoot up.' (Pratibha)

'Absenteeism' in an informal economy may be interpreted (top-down) as a lack of work ethic in 'those people', but when people's health, living and working conditions verge on the chaotic and lack social securities and justices, commitment to work becomes a moot point. Indeed, in the construction of cleaning as casual *labour*, service-providers can struggle to negotiate regular days off and the overburdened women sometimes just have to be somewhere else at the drop of a hat. The service-providers may take on a greater number of households than they can handle but then juggle between them by regularly absenting on a 'rota' basis (Sen and Sengupta, 2016) or occasionally tell white lies because a day off was needed just to recharge one's batteries. A degree of responsiveness might develop where sympathetic service-users give regular days off and accept unscheduled absences:

'I am polite with them, rather than nagging them, because there's no point. Perhaps this realisation has come [to me] with time. When you're younger ... you get after people's lives, then you realise you yourself are a woman, it doesn't matter, it's much better ... they also go from house to house, they also have a temperament, they're also human, you're also human, they also have their house. It's a monotonous job, so might as well, you know, make it a pleasant environment ... when there is a little more time maybe do it together, things become better if you do it together with them ...' (Vibha)

Responsiveness could also be thwarted in joint households because of differences in attitudes and hierarchies among the service-users themselves: a mother's efforts to forge responsiveness were constantly challenged by her daughter's proclivity towards khichh-khichh, as *Neelam*, a part-live-out service-provider, explained. The daughter lived on the first floor, while the mother occupied the ground floor of the same house:

'Her daughter, she dislikes me. But the mother, she is like a mother ... [the daughter] always speaks in a harsh way ... She talks like this to everyone. Even to her mother – you love *Neelam* more than you love me. You should tell [*Neelam*] to do this work, to do that work. But auntie-ji responds that [*Neelam*] does all the work, there is no need for me to say anything to her. … She doesn't give me a chance to rebuke her so why should I do that? Then the daughter says, but this work is still to be done, that work is still to be done. And [the mother] replies [*Neelam*] is not employed by you, she is employed by me. She will do what she can do, or she will go and take rest.' (*Neelam*)

The mental work required for cleaning was not that obvious in the Indian service-providers' work experience. Some, like Vimla's worker, took control of the work and paced it efficiently, but others said their mind dwelled elsewhere when they worked, on family issues, and so on. They still needed mental grit and discipline to:

- maintain quality in a repetitive task – a mind that is often in a state of 'tension'[12] may find it harder to maintain standards;
- maintain equanimity while working in extreme climatic conditions (for example temperatures rising to 45°C, high levels of enervating humidity, coping with the effects of lack of proper drainage in the slums during the monsoon);
- have the presence of mind to resist exploitative service-users, while harbouring ressentiment (Dill, 1988; Rollins, 1985), as *Anika* describes here:

> 'Well, what happens is, first this work doesn't get done, and you are admonished for it, then that work doesn't get done and you are admonished for that as well. They will keep quibbling about one thing or another … if they tell us six jobs, one could get left, yes? … I feel irritated, but what can I do, I can't show it. … For instance, there are four people in the house. I finish the work and come, but something will get left. And they will call me yet again "*Anika*, come back quickly, go and do that work. Don't you know how to do it? Don't you understand what I'm saying? You have a bad habit of answering back. Do you need a medicine to make you understand what I'm saying?" This is how they speak. I mean, they just admonish me. … One day, "uncle" said to me, "How long have you lived her?" I said it has been a while. Then he said "You have been influenced by the bad ways of [this city]." So I replied, "I was influenced by it a long time ago." So sometimes I answer back in jest, and this happens all the time, a bit of chicanery …' (*Anika*)

Ironically, despite the construction of cleaning as *labour* rather than *work*, many phrases used to reprimand a service-provider refer to mental ability, such as: 'Why can't you get this into your head?'; 'Is your brain filled with sawdust?'; 'Have you lost your mind?'. This clearly hurts:

> 'No, [saying it was mindless work] would make me feel bad. Because when we know we have to do this work in a certain way, it is because we have gained knowledge about it. Someone has told us that this is how you need to do the dusting, this is how you need to do the sweeping, this is how you do the mopping. Now if, in that someone tells you that you don't have any sense ... or you don't seem to listen to instructions, or you have become like "this", then one feels bad about it ...' (*Mohini*)

Several other factors contributed towards the construction of cleaning as *labour* in the Indian research site. Very few live-out providers worked in the absence of householders, and when they did, keys were left in a prearranged place, such as with a neighbour. The service-providers could not develop small-business skills, because the work was always done informally. Some communicated with a mobile phone with service-users, but text messaging was not mentioned among my sample, as many providers were illiterate.[13] In the UK, service-providers routinely messaged or emailed clients, or both left notes to inform each other about, for example, swapping routine tasks with non-routine tasks, missed out work or holidays.

The Indian businesswoman Usha succinctly illuminated the differences between cleaning *work* and cleaning *labour*:

> '... my brother has help in [the United States] ... I'm amazed by the level of quality of the work which is done ... I saw [the help working] just once, I saw, automatically, quietly [working], kitchen is sparkling, everything is in place, the slabs are clean, the cupboards also, if she has time, she's cleaning the cupboards ... And the flooring is ... and you know, the bedsheets are removed, done, machine, ta, ta, ta. Fantastic work, while here, you have to be on their heads, supervising, checking ... I mean, here in my loo, you'll find that she hasn't cleaned the shower, or the walls and I have to get it done, or I have to do it myself. But there, they all ... it's done as a routine ...' (Usha)

The difference in structure of paid-for cleaning in the two research settings, however, cannot be read as a straightforward UK–India difference. Social understandings of 'women's work' as work anyone can do cross cultures, and cleaning is also constructed as 'mindless' labour in the West. Taylorised and time-and-motion models followed by domestic and commericial cleaning firms and care agencies include strict job- and labour-intensification by task fragmentation (Ehrenreich, 2002/2010; Mayer-Ahuja, 2004; Mendez, 1998; Rubery et al, 2011; Sykes et al, 2014), a key factor in worker disincentivisation (Goerdeler et al, 2015; Oakley, 1974/1985:81). As Janet, who used agency cleaners, mused:

> '[There were] differences between individual service-providers, so there's a really thorough one who'll do my kitchen window sill, which involves taking plants and knick-knacks …, whereas another service-provider another week will … look at it and go, "Well I don't think that's in my job description" and just leave it.' (Janet)

Salzinger's (1991) analysis of the ethos of two Californian domestic-worker collectives helps to contextualise my findings. Amigos positioned domestic cleaning as a stop-gap job for newly migrated working-class Latinas with little education. Rather than making the work motivating, members were encouraged: to take on cleaning regardless of their knowledge about it and language differences impeding communication with service-users; not to resist exploitative service-users, but to charge low fees; and to do as many jobs as possible and 'move on'. Unsurprisingly, there were frequent complaints from service-users. At meetings, members talked about their life circumstances and tribulations, rather than the work of cleaning. In contrast, Choices' members were often well-educated, middle-class Latinas interested in professionalising cleaning work, rather than in 'moving on'. Regular training sessions included detailed discussions on cleaning products and methods. Members were taught to be assertive and to charge a respectable fee, take pride in their work, drop exploitative customers and impress on their service-users their expertise in housekeeping matters.

Salzinger argued that the collectives' target markets determined the construction of cleaning as *labour* by Amigos and as *work* by Choices. Choices catered to the higher end of the market: the affluent (White) American professional middle-class, for whom hiring an 'expert' cleaner was part of the contemporary middle-class zeitgeist. Amigos targeted dual-earner/single mother families or elderly retirees, who needed external help but could just about afford to outsource domestic work. Mattila argued that the increasingly short-term arrangements with live-out providers in Jaipur were reflective of modern 'market logic' (2011:190; also Sen and Sengupta, 2016). That is, to avoid paying more, service-users keep changing service-providers, and the latter also drop service-users when better-paid jobs come up. I argue that this is also part of the construction of cleaning as *labour*, rather than to do just with market logic. In my UK samples, where responsive relationships had been developed, live-out providers worked for long periods for one client within the contemporary capitalist market (range 5 to over 40 years; Figure 5.1). Similar relationships were also evident in India (also Sen and Sengupta, 2016).

Salzinger further noted that Choices' members' middle-class capital made them 'likely to conceptualize their work – even work for which they initially had little respect – in professional terms' (1991:154–155).

Figure 5.1: Length of service provision

(a) Service-users' report of time (in years) with current service-provider

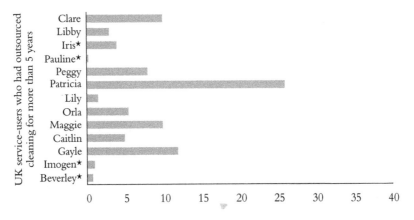

(b) Service-providers' report of time (in years) with a current service-user

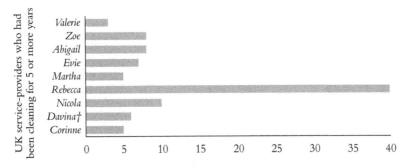

Notes: *At least one previous service-provider worked for this user for several years.
†Previously worked as employee of one household for many years.

My data suggest that the latter point is of greater significance than implied by Salzinger, who, like Mattila, places more emphasis on market conditions. The UK service-providers worked for a range of customers, from the well-heeled to those with modest means. Although they were mostly working-class women, their education and work histories (Appendix A, Table A.1) made them comparable with Choices' rather than Amigos' workers. Salzinger's and my data show that being educated does not mean one has to disparage domestic work (to be feminist); rather, educated service-providers can help to transform cleaning from *labour* to *work*.

Finally, when cleaning is recognised as clean rather than dirty work,[14] the mental labour that underpins the competence of the worker with the necessary manual skills is acknowledged, and there is no contradiction between the two views on paid-for cleaning presented earlier. That is, when service-providers claim they clean 'like they clean their own homes' it does not mean that they are doing the same work, but that they are putting in similar manual *and* mental effort, just like those who say they do not clean as they would at home.

Conclusion

The difference in structuring of outsourced cleaning in the British and Indian settings confirms Bujra's conclusion, that the link between women's paid and unpaid housework is not a total social fact:

> pre-market skills and ideologies are not transferred unproblematically to the wage sector ... what women do at work is not simply an extension of their domestic role, because domestic labour is transformed by the terms on which it is carried out. (Bujra, 2000:85; also Sen and Sengupta, 2016)

Some training appears necessary, but, as researchers such as Mendez (1998) and Lan (2006) have shown, this training is being delivered within a discourse that privileges (white) secular middle-class values and practices around domesticity as morally superior, and assumes that the work of cleaning is inscribed on the bodies of people of a particular class, caste or racial background. Thus, the training does not improve the conditions of outsourced housework and workers' rights. My research adds to existing evidence that shows societal 'norms' can – and should – be challenged, to enable workers to 'restructure the work', by rejecting 'demeaning and degrading practices' (Romero, 2002:166; see also Rafkin, 1998).

The elucidation of the structure of outsourced cleaning in the UK and Indian research sites also shows that paid-for cleaning is not inherently mindless *labour*. Rose's elegant description of how the conditions of work influence a hairdresser's ability to exercise mental skills and feel a sense of achievement (which are vital for good work), holds true for responsive domestic cleaning in the contemporary urban context as well: '[t]he more enervating and demeaning the conditions, the less opportunity to enhance one's skills, display creativity, and develop satisfying relationships with clients and with fellow stylists' (Rose, 2004/2014:50). In the next chapter, I analyse the meanings of cleaning as *work* and *labour* for the service-providers.

Meanings of Domestic Cleaning as *Work* and *Labour*

....

It was an epiphanic moment, when two sprightly White British women who had recently opened a cleaning business firmly told me they had clients, not employers. Could I dismiss their understandings of their working conditions and relationships as false-consciousness? From then on, I asked the UK service-providers and service-users how they defined their employment relationship. Later, these data informed my re-presentation of my respondents' accounts.

....

Introduction

> '[M]y assumption was that cleaning is something that enables people to get a bit of extra cash.' (Harriet)

> 'I want to put money in a bank account so that a bank can see that I'm earning, so that one day I can get a mortgage. ... So I need proof that I earn a certain amount of money. So the more that I can prove, the better for me really.' (*Jessica*)

This chapter interrogates the meanings of cleaning work for the British and Indian cleaning service-providers for their selfhood and as kin-members. It then considers the material injustices in cleaning done as *work* or *labour*. Within Douglas's overarching framework (see Chapter 2), Pollert's (1981, 1996) historical materialist analysis provided the starting point for this chapter: gender and class are simultaneously primary analytical categories, because both in private and in public, class[1] mediates gendered oppression;

this mediation is historically (Vera-Sanso, 2008) and temporally (Bailey and Madden, 2017) specific. I also refer to the Marxist feminist lens, where relevant, to aid linking my analysis to wider (feminist) research on paid domestic work. Finally, upper-class gender and class ideologies might function as reference standards not only among respondents but also for researchers, who are classed and gendered themselves. To limit the influence of my etic understandings on the analysis, I drew on Jackson's (2011) notion that reflexivity is not class- or capital-bound, and on Kabeer's (2001) conceptualisation of 'empowerment'.

The positive meanings attributed to low-paid care work have been analysed by several researchers (see review by Hebson et al, 2015). Drawing on Bourdieu, feminists such as Skeggs (1997/2002) have argued that working-class women's (mis)appropriation and (mis)accrual of middle-class feminine capital, in the presence of limited economic and education capitals, keeps them entrenched in society's basement. The sense of 'fulfilment' in their caring labour cloaks the pain of no gain in symbolic capital. Furthermore, the feminine (non)-capital drawing working-class women into caring is mediated by their social (non)-capital, with family or friends in similar jobs acting as role models (Hebson et al, 2015).

Conversely, greater education and material resources allow people to make better-informed choices, in part because they reinforce embodied capital (self-confidence/belief; Atkinson, 2010), and in part because self-reflexivity is associated with access to 'higher' symbolic capital (Atkinson, 2010; Walters and Whitehouse, 2012). Skeggs (1997/2002:161) concluded that the decisions and actions of her sample of working-class carers were about 'halting losses', rather than achieving worthwhile outcomes – where 'worthwhile' is understood as middle-class symbolic capital.

Jackson (2011)[2] argued that late-modern self-reflexivity, as defined by Giddens and Beck, is a specific, particular form of reflexivity. Its universalisation has resulted in an erroneous perception of 'reflexive selfhood' as class-bounded, whereas, reflexivity forms 'the basis of all sociality, of *being* social and participating *in* the social ... the ability to imagine oneself from the other's perspective and anticipate the other's responses to oneself' (original emphasis), but individual ability to be reflexive is limited by the always-already overarching material structures and social institutions whose effects 'transcend everyday realities'. Oppressed individuals 'often need to be highly reflexive' even if their class (and gender or racialised) position constrains 'the degree to which and the directions in which' reflexivity is realised (Jackson, 2011:16–19; also Reay, 2004).

Jackson's thesis finds purchase in published accounts of reflexivity across occupations including domestic work. Research on UK-based refuse collectors, stonemasons and academics showed that all these workers drew on the same understandings of meaningful or meaningless work (autonomy, shared appreciation of work well done and temporality – no work was always meaningful or meaningless) (Bailey and Madden, 2017). Saldaña-Tejeda observed how Mexican employers effortlessly provided a narrative 'of the self as a way to justify their privileged position', whereas domestic workers talked in terms of the constraints they faced (2015:953). But then she notes that the 'difference' in narratives might have been a product of the way both groups positioned her in relation to themselves. The employers saw her as one of them, the workers as the Other. Furthermore, looking beyond the biographies, Saldaña-Tejeda found evidence of reflexive explanations in the workers' narratives, as allowed by their limited economic and educational resources and occupation. Not only were they 'conscious about the way traditional norms, especially around sexuality, shaped their biographies but they also highlighted how things have changed … a process of detraditionalization and the way they saw themselves within it' (Saldaña-Tejeda, 2015:954). Romero was 'struck by the way' in which Chicana domestics made 'the most of their options' (2002:175). Still, Western feminist and 'development' studies often construct a singular 'Third World woman' using the lens of (dis)empowerment (Vera-Sanso, 2008).

Kabeer's (2001) incisive analysis then highlights the problems of conceptualising (dis)empowerment as a quantifiable ability to make 'a' choice at 'a' point in time. Empowerment is better conceived as a process, a shift from a position of inability to having ability to make choices that result in 'valued ways of "being and doing"' (Kabeer, 2001:21, drawing on Sen's capabilities approach). This requires access to various resources and 'the ability to define one's goals and act on them' within the constraints of institutionalised values and beliefs (Kabeer, 2001:21). Defined in such a way, any person's empowerment becomes a valid subject of study. As Kabeer points out (and Chapter 3 shows), career women often cannot deploy their resources to shift the gendered dynamics of the domestic, to stop policing their public self or to disrupt gendered ways of working, in short, 'to be and do' (see, for example, Walters and Whitehouse, 2012). Moreover, Vera-Sanso (2008) pointed out that gender-essentialist feminist research overlooks the cross-cultural, class-related issues faced by women. For example, poverty is a more likely determinant of pooling of incomes in couples than gendered power that might manifest 'differently' in different cultures.

In sum, Kabeer's (2001) understanding of empowerment dovetails with Jackson's (2011) position that self-reflexivity per se is not an inherent characteristic of privilege. The analysis presented in this chapter will bear out my standpoint – grounded in these prior works – for a single framework for studying the conditions of work in both of my research contexts.

Experiences of domestic cleaning as *work* and *labour*

I start by presenting the White British women's accounts. I consider their experiences of work more generally and the move into domestic cleaning, both as declared or undeclared self-employed service-providers. In this, I unpack the work conditions of self-employment in detail. Next, I consider the Indian women's experiences and the possibilities in domestic work in the Indian social context.

*"It's the same with any job really, isn't it?" (*Yvonne*)*

Eighteen UK respondents were registered self-employed traders (Appendix A, Table A.1). Nine were working full-time and eight were building their business. The middle-class respondents had had one or two careers previously. The rest had a chequered work history. The previous jobs ranged from entry-level and service occupations to administrative and managerial work, primarily in female-dominated areas (Appendix A, Table A.1), and changed mostly due to structural constraints (for example redundancies, discrimination against pregnant women, childcare responsibilities) and/or altered life circumstances (for example moving house, divorce). This reflects established working patterns among British working class women (Hebson et al, 2015; James, 2008; Walters, 2005; Warren, 2000; Warren et al, 2009). Several women also continually sought jobs with better pay prospects, which eventually underpinned their decision to 'go it alone' as a cleaning service-provider. There were, however, other reasons too:

> 'In my other job, you're a number in a factory with a lot of people. You can be friendly with your bosses, your line leaders, but at the end of the day, if you do the slightest thing wrong, they'd sack you straight away. Whereas this, it's different. Yes, it's a different relationship with them. So, no, I enjoy it …' (*Olivia*)

Olivia's comment shows that a key factor in work done as *work* rather than *labour* is not being just another body in the workplace (Johnson, 2002).

Nora had felt undervalued by her employing organisation in her previous caring job, and her increased self-worth and feeling of pride in setting up her cleaning business came through strongly in the interview:

> 'I wanted a challenge. Yeah! I wanted to work for myself. I'd worked on the community [health team], dealing with people, administering medication, which I had to go through a lot of training for … and … I just felt I could take it on myself to go and help people and not work for a company. A big company, that didn't really … value me [Later] … The clients made you feel valued but not the companies you work for … They have too many policies and procedures that suit them.' (*Nora*)

Nora enjoyed cleaning, but she had no illusions about it being all "good" work. A minority of her customers were not considerate, but "[t]hat's business isn't it? There are good days and bad days."

In the early 1900s, accounts of housework as 'drudgery' by some British women were contested by others, who argued it was no worse than a host of repetitive jobs in 'the office, the shop, and the factory' (Schwartz, 2015). Later, in the heyday of the Fordist era in the mid-twentieth century, Dalla Costa and James argued that the 'liberation of the working-class woman' did not 'lie in her getting a job outside the home' because '[s]lavery to an assembly line is not a liberation from slavery to a kitchen sink' (1973:35). My contemporary UK respondents also described several jobs as mundane. *Celia*, an English graduate and young mother, found her office work stifling:

> 'All work's repetitive! Well, like my last job was … I told you it was in a solicitor's office but it was the same phone-calls over and over again, checking the same information over and over again, having to go to team meetings over and over again, where you're having to discuss people who've gone 30 seconds over for having a wee, so it's the same, yeah! … whatever job we do, there's that element, isn't there?' (*Celia*)

This is not unusual. For example, see comments by checkout operators in Walters (2005) and careworkers in Rubery et al (2011) and comments in Dowling (2014). Even careers sold as 'creative' and 'elitist' include standardised deskilling work processes, and can be experienced as dull and unimaginative (Bailey and Madden, 2017; Costas and Kärreman, 2016). Mundaneness, it seems, is a basic feature of work. Autonomous working can reduce monotony somewhat, and my respondents said they varied routines and schedules when they sensed repetition.

A few respondents flatly stated that cleaning ended up being women's work:

'Because I do have a male cleaner ... And I do have to check his work, he'll do anything and work any hours that you want but you have to keep an eye on him. But, saying that, I've got five brothers, and all are really good cleaners. But my dad was in the army and we had to clean as a child ... which is probably where my OCD's [obsessive compulsive disorder] come from. But my brother, when he was out of work he worked with me and he was a really good cleaner. And all my brothers are actually really good cleaners. So I don't know, I think a man can do it, but I think it's easier for a man just to get a woman to do it and pretend that they can't do it. I think that's the problem and women do it ...' (*Tamsin*)

'... Boys can clean just as good as girls. You don't often get a male cleaner, really cause, I've never really, if someone came to me and he was a man ... I wouldn't discriminate against him, there's no discrimination in there. It is not often that you find a male cleaner, which is, uuh, they're not very domestic are they? It's a domestic kind of job ... and it is technically discriminative I suppose, because it is a ... technically a woman's world isn't it?' (*Vera*)

But I often sensed affront when I asked whether cleaning was proper work:

'No, no, it is a job. I go out in the morning and I get paid for doing that ... service. So to me that is a job.' (*Amelia*)

'you're going cleaning, it's manual labour, ... you're coming out sweating from it, ... anyone can go and sit behind a desk ... You go behind there, what do they think cleaners do? What's that they don't think is a proper job? What – because it is classed as a lower job that ... you can't have a career in cleaning? Which I'm assuming? That is what it is.' (*Vera*)

Most declared service-providers emphasised that they were neither servants nor simply 'a cleaner'. They were working women, running a cleaning business – there were differences in the structure of their unpaid and paid housework (see Chapter 5). It was demeaning when "some customers ... treat it as a joke job, like 'Oh! we'll just ring up that morning, just cancel', forgetting that it's ... your living" (*Zoe*). These women saw possibilities in doing 'women's work' as independent workers – possibilities that had been lacking in previous jobs.

The possibilities in cleaning work in the UK

> '[Domestic cleaning] is a hidden gem ... [it] has always been a pretty reliable profession. ... I know someone who has a PhD and she was struggling to get a job. And she set up her own cleaning business ...' (*Zoe*)

Cleaning provides regular work that often requires little initial investment. *Zoe's* husband joined her cleaning business when he lost his job. Ambitious *Vera* saw cleaning as a less-risky way to finance other entrepreneurial ventures. Middle-class mother *Evie's* parents had always employed cleaners. Eight years ago, she found that she needed to work, because her partner's career was floundering. *Evie* lacked resources to restart a defunct family business and rejected a teaching assistantship, because of the "ridiculous hours and pay". Seeing the demand for cleaners among her town's affluent elderly population, she opened a cleaning business.

Delap noted an increase in domestic workers during the 1930s depression (2007:82); similarly during the recession in the 1980s, women sought this work when husbands lost their jobs.[3] More recent South–North female migration has built on the reliability of domestic work. Some cleaning franchises[4] stress to interested parties that cleaning is 'recession-proof'. In fact, the story of human civilisation(s) is not about men's progressive achievements but of the continuance of reproductive work. The poignant story reproduced in the following quotation, from a study into the low-pay/no-pay cycle of life in Teesside, encapsulates effectively the long history of precarity and job insecurity of 'men's work' (Gunn and Bell, 2002; Sen and Sengupta, 2016):

> I [was] ... laid off after seven months. It was just due to the way everything went, like. He was putting in for grants to expand his business and he was getting knocked back so he had to make cutbacks himself. ... I used to enjoy getting up on a morning to go to work. It was a proper company as well so I felt safe and secure in it. I knew everybody in there ...

so it was just gutting when I got laid off. (quoted in Shildrick et al, 2012:136)

Truss et al (2013) argued that 'feminine' work involves little risk-taking, which lowers its status. But starting up and running a small business involves risks (Wall, 2015), even if it is about domestic work. *Tamsin* was employing subcontractors rather than issuing zero-hour contracts, at the risk of compromising the profitability of her cleaning quasi-agency (see next section). Key-holders risk being accused of theft. Service-providers also take risks with their own safety (see later in this chapter). Migrant domestic workers encounter risks during migration, such as safe places to live, the first job and the risks associated with doing undocumented work (Kindler, 2008; Momsen, 1999). Indeed, the decision to become a self-employed cleaning service-provider or an informal worker may involve much self-reflexivity, including rejecting 'being managed'.

Self-employment and housecleaning in the UK context

Self-employment in cleaning is often assumed to be synonymous with undeclared work, with scant research among declared service-providers (but see Hondagneu-Sotelo, 2001; Meagher, 2003). These workers might be a minority, however experiences of small groups that break the mould are important for a fuller understanding of the meanings of work (Marshall, 1995; Potter, 2015).

Martha worked as a part-time bank teller. This job involved being monitored for "how productive I am", which *Martha* found constricting and stressful:

> 'Banking can be boring yeah! … it's repetitive and there are times you do, you are told to do your job a certain way and you can't justify why you are doing it that way. It's the way you're told to do it.' (*Martha*)

Consequently, in her early forties, *Martha* opened a part-time cleaning business, to experience working autonomously.[5] While *Martha* appreciated being part of her bank's team for two days every week, the rest of the time, she said, "it is nice to just be … not in the team but just on my own. I'm responsible for the job, that is quite nice. … And I don't mind cleaning, I find it easy and I have no issues with it."

Sophie gave up her assistant retail manager post, when she realised that company policies insidiously embedded unpaid overtime into her routine schedule. Following a brief stint at a cleaning agency, she struck out on her own because:

> 'it has had a positive effect on my life, because I can work the hours I want. If I want to take a holiday, I can do without having to book with work, have weekends off, have bank holidays off, and I do actually have every other Thursday off as well, so I can, you know, choose my times. I'm a bit more in control of my *time* in general and *where* I want to go ...' (*Sophie*)

In post-Fordist times, Taylorist and neo-Taylorist forms of management and discipline have increased across occupations (BBC One, 2013; Carey, 2007; Carter et al, 2011; Cooper and Taylor, 2000; Costas and Kärreman, 2016; Jacobs and Padavic, 2015). 'Flexibility' is like a catch-22 situation, and dissatisfaction with being 'managed' was a recurrent theme in my interviews (Geary, 1992; Rubery et al, 2011; Shildrick et al, 2012; Smith and Elliot, 2012):

> 'Yeah! That's what's important for me. I don't want to work for somebody. I've done it. And then ... one of my children's in hospital, for only 10 days. But I got disciplined at work for it even though I'd worked for *every* minute I'd missed ... and I just thought I don't want to work for somebody, because my children will always come first.' (*Celia*)

In several older American studies, the live-out multi-client cleaners working informally also preferred the vendor–customer relationship (Glenn, 1986; Hondagneu-Sotelo, 2001; Romero, 2002). Yet, the employee–employer relationship is overwhelmingly accepted as the frame of reference, because it is etically seen as the most secure way to work.[6]

Glenn (1986, 1992) contended that it was the persistence of pre-industrialist personalism and asymmetry in contemporary paid domestic work that justified considering the relationship as an employer–employee type. Romero, using a Marxist feminist framework, discounted Glenn's justification; she asserted that the domestic employer–employee relationship was 'an instance of [capitalist] class struggle ... [women] employing private household workers and childcare workers share[d] the same self-interest as other employers' (2002:7–8). Romero's respondents, however, were using strategies of self-employment to improve working conditions, such as negotiating fees and benefits individually with each client. Lutz's (2011) respondents often rejected the 'employee' label; but the research team still referred to them as employees, because as researchers, they assumed that the vendor–client labels obfuscated the power–dependence equation in domestic work. Meagher (2003) acknowledged the substantive differences between 'client' and 'employer', but still used the terms interchangeably.

There are differences in employer–employee and vendor–client employment relations (Rose and Pevalin, 2005). The International Domestic Workers' Network (IDWN, 2011) and the ILO recognise these different employment relationships, and the ILO convention does not include self-employed cleaners in its remit (Pape, 2016). The UK's employment status indicator[7] confirmed my respondents' claim of being self-employed (see also Behling and Harvey, 2015), hence, my decision to use the terms 'service-provider' and 'service-user'. A key issue in (low-wage) self-employment, however, is whether a self-employed person would find the same work more attractive under conditions of employment (Kautonen et al, 2010, cited in Cruz et al, 2017:276). Thus, before considering the merits and demerits of self-employment, I discuss my respondents' reasons for avoiding cleaning-agency/firm employment.

Across cultures, feminists have shown how capitalist cleaning/care agencies have co-opted the 'wages for housework' debate to give back to women (and men) their work under Taylorist conditions, reminiscent of historical servitude. Similar to other low-wage work (Shildrick et al, 2012), through personalism and depersonalism, and working to pre-prepared scripts, domestic *work* is reduced to *labour*, resulting in disenfranchisement and exploitation (Abrantes, 2014a; Breslin and Wood, 2016; Devetter and Rousseau, 2009; Ehrenreich, 2000; Lan, 2006; Mendez, 1998; Tomei, 2011; van Walsum, 2011). Meagher's (2003) account of bespoke housekeeping services offered by Australian firms/franchises and Bowman and Cole's (2014) favourable impression of Swedish cleaning companies suggest progressive business models, in which workers' rights are protected by censoring abusive clients, through the opportunity for collective bargaining, and via third-party mediation of wages and job descriptions. About seven UK service-providers would have switched jobs, if they had found one with similar advantages. Three respondents had experience of cleaning-agency employment, and few service-users had used agencies. Many service-providers found the contractual obligations of being employed constraining:

> 'Obviously it's better working for yourself, you've got nobody ... sort of sending you wherever, you know where you're going, you know your clients and they know you, which is a lot better.' (*Grace*)

They liked negotiating with prospective clients. It was part of doing cleaning as *work*: the ability to decide which services to offer and which risks to take, and developing responsiveness by becoming partners in the vendor–client relationship rather than just 'the cleaner'.

> 'Yes, if I'm meeting new clients, I'll ask them to show me round the home and I'll ask them to tell me what they expect from me, as a cleaner. And they all differ. Nobody actually says they want me to move furniture and go behind it. Some want the windows cleaning inside and some don't at all. Some really just want it spruced up. Some are a bit more particular.' (*Martha*)

> 'Yes, I go to the house first to meet them, and they show me around the house, and they'll tell me what they want me to do, and I'll say if there's anything you want me to do differently or anything extra, just let me know, that fine, and I'll do it for you. So basically, so when I go, they'll show me round the house and then, umm, I said, right, do you want every room doing every time and they sort of like tell me everything, then they'll tell me about they're going to be in or not, and what times, and just everything like that. What's your charge and I tell them all that when I go.' (*Grace*)

Moreover, several companies follow a multi-level subcontracting business model, which comprises an informal market at ground level. Swedish companies 'may register a few workers as formal employees but simultaneously hire additional workers informally'; recruitment may occur through social networks that favour some workers and exclude others, and so on (Gavanas, 2010:27).[8] Bowman and Cole (2014) opined that with time, because of tax-breaks on outsourcing and inventive practices, the Swedish 'in/formal' market would shrink. According to Devetter and Rousseau (2009), however, this did not happen in France, where similar tax-breaks were introduced in the early 1990s. Moreover, cleaning agencies/firms are mostly for-profit and, like care agencies (McGuire and Lozada, 2017), they can close, change their name, drop workers, and so on. Blanket regulations cannot ensure quality work or unpaid overtime (Gullikstad et al, 2016) and may obstruct development of responsiveness (see Chapter 5). So while agencies or firms recognise the value of a 'regular' cleaner (Bowman and Cole, 2014), often there is high staff turnover like in other low-wage work with similar issues (Shildrick et al, 2012; Sykes et al, 2014). Companies try preventing poaching of customers, by tying workers and users into contracts. Both sides may not see such clauses as empowering, and can reflexively circumvent them:

> '[I]t was in our contracts that you couldn't pinch a client, so you had to be very careful how you said things. So I just went around saying, "I'm leaving because I'm starting my own business, so if you know anybody ..." Some clients always said to me, "If ever you leave, I'll go with you." Umm, so I didn't ask them, they asked me.' (*Sophie*)

All the registered service-providers had professional indemnity insurance. Many were Disclosure and Barring Service (DBS)[9] checked, which has become a measurable way of establishing baseline trust. But my respondents gave me thoughtful reasons why formal contracts were not always appropriate and they did not engage with them. They were not atomised workers and their job was not just to hoover and spray a lot of room freshener for effect, but to leave each house feeling welcoming and individual. Establishing rapport and, subsequently, a friendly work relationship (see Chapter 7) based on mutual trust was important:

> 'I want them to keep me because they want to keep *me* and not because they're tied into a contract.' (*Tamsin*)

> 'It should be a simple communication between people, if you like the clean, you keep the clean, if you don't, then you don't.' (*Vera*)

Valerie pointed out that contracts could be daunting for elderly clients:

> '[T]o tie an elderly person into a contract, you can't do that, like the gentleman who's just died, he'd been in and out of hospital since January, so one minute we're working, one minute we're not. So ... you can't tie them into a contract.' (*Valerie*)

Service-providers also preferred to reserve the right to drop customers. In long-term relationships, terms of service could change. Thus, usually some dos and don'ts were agreed verbally, such as a minimum of two hours' work (to cover travel time and costs), 24–48 hours' cancellation notice and advance holiday notice. These women were not behaving irresponsibly. Rather, they were participating in a considered refusal of 'good' business practices.

Four UK service-providers whom I interviewed were also running small agencies and engaging selectively with 'good' business practices, to strike a balance between growing their business and allowing their subcontractors to work as autonomously as possible. The following quote succinctly captures the essence of this 'quasi-agency' model. The owner was not sitting in an office, but wore several hats: owner, manager, hirer, admin worker and cleaner:

> 'I actually go with them ... it's me who does the induction. And I usually go with them for a few weeks on a new clean because I like to do them as well, so that if I have to stand in, I know how to do them ... This means I'm still meeting the customer as well, and sort of keeping a rapport as well.' (*Tamsin*)

A regular team of cleaners was allocated to each client. To avoid the risk of poaching, however, the owner often spent extra time doing 'customer relations', and substituted for absent subcontractors *herself*. Customers were charged the same rate regardless of whether the work was done by subcontractors or the owner (£10–11 per hour), and the average subcontractor fee was £7 an hour. Thus, the commission was not enough to pay national insurance or holiday pay, and three owners used zero-hour contracts. However, the owner paid professional indemnity insurance for subcontractors, and provided uniforms and materials. *Tamsin* also paid DBS fees. Most carried out inductions to ensure quality work, and if subcontractors reported problems, the quasi-agency owner dealt with them. Subcontractors did not participate in the initial agreement about hours of work; however, if it persistently took longer, they could request renegotiation. Otherwise, the owner did not dictate work routines to subcontractors and the customer directly negotiated with the subcontractor for small changes to the agreed work. These practices appeared similar to the actions taken by the owner of a UK care agency, whose phenomenal success and rapid growth prompted Breslin and Wood (2016) to investigate it. The founder initially put in place several rules and regulations as per the registration requirements of the Care Quality Commission to establish a reputable agency, but then permitted 'rule-breaking behaviours',[10] when formal rules seem to hinder client-focused relationships and continuity of care. Such rule-breaking did not lead to mayhem; rather, carers were self-motivated to provide high-value service.

All declared service-providers were paid by cash, cheques or direct bank transfer. Indeed, cash payment does not implicitly imply informal work or that a service-provider "does not know their way around a self assessment tax form" (Mumsnet, 2013a). A few service-providers issued receipts.

Two further issues require consideration here. First, particularly since the 2008 recession, several organisations have been co-opting the principles of self-employment to avoid fulfilling employed workers' rights (Behling and Harvey, 2015; Chakrabortty, 2016; Cruz et al, 2017; Harvey et al, 2017; Lalani and Metcalf, 2012; Rankin and Butler, 2015). Such pseudo-practices have rightly raised concerns (Barnes, 2013; D'Arcy and Gardiner, 2014; Harris, 2012; Philpott, 2012), as the pseudo-self-employed workers work under non-autonomous conditions termed 'neo-villeiny' by Harvey and colleagues (2017:19). Such individuals often earn less than employees in the same situation (Linder and Houghton, 1990). In my research, there was no third-party mediation of the (verbal) contract (except by quasi-agency owners), service-providers had several clients at one time, and they had considerable control over work schedules and methods. As a primary aim of working was to earn a living, the more successful and established service-providers were earning similar (or somewhat higher) hourly rates than in previous jobs, although everyone recognised that cleaning is among the lower-paid jobs. In Marxist terms, unlike the pseudo-self-employed person or cleaning-agency employee, the independent cleaning service-provider receives the full exchange-value of the service they have delivered.

Second, Cruz and colleagues (2017) advised caution around contemporary discourses that seek to valorise individual workers' efforts and the entrepreneurial spirit as states and large employers withdraw their social responsibilities. Fifteen declared UK service-providers had opened their business after 2008, and, thus, the same caution could be argued for my sample. However, some middle-class men and women are downshifting in search of 'meaningful' work, having failed to find self-actualisation in elite careers (Marshall, 1995; Potter, 2015; Wilhoit, 2014). Here, sociological analyses take a philosophical turn, drawing on concepts such as selfhood and individualism: 'these men and women have the access and "ability" to imagine and carry out – more meaningful – work-life trajectories' (Potter, 2015:9; also Mainiero and Sullivan, 2005; Marshall, 1995). Moreover, the direct vendor–customer relationship, akin to Marx's simple commodity production, is not a new form of work. The ideology of 'being one's own boss' existed before industrialisation and, theoretically speaking, capitalism should have engulfed self-employment (Steinmetz and Wright, 1989). But it continues to persist. My respondents were not alone in their rejection of contemporary employment and work conditions. In a survey by the Work Foundation, 73% of 1,000 people became self-employed post-2008 either 'wholly or partly' because of a 'personal preference for this way of working' rather than 'solely due to a lack of better work alternatives' (D'Arcy and Gardiner, 2014:4; also Figure 6.1).

In sum, although their wages were still comparatively low and their work stigmatised (see Chapter 7), my respondents made reflexive decisions about 'moving on' within the constraints of their social locations. Their precarity was not because of self-employment per se (see also Wall, 2015), but low remuneration due to structural factors that maintain age-old hierarchies in egalitarian societies, such as lack of legal recognition for

Figure 6.1: Reasons for choosing self-employment

(a) Main reason for choosing self-employment – by percentage of all self-employed people

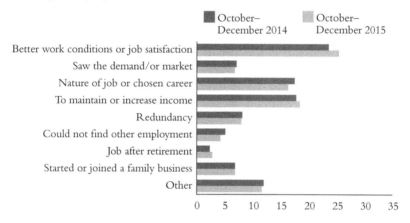

(b) Percentage of women working as self-employed cleaners/domestics choosing each reason for becoming self-employed (2014: n=111; 2015: n=101)

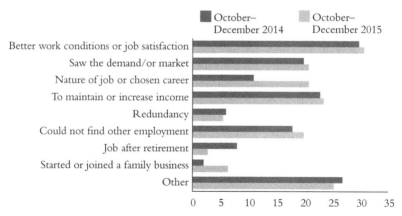

Notes: Labour Force Survey, last quarter (October–December) 2014 and 2015.
Data source: Labour Force Survey, ONS, October 2016.

domestic work and the artificial division of work into high and low status based on 'skill' and the mental–manual divide (see Chapter 5).

The presence of dependent children or personal status had no association with the likelihood of declaring the income (Appendix A, Table A.1). The older declared service-providers started with the intention of doing something for themselves. Still, eight women chose to work informally, and this pattern of working forms a significant part of the sector.

Cleaning on the side in the UK

Gregson and Lowe (1994a) conjectured that abundant feminine but limited education and financial capital (thanks to the structure of the UK's welfare system) pulled older working-class women into informal cleaning jobs to avoid poverty. My sample included women who challenged this generalisation. Consider the choices made by *Martha*, the bank teller introduced previously, and *Charlotte*, a farmer's wife. *Martha* could have justified not declaring her cleaning income on the grounds that she was a divorcee with two dependent children and had lost out on earnings previously as a part-time working wife. But *Martha* was not doing cleaning work to just make up lost income, she was doing it for herself, for her self-worth. *Charlotte's* four-bedroom family home appeared as well furnished as *Martha's*. She juggled three jobs: farm admin and an antiques business, which she declared, and cleaning, which she did not declare. She said it was her way of doing 'right by her family', for instance, buying her children good Christmas presents:

> 'I wouldn't do it [if I had to declare it] because it wouldn't be worth it. Because the way we are with the books, with the farm, everything is above board and I have a certain amount of money out of the farm – I don't have it, but it's said that I have it and it goes back into the business ... [so] we'd end up paying much more [tax] than I'm earning [from cleaning].' (*Charlotte*)

Several others were also working underhand to partially circumvent the tax system: *Corinne* had been a teacher, but her pension and income from child-minding was not enough for her to have a quality retired life; *Nicola* had been a supply teacher while also cleaning to support three children as a single mother; *Carrie* had been a university student. But underhand payment does not make the work demeaning or *labour* per se. Many of these women appeared committed to doing a professional job in a similar way to the declared service-providers, and their accounts contributed to my delineation of the structure of paid-for housecleaning in Chapter 5.

"They say majboori[11] has no boundaries" (Anika)

Most Indian service-providers were working to make ends meet and educate their children, with the hope that their lives would be better (Banerjee, 2015; Coelho, 2016; Ray and Qayum, 2009/2010; Sen and Sengupta, 2016; Singh, 2001):

> 'I haven't liked any of my [about ten] employers. We are just "passing time" ... They say majboori has no boundaries. And that's it, we are just working out of majboori. Otherwise, the best place is one's own home. But we couldn't manage by being in our own house [in our own village], we had to migrate. We have come to fill our stomachs. Otherwise, we don't have any home here, or house, or anything. That's it, we just do the jhaddhu-pochha[12] and survive.' (*Anika*)

> '[In the village] we had great difficulty making ends meet. My mother-in-law was alone, so she could not look after our children and me as well. We need to think about the future, that our children should study and be upwardly mobile, they bring pride to the family name. If they work like us, doing jhaddhu-pochha, then what will their life be? That is why I'm doing it ... for my children.' (*Madhu*)

In India, although women from poor and vulnerable groups are more likely to work (Desai et al, 2010; Raghuram, 2001), several respondents did not see their work as integral to their selfhood (see also Bali, 2016; Mattila, 2011; Ray and Qayum, 2009/2010). However, these women were not being unreflexively pushed into domestic work simply due to their lack of middle-class/caste capital or the failure of patriarchy's[13] promise (Ray and Qayum, 2009/2010:26). A key factor in the class–caste oppression of these women is the class–caste oppression of the men in their social world (Bhasin and Khan, 1986/2005), which is often invisibilised by the hegemonic–pathological dichotomisation of middle-class and working-class masculinities (Vera-Sanso, 2008). Nearly two thirds of the Indian service-providers said their 'failed' breadwinners were concerned about their family's welfare (Figure 6.2). But like themselves, the men's limited education and cultural/social capital meant hard work

Figure 6.2: The need to work disaggregated by husband's breadwinning ability as reported by the Indian service-providers

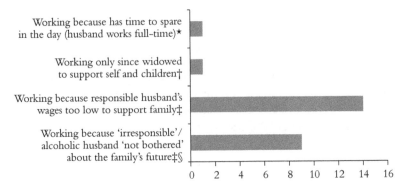

Notes:

*Asha had not done paid work when her husband had been alive.

†Divya had spare time in the day when her child was at school as her 'home' became converted into her husband's ironing shack.

‡Kalpana is included twice, since her first husband was an irresponsible alcoholic but her second husband was a responsible low-wage breadwinner.

§Two of the women with alcoholic husbands were now widows. Both husbands had died young, probably due to their alcoholism. The women had continued to do domestic work in preference to going back to their village and doing other work, to enable their children to avail themselves of the greater educational opportunities available in cities.

was rewarded with dismal wages that have remained static or have declined in recent years (Bremen, 2013; Gill, 2009/2012; Kundu and Mohanon, 2009 cited in Sen and Sengupta, 2016:27; Vera-Sanso, 2008).

> 'No, ... we both need to work. By pooling both our incomes we will be able to do everything easily, food, our other expenses, clothes for the children. He is also uneducated, so when he came from the village, someone helped him get work for Rs1,200–1,300 [£12–13 per month]. Then slowly, slowly, as he worked, he came to know more people and he used to tell them, if you know of any work let me know. In this way, he moved on to other work and finally to this shop.' (Sanvi)

> '[W]hen my husband can't earn enough, then both of us have to work – otherwise how will we cover our living costs? ... Who can bring up four children by oneself [in this city]? ... Nowadays one doesn't earn anything driving a cycle rickshaw ... the customer prefers the tempo [autorickshaw] or then people have four cars in their houses ... [So] I came

here, so I will be able to bring up my children, and when they grow up we will have support in our old age.' (*Neena*)

Thus, bitterness about failed patriarchy often was not an 'anti-men' tirade. As *Rashmi*'s response to my question about her husband's contribution to housework indicates, it was about the crippling of both men and women by the hegemonic institutions of class and caste:

> 'No, I don't let him sweep. He is like me in constitution. Do you know what daily manual labour is like – it is such hard work. He is like me, thin, very thin, his stamina is poor. ... He is also very thin. But like if I am ill, and I am not able to look after the children, he will cook and feed everyone.' (*Rashmi*)

These husbands worked long, six- or seven-day weeks, often doing physically and mentally gruelling work in poor, unhealthy environments (Bharati and Tandon Mehrotra, 2008; Bremen, 2013; Soni-Sinha, 2006). Roy's ironic observation of the material reality of the digital superhighway succinctly illustrates how the condition of 'servanthood' still extends far beyond the domestic sphere: 'Every night outside my house in New Delhi, I pass this road gang of emaciated labourers digging a trench to lay fiber optic cables to speed up our digital revolution. They work by the light of a few candles ...' (Roy and Barsiaman, 2004:30). Such men, then, are vulnerable to alcoholism and other addictions, but how valid is the stereotype of 'irresponsible' working-class masculinities?

> 'I have lived in jhuggis,[14] I have slept on the bare ground, on mounds of pebbles. ... Somehow we have to pass our day. My [alcoholic] husband is also uneducated. ... He doesn't have brain either. Like, I have this much sense that we *need* to work *this much* to educate our children. My husband says, never mind, if they study, it's okay, if they don't, they will continue to live in poverty like us. What is it to us? And I feel that my children should earn enough to eat well, dress well, so I want to educate them well. So whether my gharwala [householder] earns or not, I am earning, I am doing it for my children, I am determined to do it.' (*Anjali*)

The reported prevalence of alcoholism in my sample (Figure 6.2) was largely similar to that reported in previous studies carried out in the wider region in which my research site was located.[15] Many poor men recognise that illiteracy is equated with being 'naturally deficient and shiftless' (Bremen, 2013:91) and their powerlessness in changing their class position. Thus, the pressure to marry, have sons and provide for them while being unable to earn a family wage sometimes means 'harsh consequences for their families and themselves' (Palriwala and Uberoi, 2008:43; also Bremen, 2013; Soni-Sinha, 2006; Vera-Sanso, 2008).[16] South Asian women are not 'naturally' immune to substance abuse: they are less likely to succumb (Benegal et al, 2005; Hettige and Paranagama, 2005), because 'good' women go straight home after work.

Overlooking these factors risks conflating gender with women (Vera-Sanso, 2008) and missing out a key issue in paid domestic work. That is, all Indian service-providers hoped their children would not follow in *either* parent's footsteps: if they did not want them to be exploited, demeaned domestic workers, they also did not want them to be exploited, demeaned dhobis, floating agricultural or daily labourers, or gardeners like their husbands (Bali, 2016; Singh, 2007). This analysis shows that for a fuller understanding of the meanings of domestic work for Western working-class women, in subsequent research, the meanings of Western working-class men's work experiences for the women also requires elaboration. Differences in conditions of work mean that my findings may not necessarily be replicated, but it would further help contextualise domestic work as an occupation.

Earning their own money gave some of the Indian women more control over their own life (see also Sen and Sengupta, 2016):

'I started to work because my husband's income was not enough to make ends meet. He earns Rs 4,000 [per month]. In Rs 4,000 neither are we able to eat three square meals in a day, nor are we able to pay for our children's education. If we both earn and pool our incomes, we can manage nicely. I don't have to ask anyone for money and nor do I lend anyone money. There is a balance.' (*Urvashi*)

Practically all the Indian women had no prior work experience. Yet, they did not do paid domestic work because the only capital they possessed was feminine capital. Rather, their *labour* was commonly exploited based on socio-religious ideologies that inscribe 'polluting' manual labour on their bodies because of their caste and class position (Chigateri, 2007). Some respondents had considered alternatives. But unlike housework, which could be learned on the job, home-based tailoring, for example, required prior training. Also, in *Chetna*'s experience, tailoring was irregular work, and the piece rate was too low to make a reasonable income after overheads. Roadside hawkers are often 'shooed off' by local officials and their wares confiscated. *Brinda* had thought about becoming a fruit and vegetable vendor, but she could not afford the initial investment. Elsewhere, employees, particularly those doing housekeeping jobs, have reported a preference for domestic work due to the harsher conditions of work in their organisations (Coelho, 2016). What possibilities were there, then, in domestic work for these women?

Possibilities in cleaning work in India and employment status of the service-providers

Domestic work often provides 'the most stable component' of the income in poor households (Sen and Sengupta, 2016).[17] In my research, the work required no investment except travel costs, as service-users provide the materials. Many women returned to their village for two to four weeks every year or so. During this time, their service-users would use other providers. When the women came back, previous service-users could refuse them work if they were satisfied with the substitute's work. But steady demand meant that they could usually find other clients or substitute themselves. But this is not a 'possibility' as in the UK. Rather, the situation in the two sites shows that some material investment, such as indemnity insurance and responsivity, is necessary to transform cleaning from *labour* into *work*.

As regards employment status, Indian legislation defines live-out domestic workers as 'part-time' waged employees (even though many work the full day) in the informal sector – that is, waged employees without recourse to social protections arranged by the employer (Sen and Sengupta, 2016). Ray and Qayum (2009/2010) used the term 'servants', because the 'employers' they met referred to their service-providers as such. Mattila (2011) preferred 'workers', which was commensurate with her Marxist feminist analytical framework, but she was sometimes compelled to use 'maid' because that seemed more appropriate. The service-users I interviewed used all three terms. While transcribing, however, I noted that in reply to my question regarding clients, the service-providers often replied in terms of the number of houses they had 'caught' ('khothian pakadi hai') and referred to the service-users simply as kothiwaale (householders). Moreover, while telling me why returning in-country migrant service-providers might have to find new work, *Divya* said: "it was not a sarkari [public service] job, it was private. Kothiwaale could use anyone's services. *She* [the substitute] has to earn, I have to earn.' *Divya* was conflating private–public sector division with self-employment–employment division.

Sen and Sengupta also argue that it is a 'contractual relationship rather than a relationship of servitude' (2016:138), because it involves bargaining, awareness of 'unfair' demands, calculation of advantages and disadvantages of doing the work, and decisions about the households in which to work. The work happens informally because 80% of paid work in India happens in the informal sector (NCEUS, 2008, 2009) – from the 'backyard industries' (the core production units of formal organisations in several industries) to small manufacturing enterprises to domestic work (Raju and Jatrana, 2016a). Informal workers as a whole encounter employment insecurity (because they can be hired and fired at will), health insecurity (due to lack of decent work conditions and healthcare access) and social insecurity (due to inadequate state welfare support) (NCEUS, 2009; Neetha, 2016). Given this background and the lack of experience in other jobs among my Indian respondents, I decided to use the same terms for both my samples.

As in the UK, no Indian service-user issued a contract. Contract-less work arrangements at the bottom end of the informal economy are common in many industries (Raju and Jatrana, 2016a). Also, when one party is illiterate, the legitimacy of the contract is questionable. No Indian respondent had worked for a cleaning agency, which were relatively sparse in my research sites. For concerns around cleaning agency employment within 'cultures of servitude', see Lahiri (2017), Neetha (2009), and Neetha and Palriwala (2011). Tandon's (2012) comparative analysis showed that private workers in Delhi: were more likely to be self-assured (whereas agency workers were self-effacing); earned almost four times the hourly pay of an agency worker; were better able to negotiate time off; and had greater access to supportive social networks. The agencies usually contracted a worker with one service-user for a year, after which they were deployed elsewhere or sent 'home'. If the client demanded the same worker, they had to pay more for the now 'trained' worker.

Worker collectives (Tandon, 2012) and organisations such as the Self-Employed Women's Association (SEWA) (Bali, 2016) provide training and aim to raise workers' self-esteem and confidence, suggesting that collective formalisation of the work would improve work conditions (Tandon, 2012; see also Estey (2011) for a Western context). As regards self-assurance, my respondents appeared on a spectrum, with those with longer work experience more likely to appear more assertive, although this attitude also appeared to be shaped by their responses to other life tribulations. Some were clearly more able than others to choose and give up on more exploitative service-users. None of the women I interviewed appeared to belong to a collective, but some gave me the impression that they might have benefited from such an approach.

Isolation, safety and physicality

Sheila missed having work colleagues but not enough to go back to waitressing, which she had found dehumanising. She put on the radio or television, to keep her company, while she worked. Some of Meagher's (1997) respondents preferred the isolation of housecleaning to doing emotional labour in face-to-face service jobs. But working alone was not always disadvantageous for the service-providers. *Jessica* and *Charlotte* liked the quiet time on their own. In their lively households, no two days were the same and they had little time to themselves.

Many UK service-providers had some customers who were at home when they worked, often offering a cup of tea and a chat before they started working – although service-providers were conscious of the time-bind (see Chapter 5). It was also in this context, when service-users were around, that I was told about a few instances of risks to safety. A retired married man had made several passes at an older service-provider, if his wife was out of the house. She almost gave up the job, but then decided to stand up to him and continued. In another instance, men had been around in an apartment being cleaned by a pair of service-providers, who felt uncomfortable in the situation and the quasi-agency owner promptly terminated the agreement. Another single man also made his service-provider feel uneasy, but she continued to work until he moved to another town, perhaps because he was her first client and she was not yet in a position to choose her clients. There were no incidents reported when women worked in their clients' absence.

The Indian live-out workers mostly worked when service-users were at home. Those working for dual-earner households often started very early in the morning, because female service-users who "go out to work" themselves often preferred to have the domestic work done before they leave the house. No-one reported any safety issues, with a few even saying that men tended to "leave the room they were working in". Women might be reluctant to talk about this issue for fear of compromising their respectability (see also Sen and Sengupta, 2016; Mattila, 2011:79; Ray and Qayum, 2009/2010; Tandon, 2006). To the best of my knowledge, there are no data comparing the safety risks for live-out, part-live-out and live-in domestic workers in my research sites. A few women talked about experiencing domestic violence, and one hinted at sexual transgression within the family rather than at work. Cleaning done as *work* would involve adequate safeguarding, including for the self-employed worker.

The physical demands placed on domestic workers are historically linked to classed and raced notions of the Other body as non-consequential (De Casanova, 2013). Occupational hazards range from skin problems to respiratory conditions to musculoskeletal wear and tear (Chatterjee, 1990; Smith, 2011). Few UK service-providers mentioned prior health problems, and most travelled to work by car (Appendix A, Table A.1). They used gloves when required and those with sensitive skin used eco-friendly products. Generally, they would not move heavy furniture and most worked from the upright position. Modern cleaning products reduce elbow grease somewhat. A full day's work was no doubt physically tiring, with some UK service-providers organising schedules such that the work was not 'strenuous all of at once' (*Sophie*). They said other jobs, such as childcare, retail and care work, also involved considerable physical labour (see also Hughes et al (2017) for physical issues in refuse collection).

The physical tiredness could be worse when other aspects of life were wearing one down. For example, *Nora*, who had gained much in self-worth since opening her cleaning business with a partner, said: "It's improved my physical health, yeah! Because I had a slipped disc, sciatica, down my leg. Because it's more physical and I'm moving about a lot more, it's been a lot better. So it is good if you keep busy and exercise ... ." But *Angela*, who was doing the work because of a lack of opportunity to do carework, also had a bad back, and indicated that the work worsened it. Her preferred choice of work, though, would have also been equally physically demanding (care work, see Stacey, 2005). Tiredness in cleaning work could be outweighed by autonomy and understandings of 'busy' as doing manual work rather than as a virtue linked to long hours of sitting in an office (Gershuny, 2005): "I'd rather be doing something physical than working in an office, and sat and being miserable ..." (*Grace*).

Indian domestic workers are often chronically anaemic or under-nourished (Bharati and Tandon Mehrotra, 2008; Chatterjee, 1990; Duggal, 2010; Singh, 2007). This was one reason why Pratibha gave up outsourcing:

> 'One has to be extremely insensitive to ignore and overlook the human problems with which they are beset. And if you choose to address their physical and social problems it is almost impossible to make them work hard to keep my house spick and span.' (Pratibha)

Many of the service-providers I met in India appeared to fit the previously published portrayals of domestic workers. They either walked or cycled to work. They mostly squatted or bent down to sweep and mop, and sometimes to wash clothes and dishes. None mentioned using gloves, and some women had developed skin problems following prolonged contact of hands/feet with modern detergents and water (see also De Casanova,

2013; Singh, 2007). Coelho (2016) noted similar problems among commercial cleaners in India. Still, some Indian women said domestic work was less strenuous than other manual work available to them, for example agricultural labour, commercial cleaning or factory work, which may still involve labour-intensive methods (Coelho, 2016; Hawksley, 2014; Singh, 2007; Vasanthi, 2011:85).

Overall, in the modern urban context and in the absence of abuse, the physicality of domestic labour was of concern when:

- the worker's health was already compromised;
- the amount of work – or the pace of, or method of, doing the work – put undue strain on the worker (De Casanova, 2013; Glenn, 1986:148);
- the work is done under duress or mental stress due to other aspects of life.

The physical effects of housecleaning as a long-term occupation in good conditions of health and work needs further research. This would also require bearing in mind that they would most likely also be doing their own housework. There are three issues here, which remain under-researched:

- First, outsourcing cleaning to a live-out service-provider once every few days does not mean that service-users do not do any housework in between. Even in the daily whole-house cleaning scenario in India, there are many aspects of housework that could be done oneself.
- Second, there has been little research on the impact of men's paid work on their availability to share housework with spouses/partners working as cleaning service-providers. Many low-paid men work long hours. Single women might not have a choice. *Yvonne*, for example, had outsourced her own cleaning to one of her subcontractors.
- Third, cultural factors impact in complex ways. *Sheila* had in part been inspired by her father (who was a laid-off printer turned cleaner) to open her own cleaning business. Still, she did not let her partner do much housework, as she was "good at it". *Tamsin* was a compulsive cleaner. Even though she said her brothers and father were all good cleaners, and one brother had worked for her, she would not let anyone else, particularly a man, clean her house. In India, some men did the 'outside' work: the groceries, fetching water and firewood, taking children to school. Those who had lived alone, for instance, when they first migrated or when wives were away, then could have done 'inside' work as well (Gamburd, 2003; Soni-Sinha, 2006). As *Jyotika* explained, it was not doing housework that was the problem for her

husband, but to be seen doing 'inside' housework when *she*, the wife, was present. Mothers might collude with patriarchy, by not letting their sons do housework:

> '[When I first got married] if by chance I asked him to do something in front of my parents-in-law he would not have done it. As such I didn't tell him to do things that time but even now when we visit his parental home, even though my mother-in-law is no longer alive, he would not do it if I asked because what if someone else saw him? They would laugh at him and say "Oh! look he's doing his wife's work".' (*Jyotika*)

Also, as discussed in Chapter 5, paid housework is not always seen as an extension of unpaid housework by service-providers. This raises the question, then, about the meanings of cleaning work for selfhood.

Domestic cleaning and empowerment as 'process'

Kate mustered much courage to open her own business:

> 'And then I like cleaning. ... I wanted to do it for a while but I just didn't have the guts to start up. And I've tried looking for other work but couldn't get anything. So I thought I'd just try ... set up on my own.' (*Kate*)

While UK respondents reported being inspired by others in their social network, this was not always disempowering. Some had friends who helped them think about cleaning in terms of *work* rather than *labour.*

> 'People always like first want to know why you don't charge hourly. That's always the first question. But the reason I didn't charge hourly in the first place was because my mum's really good friend is a cleaner, so before I set it up like I met with her, and got loads of advice. And she said to me, she said don't, just don't charge ... like have set prices. Go in, have a look, she said otherwise people will just take the mickey out of you, you'll just be on rubbish money, and it's just not worth doing.' (*Sheila*)

Ruby's friend guided her on setting up as a business, on insurance matters and designing marketing flyers. Other channels of support included advice on starting up a business provided by local councils, banks and/or the internet. A service-provider started a discussion thread on Netmums (2009–2014) "to swap tips with others who have a similar business … ideas of how to … increase business, how to deal with difficult cleaners or clients, just generally exchange ideas". Besides help in finding the first job, cleaners' networks also signpost exploitative service-users (see also Dill, 1988; Hondagneu-Sotelo, 2001; Momsen, 1999; Romero, 2002; Salzinger, 1991):

> 'There's also a cleaners' network, and it gets around "I would not work for that family. They expect you to do so much more, they're late to pay you" or "I will write you a cheque", but the cheque does not clear or you turn up and they've left you – the house is disgusting, you've got two hours and there's at least eight hours work there. You do what you can do in two hours and go – "It's not good enough, we're not paying you." Word gets around and you don't work for those families.' (*Nicola*)

Many UK respondents drew on their education, training and prior work experience to transform 'pushing a hoover around' into proper work. My small sample's experiences are supported by a British Household Panel Survey-based study aiming to capture the effect of broad social structures on pathways to business creation (Jayawarna et al, 2014). Despite the study's broad conclusion that people in privileged locations were more likely to start a business which succeeded, the authors noted:

> [e]ntrepreneurship also involves skills that are not commonly developed in education … There may be a pathway in which under-privileged children create businesses due to application of entrepreneurial competences developed from families and communities rather than education. … Overall, it seems that getting a good level of education early in life is fundamental for start-up. We did also find a positive relationship with higher school leaving age, but this may include vocational education (human capital specific to businesses) rather than general education. (Jayawarna et al, 2014:300–301)

Some UK respondents had websites, others used Gumtree and Facebook to find clients. When *Grace* overheard people sitting at a neighbouring table in a restaurant discussing outsourcing cleaning, she handed them her business card on her way out. Many registered self-employed women identified themselves as business-owners rather than 'cleaners', and some had accountants and ambitions to grow their business in cleaning or other areas such as sewing and alterations.

It was not all plain sailing, however. There was competition from undeclared cleaners "out to make a quick buck" (*Jessica*), as well as cleaning agencies, and a few were clearly struggling to set up. Most had to contend with the time-bind, and there was the social stigma of being "just a cleaner" and being treated badly by some people (see Chapter 7).

Some women said that if their children did the work as a cleaning business, they would encourage them:

> 'I'd have an issue if ... she just thought it was an easy job and had no aspirations with it. If she said I'm going to set up my own cleaning company, I'm going to work X amount of hours and here's my plan, I mean, I'd be really proud of her!' (*Celia*)

Celia was a graduate, but a few others justified their own lack of higher educational engagement in terms of "It isn't for the likes of me", a typical response that is interpreted sociologically as reluctance to acknowledge, or unawareness of, the real cultural and economic barriers facing working-class people (Atkinson, 2010; Johnson, 2002, see Chapter 1) or belated recognition of a missed opportunity.

To understand this better requires examination of the Indian context: the service-providers here were acutely aware of their own and their husbands' illiteracy as a consequence of their social condition as well as its role in shaping their lives (Jeffrey et al, 2004) – there was no 'misplaced' sense of individual lack of engagement with education. Rather, a desire to educate children was a strong motive for seeking paid work in the urban domestic market, as educational opportunities were better in urban than rural areas (Neetha, 2004; Ray and Qayum, 2009/2010; Sen and Sengupta, 2016; Vasanthi, 2011). Some comments revealed the heightened reflexivity of the under-privileged self (Jackson, 2011). Again and again, I heard the English word 'tension' and the phrase 'bus timepass kar rahein hai' ['We are simply passing time']. 'Timepass' is 'a sign of resentment and ... an expression of pain' used to indirectly question injustices related to caste/class location (Jeffrey et al, 2004:981). 'Tension' indicated awareness of everyday economic and social pressures: fragile daily lives, including protecting children from substance abuse, financial debts, and so on (see also Sen and Sengupta, 2016). Moreover, as the following remark indicates, the absolute need to work, but as *labour* rather than *work*, and showing servility, formed part of a wider shared oppression (Bremen, 2013; Khare, 2001):

'Nobody thinks about the poor. … I have a lot of trouble with my eye. But [private] laser treatment requires a lot of money. That is the problem … [my husband and I] don't have that kind of money. And in the state hospital also, nobody heeds us. Nobody listens to the poor … you sit there and you keep sitting, [waiting in the 'so-called' queue], the high-status people are looked after, nobody asks after the low-status person. We get knocked about …' (*Rashmi*)

As regards social and feminine (non-)capital, community networks are the primary site of advice and support for the live-out worker. For instance, the decision to migrate to a particular area is facilitated by prior knowledge about it (job opportunities, wage rates, living spaces, and so on), gleaned from people from the same village (usually extended family) who migrated earlier. Women already doing paid domestic work influence other women's decisions to take up work and often help them to find the first job and to negotiate fees, and networks of domestic workers might take control over servicing particular residential areas (Srinivasan, 1997). They might cover each other's work, so that service-users do not look elsewhere when they go back to their village and help each other with childcare, which Raghuram (1999) argues is not useful, as it hampers gender equality. My data show that concerns around men's domestic contributions need to consider the role of debilitating normative definitions of masculinity and their work experiences (see the earlier discussion in this chapter).

For several women, doing paid work made little difference to their own life: they could have two square meals a day, or/and their children had access to somewhat better education. But the women with empathetic service-users, less-volatile domestic circumstances or whose husbands were supportive and shared their hopes for the next generation, articulated a sense of their own selfhood,[18] even if materially they were not significantly better off (also Lahiri, 2017; Sen and Sengupta, 2016). *Kalpana*, who was also a survivor of a suicide attempt due to the domestic physical and mental abuse mentioned earlier and now happily married to her brother-in-law, specially dressed up to meet me, and scoffed when I said that this had not been necessary. *Urvashi's* critical observance of every detail of her service-users' lives unnerved me. Such women selected service-users reflexively, and were conscious of having moved beyond their prior, more-constrictive rural life (Lahiri, 2017; Sen and Sengupta, 2016; Srinivasan, 1997:94):

'In the village we have to wear saris, do farm labour and then sit inside the home. We also have to wear a veil over our faces.

When the village women see suits [salwar kameez] they make
fun of us – hey what are you wearing? ... So it is nice here. ...
[In the village] people are narrow-minded. We can't wear a
suit in the village. I wear a suit to travel but then I change into
a sari before entering the village.' (*Neena*)

Through their access to middle-class private spaces, like *Urvashi*, they
observed how the other half lived, even if their squatting position made
them 'invisible' to those people. Western manual workers may also be
insightful about how they are positioned vis-à-vis the middle-class by the
middle-class. *Abigail* had been very conscious of how, in some households,
she had been made to feel as 'just a cleaner':

'... I have found that certain people I took the job on for when
I first worked, thought I was a bit ... I'd no education at all ...
and made me feel that way. And one of the children actually
said my mum said you're only in this job because you've had
no education. Made me feel a bit uncomfortable. I'm not as
qualified as some of the people I work for or ... but I think
that is a bit distressing ... And I couldn't say nothing to the
child because it wasn't the child's fault. And I thought do I
say something to ... the lady I was cleaning for to say that
wasn't nice? ... we had a good relationship in the end but I
still never mentioned it to her that she must've said that to
her daughter.' (*Abigail*)

In both social contexts, however, reflexivity was limited by the hegemonic
middle-class values and beliefs that are accepted as 'total social facts' for a
'good' life (Ilaiah, 2005/2017; Lucas and Buzzanell, 2004; Torlina, 2011).
As Patricia spontaneously noted, when trying to appreciate the work:
"There's something satisfying about a clean house after you've done it.
That's true. But there's not going to be much of a sense of development
in it." These norms, when applied in a situation of social exclusion and
poverty, result in the continuous chasing of losses, a life starting and
ending in the hamster's wheel (Skeggs, 1997). Thus, it was hard to hear
the Indian women's hopes about the power of 'education'. The education
available to their children is often poor quality.[19] Later, many encounter
disenchantment in the highly competitive, limited and plutocratic job
market (Chandra Mohan, 2015; Cross, 2009; Jeffrey et al, 2004, 2005;
Lahiri, 2017; Mayyasi, 2013; Sen and Sengupta, 2016; Singh, 2007). My
respondents also hoped that their sacrifice would be rewarded by filial
care in old age:

'If we can educate our children, they will support us in our old age. They will earn and give us food, isn't it? But if I'm not able to bring up my children, then what will happen? The neighbours aren't going to feed us. … I have brought up my children, my life has passed.' (*Neena*)

However, the pressure to marry and have children (sons) often makes this difficult. For instance, *Bela* and her husband, a dhobi, both of whom were around 60 years, were still living and working in the 'ironing-table-converted-to-shack-at-night'. None of their four married children earned enough to also care for their parents.

Patricia's comment thus falls in the trap that Kabeer (2001) cautions against: seeing empowerment as simply a state of being 'aspirational' and middle-class. But some middle-class people themselves reject notions of self-actualisation as a property of high-status paid work. They seek it either outside work, because they can 'afford' to (Hebson, 2009:35–36), or in 'low-status' work (Mainiero and Sullivan, 2005; Potter, 2015; Wilhoit, 2014). Such decisions are not considered instances of volitional disempowerment; rather, the process of rejection of the 'position of power' is read as an 'opportunity'. The UK service-providers' decision to do housecleaning might not propel them into positions of power. But given their attempts to do the work as *work*, should their claims of self-development be measured differently because of less access to material/cultural capitals? An affirmative answer to this question implies that middle-class status is a 'natural' resource, even though it is a product of historical social changes. The Indian women's association with their paid *labour* was, as shown earlier, almost universally linked to their maternal role.[20] Although some had gained in embodied capital over time, and many were making decisions such as using contraception, rejecting child marriage, giving up exploitative employers when they could, and taking control of household finances (Kabeer, 2001; Vera-Sanso, 2008), in both familial and work contexts, many still seemed largely to remain subordinate (Gopal, 1999; Neetha, 2004; Sen and Sengupta, 2016). A major reason for this is the low material and cultural value accorded to manual work.

Material injustices in outsourced housecleaning as *work* and *labour*

'I think things could be better for this profession as a general – this is not just for myself but for cleaners in general – if the customers would definitely give you more time to clean properties, and I think also if customers would be aware of why you have to charge them, because I think some do feel that you're a bit expensive. But they're not taking into account any of your costs, you have to advertise, you have insurance, and your cleaning materials ... they just look at it as a set price ....' (*Zoe*)

'I'm sort of, I've been having a think about that, it'd be about £8.50 an hour, which is, it's above the minimum and it's above the living wage. It isn't a fabulous number, but if I paid Sandra £10 an hour it would be better and I may be moving to that by the end of ... the point is that if I start feeling guilty as an employer, which I'm capable of doing, I think then where do I stop? What should I be offering?' (Maggie)

A key factor for declared UK service-providers was that housecleaning, although low-paid, was still better remunerated than much other work. *Evie* had trained as a teaching assistant, but she changed her mind when she saw a friend doing "silly hours": that is, "pay is awful and she ends up doing extra hours that she doesn't get paid for, which ... doesn't make sense to me". My interviews, as well as the internet discussion started by a cleaning service-provider (Netmums, 2009–2014), revealed both material and cultural dimensions to the valuation of housecleaning services offered by a self-employed person. Here, I focus on the material dimension.

In Marxist terms, self-employed providers who sell services produced by their own means of production are termed 'petty-bourgeoisie'. They receive in fees the exchange-value of the service provided (Steinmetz and Wright, 1989). Practically, though, describing as 'bourgeoisie' individuals doing work that is historically and contemporaneously low paid and stigmatised – perhaps for only part of their working life, and that is dependent on others' custom – risks deepening their 'atomized disempowerment' (Linder and Houghton, 1990:734). But bearing in mind that this theoretical category straddles traditional class categories derived from waged factory work (Steinmetz and Wright, 1989), one can usefully unpack the singularities of exploitation of a proletarian petty-bourgeoisie group, without compromising their self-employed status.

Whether the selling of a service is analysable in terms of capital depends on 'its location in the circuit of capital and its relationship with the production of surplus-value' (Tregenna, 2011:297). The services sector can, thus, be divided into three groups of activities, of which two lead to surplus-value and form part of the 'circuit of capital' (those producing commodities, and logistics and transport services). The third group, personal and domestic services, is 'exchanged against revenue rather than against capital ...' and thereby threatens the circuit of capital (Tregenna, 2011:297). From a feminist perspective, however, domestic and personal services have 'exchange-value', and a self-employed service-provider receives this in full, whereas for an employee it is partly appropriated by the employing organisation. Except Janet, all the UK service-users preferred to use an independent service-provider, based on their conscious belief that domestic workers should receive the full exchange-value of their labour, which includes not only a clean house but also improved quality of life for the service-user. However, because the service depletes capital, the amount of which varies among service-users, translating this belief into practice is not a simple matter, regardless of cultural context:

> 'We didn't negotiate! She just said what she expected ... it was slightly ... more than what I had been told, and I thought it was absolutely fair. If anything, I do think it's underpaid ... I would recognise them as skilled, and I don't think, you know, there's wider recognition of the types of skill involved in cleaning. Umm, because definitely you can do it well or badly and they do it very well. So, but on the other hand I'm not going to turn around and say do you want £15 an hour instead. I don't want to do that. But I get quite annoyed when people sort of assume it shouldn't be paid for.' (Pauline)

The UK service-providers charged from £7 up to £15 or more an hour (average £10 an hour; see Figure 6.3) with no regional differences. This is similar to the fees reported in internet discussion threads (for example Mumsnet, 2014i). As *Zoe* pointed out, in a labour contract relation (ONS, 2010), an 'employing authority' makes assumptions about use/ exchange-value, based simply on physical aspects of the work, or factors that have little to do with the work itself: 'going rate', gender, or class-related or feminist 'guilt' about outsourcing 'dirty' work in ostensibly egalitarian societies (see also Jones, 2004). Service-users who check their neighbourhood 'going rate' may not realise that the same rate, applied to two different households, can lead to different outcomes for one service-provider or two different service-providers working for the same two households. A bigger or dirtier house means that cleaning cloths wear out faster. Service-providers working in the same area may have different travel costs, depending on the distance travelled, wear and tear of vehicle or public transport costs.[21] The highest hourly rate, however, was paid by Lily, who wanted 'to be honourable' with someone doing unskilled

Figure 6.3: Hourly rates for outsourced cleaning in the North East, North West and Midlands regions of the UK (spring 2014)

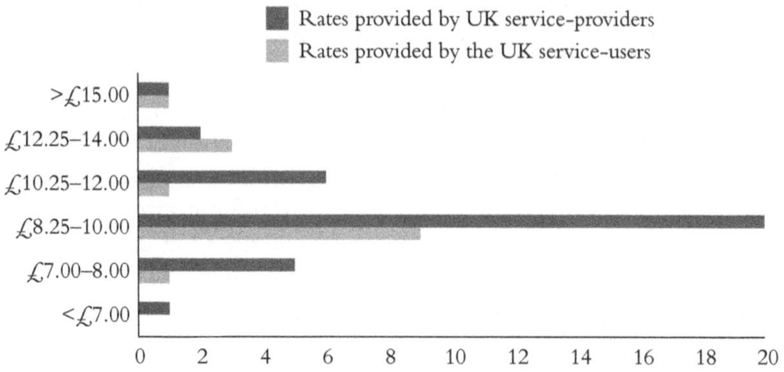

- ■ Rates provided by UK service-providers
- ▨ Rates provided by the UK service-users

Notes: Since some service-providers charged different rates for new and old customers, the total of the entries for service-providers in the figure exceeds the sample number. *Sheila* had the highest rate and worked for a flat fee. For comparing with the other rates, she told me she charged £40 for a smallish flat that took her about 1.5 hours to clean. I have put this as >£15 to allow for errors in estimates.

and demeaning work. Others paid more than the minimum wage, in an effort not to exploit the service-provider. But, as Pauline said, most were unwilling to pay significantly more for this work, and simply paid the amount quoted by the service-provider.

My respondents mostly used an hourly rate and often did not charge for small periods of overtime, tending to inform the client only when their overtime approached 30 minutes. As self-employed workers, they did not expect to be paid for time off. Some, however, had started to charge separately for tasks that can take almost the whole of the allocated time, such as oven cleaning. In *Sheila's* experience, these problems were overcome by charging flat fees (as advised by her mother's friend), and she was earning considerably more than the rest. A service-provider on Mumsnet also commented that a male service-provider in Harrogate, North Yorkshire, who charged by the job, was earning "about £18" per hour (Mumsnet, 2013a). Romero (2002) showed that charging by job work rather than an hourly fee was an important factor in how the Chicana workers in Denver were modernising domestic service. However, Patricia paid a flat fee to *Enid*, and this translated to around the lowest hourly rate in my samples. Since I did not have enough flat-fee accounts in my UK sample, I cannot comment further on how this form of payment might counter material injustices.

The Indian case, however, showed that the flat-fee method would benefit the service-provider only when cleaning is done as *work* rather than as *labour*. Live-out Indian service-providers, who usually work six

162

to seven days a week for each client, are paid by the job, commonly on a monthly basis. I have not included the data here, as there was wide variation in the rates, which is in line with previously published accounts and has been attributed to work fragmentation (see Chapter 5) and influence of the general socioeconomic status of a residential area on the 'going rate' (Neetha, 2008, 2016).[22] All these factors, operating in a 'culture of servitude' with vast social distances between the service-providers and service-users, considerably reduce the negotiating ability of many workers around, for instance, the number of rooms or household members (which impacts on the number of dishes to be washed or the amount of laundry) (Archarya and Reddy, 2017; Lahiri, 2017; Neetha, 2008, 2016; Sen and Sengupta, 2016):

> 'I personally feel we are underpaying, because the work that they are doing – but again, you are governed by the market … the number of times I get cursed by my neighbours: "You are paying more so they are also demanding more from us." … That is why … I'm helping in kind. Giving bags, books, pens …' (Kajal)

> 'Dekho aisa hai ki – ek to [See it is like this – first] it's because of the market forces only, because here the workers are available at lower rates. And they also have no option … So that way we are actually exploiting them. I am not being shy in saying this because … now I'm alone, I'm paying Rs500. But even if I had my family here, they would be paid … maybe another 100 rupees a month, which comes out to be Rs20–23 for [about] … one and half hour's work each day. So, I find it is low paid, … [but] because they are accepting it, we are doing it because it suits our pocket, and finally we are doing it because lots of people are available.' (Lata)

Several Indian service-users said they paid more than the 'going rate' as well as, for example, for their service-provider's children's education or healthcare. The monthly pay pattern meant that the few days off per month were often paid for,[23] but this is more so in theory because of the low fees: that is, when the fee is low, workers' rights such as being paid for time off makes little difference to their standard of living. Cooking and childcare were valued higher than cleaning, in the instances where I was told the rates paid to these workers. Three of the six part-live-out workers were provided with accommodation in the outhouse and utilities in exchange for their work (Raghuram, 1999:217). Their husbands' income covered other expenses. As in the UK, the assumption in India that anyone can do this work also means that supply levels are continually replenished by people denied other work for a variety of reasons, and newcomers often undercut wages to gain a foothold in the occupation. As in other industries (Desai et al, 2010; NCEUS, 2008, 2009), women are paid less than men in domestic work (Raghuram, 1999; also personal observations), but when the men's wages are also too low for a meaningful existence, the 'gender gap' seems a futile concern (Vera-Sanso, 2008). That is, such material injustices are not peculiar to domestic work and are compounded by the fact that they occur across the low-wage sector regardless of the form of employment relationship and social context.

At the time of the interviews, most UK service-providers were reluctant to raise fees annually, because of austerity cuts and pay freezes. Some quoted higher rates to new customers and then dropped lower-paying ones. They offered different cleaning packages to avoid working overtime (basic clean, deep clean, separate oven cleans, and so on), some more successfully than others. The Indian women's penurious circumstances made them less shy of asking for a raise regardless of wider economic concerns. Again, some dropped exploitative service-users, when an opportunity arose.

A key point here is state welfare provision, which made a difference to the quality of life experienced by the two samples of service-providers, even though both were low paid in their own wider cultural context. In the UK, today's working-class living standards are the legacy of 20th-century workers' labour right struggles, the establishment of the welfare state after the Second World War, and significant state and local government investment in basic civic infrastructure and social housing, with slum clearance in several stages, commencing in the 1930s and extending into the early 1980s. These developments were not without problems, but there continues to be free access to comparatively better-quality school and further education and healthcare, and other state welfare support measures, although state investment in social housing has diminished considerably. Still, the 20th-century developments meant that many service-providers could take holidays within the UK or abroad. Some service-providers could then also argue that their work had made them 'independent', because they no longer needed male support. A woman's private dependence on a man is clearly different from public welfare dependency. But even in the British welfare state, the population is divided into support-receiving and support-contributing factions, because low incomes more generally do not constitute a 'living wage' (Shildrick et al, 2012).

India also offers some free school education (until Class 8) and subsidised higher education, and has a raft of welfare programmes. Many of these remain poorly developed and even the most vulnerable can prefer privately delivered services, for example education and healthcare, if they can access them. At their economic level, 'going on holiday' largely meant visiting their marital/natal village of origin (some were paid for this time and others were not) and depending on loans, advances and other goodwill payments by their clients (see Chapter 7).

No UK service-provider referred to pensions, when I asked about disadvantages of their work. Pension is a key part of workers' rights and is necessary for a decent standard of living post-working life. However, at the time of writing, the issue of pensions for independent cleaning service-provides seemed part of a more widespread problem. The majority of self-employed people in the UK do not have private pensions, and there appeared little difference in pension concerns between self-employed and employed low-wage earners (Blake, 2016; D'Arcy and Gardiner, 2014; Hu and Stewart, 2009; Warren, 2000). For instance, *Vera*'s pension entitlements linked to her wage of £15,000–£16,000 per year for work she had enjoyed would have been meagre. She saw greater benefit in being able to claim her petrol costs against her self-employed tax return, which she had not been able to do as an employee. The gender pay gap, family responsibilities and situation after divorce also impact on women's pensions. As mentioned already, with two failed marriages, *Corinne*'s pension, accrued during her long-term teaching career, was insufficient to maintain her chosen lifestyle, which is why she was working as a (declared) childminder and (undeclared) cleaning service-provider.

In India, only 12% of the active workforce 'has a formal pension or social security plan' (Joshi, 2012:n.p.; see also Hu and Stewart, 2009). Some women had set up pension plans with the help of empathetic service-users, but these would not have raised their standard of living significantly.

In sum, there are several levels to the concerns around remuneration in outsourced cleaning. According to Pape (2016), the ILO convention does not apply to self-employed service-providers and, as Cruz et al noted, 'straightforward arguments for the use of [existing] individual labour law claims' (2017:275) are problematic, when people clearly indicate that a high degree of autonomy at work is important for them. Another illuminating example is Meagher et al's (2016) discussion of differences in Swedish and Australian care workers' perceptions of their work. The thrust of that analysis was macro-level comparative institutional theory, through which differences in the structural make-up of the two market economies (Swedish socialist/co-ordinated versus Australian liberal) were shown to be responsible for the differences in the way caring work was experienced in the two countries. The Swedish employment conditions on paper were much better, but the Swedish workers were less satisfied. While they did more personal (body) and professionalised work (for example giving injections) and had guaranteed rights such as holiday pay, they worked longer and inflexible hours, and more often reported that they could not deliver the care that a client needed; in turn, the client also usually had many different workers visiting them. The Australian workers had comparatively poorer employment conditions, but were more satisfied with their work. They had greater autonomy and work–life fit, and engaged more freely in the social aspects of their work.

Given that payment for domestic (and care) work depletes capital, then how does one assure 'independence' without state support, or is the latter inevitable? I would argue that making cleaning *work* rather than *labour* will require a staged approach, in which as Fraser (1996, 2013) argued, the politics of distribution is intricately linked with the politics of recognition (see also IDWN, 2011). Thus, a full exposition of my argument requires further analysis of the cultural dimensions of contemporary urban housecleaning done as *work* and *labour*.

Conclusion

By using a single frame of reference in this chapter, I have shown that the meanings of the same work for the respondents in the two research sites indicate that the problem with service work such as housecleaning is not commodification per se, but the way the work itself – as well as work more generally – has been commodified. The material concerns outlined here, however, are underpinned by cultural injustices, which are addressed in Chapter 7.

The Occupational Relations of Domestic Cleaning as *Work* and *Labour*

Bhavna lived with her mother in the family home. Bhavna's mother managed the household with the help of domestic workers. As Bhavna talked about her relationship with the workers, the contextual nature of institutionalised misrecognition became apparent:

> '[I]n India, it is very different. It is not possible to eliminate that kind of social thing … A good friend of mine … is a house cleaner in [the US] … I met her when I went [there] … we hug … I mean, she's just like … you and me, … she's absolutely equal, my equal, there's nothing like she's a house cleaner … But in India it's not possible … because it is so deeply embedded in the social structure here … abroad the living standard more or less is the same everywhere … even the cleaners, everybody has good living standard, everybody has a car, everybody can go to the same restaurants … But here, the difference in money is so much, so extreme, and then people think that money brings them power and that gives them power to be able to say anything to them. … [So] if I invite him to have lunch with me, he'll stop working for me. I can't ask him to do any other work for me.'

Introduction

Two factors informed the analysis presented in this chapter, which builds on and adds to the already extensively elucidated socio-cultural processes of power that shape occupational relations in paid domestic work (see Chapter 1). First, the UK respondents' class identities were not in absolute opposition. Five service-users were first-generation middle-class, and Libby's service-provider also worked for her (still) working-class grandmother, who had herself been in domestic service. Four service-providers identified as middle-class. In India, upwardly mobile lower-caste people also outsource domestic work. Second, as the quotation from a conversation with Bhavna, a freelancer in publishing, illustrates, the intersectional influences of gender, race, class/caste, and our relative valuation of housework shape the cultural injustices experienced by the cleaning service-provider.

Fraser (1996, 2013) has argued that material and cultural injustices are mutually constitutive and their simultaneous redress is necessary for people to function as 'full partners and participants' in all their social relations – 'formal legal equality' is not enough. For participatory parity there has to be 'freedom from deprivation and from the sort of dependency that renders one susceptible to exploitation', a condition that is inevitable when 'great disparities of wealth and income' are normalised (Fraser, 1996:32, 48–49, 54) – a process that includes institutionalisation of cultural markers of status. Such an approach suggests that transformative measures for redressing distributive injustices require coupling material solutions with non-identitarian recognition; that is, de-differentiation of social groups along all axes of subordination in both public and private spheres.

Remedial measures that rely on putting people into boxes leave in place the power relations behind the injustices. Using a medical analogy, such affirmative strategies simply treat the 'symptoms' rather than the underlying pathological process, whereas transformative strategies aim to tackle the core pathological process to ensure participatory parity. The cross-cultural applicability of this two-dimensional approach to social justice has been demonstrated (Australia: Meagher, 1997, 2003; India: Chigateri, 2007), and sociologists more generally have highlighted Fraser's argument (Crompton and Scott, 2005; Devine and Savage, 2005; Lawler, 2005; Hebson et al, 2015).

In this chapter, I describe how the respondents constructed their occupational relations, the cultural injustices evident in the interactions, and how service-providers negotiated these injustices when doing cleaning as *work* and *labour*.

Occupational relations: "ultimately you're there to do a job" (*Zoe*)

In the UK, where workers' struggles in the industrial pre- and post-war periods had led to some breakdown of class hierarchies (Gunn and Bell, 2002), most respondents said they had "friendly work relationships". That is, the client treated the service-provider as equitably as possible in a structurally unequal situation, for example by being courteous and doing pre-tidying. Two UK service-users and two service-providers said they were friends with a provider or user, respectively. Other data lent credence to these claims. Una's first service-provider had been a relative and Peggy's had been a neighbour (see also Metcalfe, 2013). *Nicola* currently cleaned for a neighbour and *Carrie* for her sister.

Most respondents, though, had different relationships with different service-providers/users, shaped by micro-level factors, such as assertiveness and sense of self-worth in the service-provider, degree of responsivity or shared interests outwith the work relationship, as well as macro-level, socioeconomic, cultural markers of class (Figure 7.1):

> 'my background ... wasn't [as] working class as hers ... she's a sort of archetypal ... [Northern] woman who's managed to get rid of her husband, bring her kids up, ... will sometimes come out with views that are quite bigoted ... you hear a lot of what she's read or heard about on the radio ... but I suppose I tend to be a bit more liberal and middle-class ... [and] sometimes ... I just want to get on with my work on a morning ... she likes going out and going on holidays where she'll probably be going and drinking quite a lot and have a great time ... I would like to go walking in the countryside ...' (Peggy)

While Peggy was one of a selective sample (see Chapter 2), the service-provider respondents worked for a range of clients, and many asserted that they participated in defining the depth and nature of the relationship (also Lutz, 2011:58):

> 'The ones that are always in ... they lock themselves away in their bedroom! The one that I go to twice a week, yeah, me and her have a natter when I get there ... [But] they would never be ... somebody whom I would become friends with, because they're not ... my type ... then the ones that have been there the longest, their home is ... probably the most

Figure 7.1: Relationships between service-providers and service-users

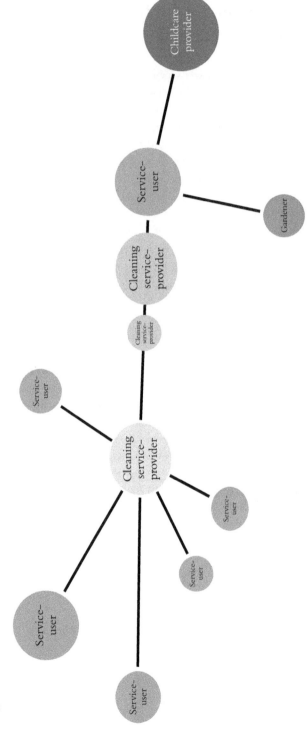

(a) **Perspective of a cleaning service-provider**

(b) **Perspective of a service-user**

Note: The lines indicate the length of the time of service provision, and the different sizes of circles indicate the level of the relationship.

similar to my home and it's got a few old things and … when we were going to an old penny arcade auction and I told them about it, they went as well.' (*Charlotte*)

In the most superficial relationships, the user and provider rarely met, with communication being limited to notes and texts about service requests or requirements. Some service-users said they had a *friendly* work relationship,[1] that is, they situated the relationship fully within the 'intimate' private sphere:

> 'So actually I would feel much, much closer to *Rita* actually
> – and I think our relationship is very different. … this
> thing about the nurturing-ness and the taking care and the
> intimacies …' (Clare)

Such service-users then get 'caught between the reciprocity of care and the desire for depersonalisation' (Molinier, 2009/2012:113), a tension that is claimed to be unique to domestic work relationships, as Clare suggests, even though intimate interactions can happen in any workplace. Other service-users[2] and the declared service-providers described a friendly *work* relationship. *Tamsin* encouraged her subcontractors to talk to clients, while cautioning: "there's a fine line though, … you got to be careful because there's that line that you're still working for someone". These service-providers could also gain from service-users' ignorance of their private life:

> 'I have actually reduced people's hours because they mess me
> about, like she was a four-hour client, and she used to just
> cancel at the last minute, and she was four hours a week, so
> I did actually find client number 9, and I told a bit of a fib
> actually, I told her I had to be somewhere, so I could only
> do two hours. Because it's a lot of money – when you're self-
> employed – to just lose at a moment's notice. So, you can, you
> know, you've got that power to rejig, yeah!' (*Sophie*)

A few UK service-providers talked about discovering pleasure in 'helping' others. This is a common finding in care work more broadly (Hebson et al, 2015), but in both contexts, this was done within a framework of provision of service as *work* (IDWN, 2011). For instance, website blurbs of my respondents mention 'helping' clients, but through the provision of a *professional* service.[3]

The Indian service-users who had a live-in worker were more likely to talk about that relationship. Due to fragmentation of work, live-out workers may spend only a little time – often less than an hour – in one client's house. Few respondents, however, described a 'friendly work relationship'. Although many service-users referred to their providers as 'domestic help', the terms 'maid' and 'servant' could also slip into the conversation. Many service-providers referred to service-users in a detached way – 'kothiwaale' (see Chapter 6). They also indicated that they could be perceived as the Other ('these people'): their presence might be ignored, or they could be patronised or treated unkindly in the presence of others:

> 'I say it that these people are good. They give you food and drink, treat you respectfully, recognise that you have come to work. I mean they don't think that I am their servant. ... As such now the nice ones are in one place now, who value me a lot. If occasionally I suddenly need two to four thousand rupees, they lend it to me [and cut it out of my fee over time]. They also give me clothes ... They also give me food, I mean, they don't stop me from eating anything, in fact they say, eat whatever you want to eat and I take some food and eat it. In other houses, I am just there to work and go. They only recognise their own as their own. She is the kaamwali [woman who does the work], why do we need to make small talk with her. I mean they talk like this. They are high-status people and they like to talk high-status talk. Who will talk to us? Low-status people that we are. Do your work and leave. They behave like this, retreat behind a barrier, why have anything to do with "these people"? Do you work, leave, run off.' (*Anjali*)

> 'I am like this, that if you ask me to stand the whole day I will. But when she asks me why have I not done this work, I don't know what to say. What should I say why it was left. Then when she says do it now, I feel a bit humiliated. Also like when guests come and she tells me to clean the table in front of them I feel bad because it implies I haven't done my work properly and I feel demeaned. We are also human ...' (*Mohini*)

Some women's awareness of the public–private continuum in their status (see also Sen and Sengupta, 2016) may have made it difficult to separate out the subordination in the work relationship:

> 'We [women] just have to listen to all admonishments and bear up – admonished by the big house and admonished by

our husbands. Isn't it? We have to bear being admonished by everybody, what can we do?' (*Anika*)

In this social situation, I discerned two kinds of user–provider relationship. In the first, a mutual tension was palpable as service-users tried to assert their 'employer' status, or service-providers tried to assert their service-provider status:

'This was one interview where the employer had to answer more questions than she could ask, because the would-be employee knows the indispensability of her position and takes full advantage of that. I have been asked about the number of rooms in my house, number and age of family members, frequency of arrival of guests, types of gadget in my house, availability of colour TV and cable connection. After this, haggling over wages, mutual agreement on service conditions, holidays allowed, festival bonus, increments and time slot, ultimately completes all the rituals.' (Pratibha)

'And money – if they are asking for more work and suggesting less money, and I am saying that this much work will mean this much money, and if they say you are asking for too much, I don't like it [and I don't work there].' (*Jyotika*)

The second was a benevolent patron–client relationship[4] (Tellis-Nayak, 1983), in which clients often communicate using a respectful tone:

'[T]he economic difference makes that huge, everything else becomes different, so your take-off point becomes very, very different ... because they don't have the means, they are not educated ... their awareness snowballs into so many other things ... but, you know, ... I realised that, with my mother gone, certain womanly issues ... you can actually share with them ... the kinds of maybe bodily changes that you may experience ... the larger philosophies of life or values of life, ... and they themselves say that, you know, you should do this and you should not do this, you know, they also, you know, give you advice yeah!' (Vibha)

'They treat us kindly, they respectfully offer us tea and water. On every major festival they give us new clothes, we don't need to spend our money on clothes. And if they ever see us outside the house, from the back or from ahead, they acknowledge us respectfully: "My *Urvashi*, where are you going?", "Beti [daughter] where are you going?". Now, who asks after someone like this in a city? But they ask us. That's why I feel that this is like my family. In all four houses. [Lotika: have you ever worked where you have not felt like this?]. No, because I've been working in this area of 12 years and I know [this part of town] – what is happening around. When you get out of your home, you learn to become worldly-wise [through the cleaners' network], so why I should I work where I know [I won't be treated well].' (*Urvashi*)

The considerate behaviours described by *Urvashi* could be constrained by practices of separation; that is, *Urvashi* was unlikely to sit next to her client, while having the cup of tea she was given by her client. As higher-caste domestic workers may not be excluded from such hierarchical practices and they occur in other social contexts too, they are articulations of the broader pollution ideologies (Douglas, 1966) that underpin caste, race *and* class-based discriminatory practices. Again, these data refute the idea of 'intimacy' in domestic work relationships. Hence, I do not consider in detail the 'pragmatic intimacy' approach suggested by Sen and Sengupta (2016).

Overall, this analysis shows that a friendly work relationship appears necessary in order for cleaning to be done as *work*. At present, however, the persistence of cultural injustices impedes full participatory parity for the service-provider in both the cultural contexts presented in this book.

Cultural injustices in outsourced cleaning and wider occupational hierarchies

The UK context

A moral disproval around outsourcing of housework pervades some quarters of British society, related to understandings of housework as low-status/low-value work:

'I think it is degrading to the individual to have to clean up after somebody else. So in a perfect world, everybody would feel equal and be treated with equal respect. And just the nature of the job prevents that really. Yes, umm … also it can give you an inflated view of yourself. That you could make a place quite messy and dirty and not have to take responsibility for that.' (Phoebe, a public-service administrator)

'Well I was working for an agency. When I first started at the agency, the majority of the jobs were social services jobs, which were given to us by social services. So they were fine, I didn't mind them because it tended to be elderly, disabled people. They were very embarrassed to have you there, they didn't really want that help but they had no choice because they were physically frail. And they were lovely. And they treated me lovely. I mean they were always telling me to stop – used to say, "Sit down, come and sit down, and have a cup of tea." You know! And they were really nice.' (*Georgia*)

When Beverley invited *Natalie* to a house-party, *Natalie*'s daughter joked about "going to the big house". Beverley then said, "Because I think she was aware and I was aware that people would ask her 'How do you know Beverley?' and she'd say, 'I'm her cleaner' … I said you're my friend, end of story." Such constructions of equality by the service-user[5] – or even co-constructions (if *Natalie* had a role in the origin of the decision) – impede participatory parity, because *Natalie*'s work was not acknowledged in that construction. Some class-conscious service-users practise 'parallel houseworking' (that is, doing some other housework as the cleaner cleans). This is not possible in many situations, for example in restaurants, hotels or paid childcare. An argument used to differentiate between the (im)morality in servicing within and outwith the home is that in the former case, the person paying for the service is directly hiring the worker:

'[I]t's more like we all have jobs at the university but some are more socially valued than others, so I feel uncomfortable about the fact that the world works like that, but less like I've actively helped create that situation.' (Felicity)

Pauline described how her current service-providers' demeanour and work attitudes had squashed her guilt:

'They struck me very much as professional women, that they'd decided [cleaning] was going to be their job. That they had certain expectations and really were quite clear about it. And I much rather prefer that, I felt much happier with this sort of arrangement … I feel like we're equal partners in this job, or in getting this task done … they don't make me feel like an employer.' (Pauline)

The remaining UK service-users said that outsourcing cleaning was a way to share their wealth with their wider society, similar to outsourcing of other work such as gardening:

> 'As far as I'm concerned, I work very hard. I earn a lot of money. I pay tax on the money. If I can turn some of the money that I earn into jobs for other people locally, I'm very happy about that. I don't think that they're being badly paid or badly employed, well, umm, the gardener gets £15 an hour, cleaner £12 an hour, dog walker … it was £11 for a walk, it might change into £12 for him. It's not a lot of money but it's helluva lot more than minimum wage. A lot more than people without professional qualifications would be earning. And provided that you can give them some security, some paid holidays then they can actually earn a decent wage. … And that's the way I think about it – I may be naïve, but I've never thought differently. If I was looking for people, and wanting them to be paid the lowest possible amount of money and treated them badly then I would find that was in conflict [with my feminism].' (Orla)

Notions of a fair price for cleaning were often rooted in mainstream social constructions of housework as 'unskilled' or 'low-skilled' work. As Tanya said, the work was "sort of just an entry level thing isn't it?" Samantha had paid the minimum wage, because "there are people in the labour market, who are wanting to do that work, or don't have the skills or qualifications to do other work and, therefore, they're filling that gap …". Imogen ruminated:

> 'So perhaps you could say well, it's not fair you know, here you are as a professor, you know, earning sixty something thousand [pounds] a year that you're hiring someone else to do your cleaning for you and you're only paying her nine pounds an hour … is it an argument that I accept morally? I think that people should be paid a fair wage and the minimum wage is not high enough. And I think that wage should be influenced by the skills you have and the tasks you do but also, but also, you know that, that there should be a living type wage …' (Imogen)

This problem also exists in the public sphere because, as I mentioned in Chapter 5, skill is a shifting concept. Commercial cleaners directly employed by public sector organisations in the UK are paid better (£6.30–£9/hour) than private-sector employees (£5–£7.50/hour) – this is not because of 'skill' differences, but because public-sector organisations are more likely fulfil workers' rights (Sykes et al, 2014).

Regardless of their moral stance, all academics except Janet preferred independent service-provision, as they were concerned about agency exploitation of workers (see Chapter 6). Yet, some were uneasy around the legitimacy of low-wage self-employment in domestic work, because of social understandings of housework as 'dirty' work or because they deemed that such service-providers were missing out on workers' rights:

> 'I've treated him as a small business, rather than me as an employer. So I see him in the same way that I would the gardener who goes and does Alec's ... But actually a social injustice perspective might turn that on its head and say I am an employer, what about things like sick leave and paid holidays and you know, national insurance and stuff. So in some ways I would say I haven't taken the social injustice view far enough probably.' (Felicity)

When I remarked that Felicity's service-provider was a small business, her reply revealed that since she considered cleaning 'drudge work', she could not reconcile herself to *Gary's* self-employed status, regardless of his opinion:

> '[One might want to question the] UK way of thinking about small businesses ... given the power dynamics in the way ... it is different being a remedial massage therapist, for example, who can charge me £33 an hour and can tell me through his business when he's put up his fees than being a self-employed cleaner who's considered pretty much at the bottom of the pile.' (Felicity)

When Clare's self-employed service-provider, *Rita*, refused her offer of a raise and holiday pay, Clare felt uncomfortable. *Rita* cleaned Clare's house on Mondays and Clare circumvented *Rita's* refusal, by insisting on paying her for bank holidays, while bearing the inconvenience caused by *Rita's* right to take holidays as *she* pleased. Moreover, service-users sometimes tolerate poor-quality work, either because housework is not perceived as 'proper work' or in an effort to avoid confrontation –

with the equal-yet-unequal service-provider. The service-providers, however, said that a good provider–client relationship included feedback on quality of work:

> '[A good service-user is] somebody who would treat me as – I wouldn't say an equal – as comfortable when I go in their house. And I could be able to say something that wasn't right to them and they could say it to me without feeling uncomfortable.' (*Abigail*)

So, when service-users avoid doing this, they reduce the provider to 'just a cleaner'.

Some service-users expressed uncertainty about their own status as employer or customer. Imogen always took out third-party insurance herself. Given that all declared traders in my research had the necessary insurance, perhaps this might not have been necessary with her current service-provider. Gayle was of the opinion that such matters only came into question with cleaning agencies, and not with the sole trader:

> '[*Amber*] comes sort of out of the what I would say was "an old-style cleaner". She made her services available to individual people through personal contact and, and knowledge. She's, she's not part of a company that, you know, come and deliver ...' (Gayle)

For Gayle, any sole trader was "old-fashioned", a label that the majority of my service-provider sample would have protested against. *Sheila* said customers were 'bemused' at being provided with receipts for payment:

> 'I did [provide an invoice] at first, however it didn't quite feel right and people seemed slightly bemused as I handed them a handwritten receipt so I just decided to stick to keeping all my own records on a daily basis. If somebody requests an invoice, which does happen occasionally with one-off customers, I send them one via email.' (*Sheila*)

Many service-providers were not averse to the idea of outsourcing their own cleaning. A few did not do so because they were fussy about their own standards or because they had subscribed to the 'failed woman' myth – that if a woman does not keep her house well herself, she is a loser as a woman (see accusations in Mumsnet, 2012a, 2013a, 2014a,c,f,l):

'I'd love to! I'd love to [outsource my own cleaning]. I just …
I keep saying I'm going to get one of the girls to come in and
do it for me, but then I keep thinking when me and Gaby
come home, like today I was at home at half past ten, so there's
nothing stopping me really from – it's about being idle isn't
it really?' (*Valerie*)

Jessica had outsourced cleaning in the past, but had not been happy with
the work of the cleaning agency staff who had come. Thus, presently she
preferred to do it herself. Such data show that the service-users were in
various ways inadvertently retrenching the social attitude that housework
is low-value 'women's work', but these were not distinctive actions on
their part, peculiar to the domestic sphere.

As regards the UK service-users' workplace, the contemporary
restructuring in many Western organisations, including UK universities,
appears to reduce hierarchical ways of working. However, administrative
staff still provide support to academics and other senior staff (as a 'wife',
see Chapter 3 conclusion). Their contracts are primarily labour or a mix
of labour and service contracts (Rose and Pevalin, 2005), and they often
have to be available in the office in 'usual' working hours:

'[W]hat do you call the relationship between academic staff
and professional, technical and secretarial staff? … you can say
it straightforwardly there's a hierarchy and the academics are in
charge except it doesn't always feel that way! But it's still the
case, the academics … come together to buy presents for the
office staff at Christmas, so this, I think is an … an interesting
dynamic, cause it is a kind of … thing you do for a subordinate
isn't it? Even though quite a lot of the time we would … I'd
like to *think* we work together as … colleagues, and … asking
somebody to do something as a favour goes both ways, but
then the academics are paid quite a bit more!' (Tanya)

As Tanya says, people appear to be working *with* each other, rather than
within a hierarchical order. Everyone is a 'colleague', and those higher
up the pecking order may find it "easier to work with people when …
they have a sense of that, of their own job and are prepared to set limits
and tell you, you know, 'No I don't do that' or something" (Patricia). At
the bottom of the system, cleaning – alongside catering, portering and
trades – is often outsourced and subject to the vagaries of the low-paid
'marketplace', and these occupations are not included in all-staff email lists
or organisational-wide consultations. Most administrative and outsourced

occupations also remain gendered (for example, administrative staff and cleaners are more likely to be women, and porters and other ground staff are more likely to be men). Cleaners float around departments and buildings, working in strict time-and-motion shifts, commonly early morning and late evening, leaving them little opportunity to engage with other staff or to be part of the departmental team.

Most service-users said they acknowledged the office cleaners when they saw them; a few had become friendly. The boundaries of these 'friendly work relationships' were set by the service-users "against the background of being *frightfully* careful not to be patronising" (Patricia). Clare often had a quick chat with her office cleaner, but one morning when the cleaner sat down and appeared to "get cosy", she became worried. Cleaners are not usually invited to departmental events or parties, and gift-giving at Christmas is often an unequal exchange – as Tanya says, we give them something but nothing is expected in return. Indeed, class continues to inform social practices in the UK (see also, for example, Jones, 1997; Skeggs, 1997, 2004).

The Indian context

No Indian service-user expressed guilt about outsourcing, except the two who eventually gave up. Pratibha stopped when she had started feeling uncomfortable about outsourcing housework to undernourished women who often did not turn up (see Chapter 5), and Bindu became increasingly aware of her service-provider's struggle to earn:

> '... and after a while actually I found it a little bit exploitative, honestly too ... although I was paying her more than what other people around me were paying her, there was some ethical questions, because she was already employed as I came to know later on ... and she was doing this job to supplement her income ... which is understandable because she came from a very low-income group, and ... I used to feel actually quite guilty every time she would pick up the bucket ... I would fill the water for her because I didn't want her going into my bathroom ... so I would half the times end up going around the two rooms with her and helping her do things, and I realised that it's not working out for me ....' (Bindu)

Most commonly, outsourcing was justified in terms of helping a needy, uneducated person, often facing many challenges, to earn a living.

Sometimes this was done within a discourse of 'mutual' dependency. That is, in return for the service-providers' help with domestic *labour*, besides cash payments, many Indian service-users helped them in other ways, such as providing interest-free loans, paying for medicines and children's education, and providing guidance on saving money:[6]

> 'Suppose I have a lot of … if I can afford it, why not to hire a person so that that person can also get employment. After the Sixth Pay Commission, you know, our salary shot up … so I have a very good salary. On the other hand these women are very poor … So, if I can employ a person why not? They will also get something out of it. Not only in the form of cash. Like, when she is at my home, she will have tea, I will give her fruit, some lunch …' (Kajal)

As Tellis-Nayak (1983) has argued, 'mutual' dependency is rooted in feudalistic patron–client relations.[7] This is clear in the following account, where even though the service-user is showing a change in her thinking, the idea that some dependency is acceptable remains:

> 'I've never thought about [guilt], no, I would say I am creating a space where that's her domain of work … I used to always cook myself earlier, and I realised with one of them that it's very important for them to cook. … Interestingly, I've really learnt a lot in the manner of how to deal with them also. You know, instead of saying 'ki bachhe hain' [they are children], one would also view them as lesser privileged, one is kind of doing things for them … But I feel that if supposing she was not working for me, and I was not giving her this kind of, so to say, whatever freedom or comfortable place – she says she has no light in her village, that's why she comes back, she doesn't have a room – I've built a special room for her and a bathroom for her. And that's for her, it's her space. And the way she wants to keep it … except that I don't buy her a separate TV because I know what she's going to do, and in summer she comes inside and sleeps in the AC. So no, I'm not guilty about that at all. In fact I think it's an opportunity for them, in fact they all learn so much in our homes …' (Navita)

No service-provider in my sample, however, framed their dependency in 'mutual' terms (see also Kordasiewicz, 2015). The service-users, thus, appeared to miss the point that their benevolence was legitimising the maintenance of social hierarchies. Moreover, regardless of framing of justifications, many occupations in India still remain caste-segregated (NCEUS, 2009; Raju and Jatrana, 2016a). Yet again, these issues are not unique to the domestic sphere.

As in most Indian public service or private workplaces, cleaners form part of the low-ranking workforce in universities. These workers frequently serve refreshments to other staff and their visitors (for example me) or lay out the boss's lunch and so on:

> 'the interaction [with cleaners] is [may be] not so much, it is less. But they know what I want – because the cleaner knows that whenever I have water, I like it to be lukewarm. So he keeps the water [ready] before I come.' (Sarika)

During departmental or wider celebratory events, cleaners may be the last to join in and then sit separately. The boundary between cleaners and the rest is not a sharp boundary, as hierarchies are complex and evident at each step of the ladder. As Meenakshi showed me around her institution after the interview, several students touched her feet, while she called them 'children'; the students were showing her the same respect they would show to elders in their family. Caste, too, continues to shape public social relations:

> '[I]n the university I find there are people, even at the higher level who very openly refer to these kind of things. We had a senior person here who would all the time say to one of the clerks "Panditji, Panditji". So I said you should not say "Panditji" because it is a caste address and the constitution actually forbids us to do this. But this [kind of talk] "Yeh to baniya hain so yeh aise hi karega" [he is a Baniya (another caste address) so he will behave like this] ... it is done in a sporting way, they don't even realise it that they should not be saying it ...' (Pratibha)

This analysis challenges Bhavna's broad comparison (see the beginning of this chapter) of East–West differences in attitudes and behaviours towards cleaning service-providers as the reason for her shifting attitudes in the two spaces. See also Grover's (2017) research on how some people from the more 'advanced' societies, such as the UK, negotiate their imagined egalitarian selves in obviously hierarchical societies such as India. It was common among the foreigners to outsource domestic work, but the workers mostly came from a particular social location. They were better educated than the average Indian domestic worker and spoke English. While these workers often did not experience the cultural injustices discussed here, their better treatment did not extend to the material aspects of the work. While Westerners are often paid more and receive greater perks for the same work as their Indian counterparts, they may not pay their service-users a proportionally greater amount. They also pay much less than they would in their own countries for the same work; that is, they do not follow the labour rights of their own countries while in India (also Lahiri, 2017:192). Moreover, these arrangements are considered temporary – employers do not pledge lifelong job security to their Indian domestic workers (Grover, 2017).

The common ground in the cultural injustices in the UK and Indian cultural contexts

In sum, while there are clearly inhumane service-users, some follow social norms more reflexively and try to grapple with injustices on a personal level. My UK respondents, either explicitly or implicitly, often appeared to draw not only on feminist understandings but also on wider sociological/social trends towards living in a more egalitarian society by, for example:

- deciding to use the services of an independent service-provider, which was mostly due to their conscious belief that any person doing domestic work must receive the full exchange-value of their labour (Janet, who chose an agency, said that her decision was based on the belief that a worker's employment rights were more likely to be realised if they were an employee);
- deciding to pay more than the national minimum wage or the going rate;
- having a friendly work relationship with the service-providers;
- using a male cleaning service-provider;
- reinvesting their wealth in the local economy;
- tidying up beforehand or leaving the toilet essentially clean.

Middle-class Indian women's liberation is, in part, historically rooted in the social reform movements of the late 19th century, in which the focus was often reform (of women's oppression) within the family, rather than as intersecting with caste oppressions in the wider society (Ambedkar, 1916/1979/2004). Still, my contemporary respondents' description of their actions often appeared to be influenced by an awareness of gender sensitisation and/or a general humanitarian consciousness by, for example:

- paying more than the going rate and raising rates annually;
- allowing days off without forfeiting pay;
- helping the worker and their family in various ways, including: trying to ensure that the woman had a proper meal by providing this at her workplace; giving advice on how to set up saving accounts; and giving advice on how to do this while living with an irresponsible husband (Seema's long-term, live-in housekeeper had, in her view, gained self-esteem through Seema's advice and support, and had also purchased land and built a small house);
- resisting the requirement to distance oneself from manual labour as a marker of their middle-classness (in the case of Pratibha and Bindu) and also by doing the work herself when her daily service-provider was unable to come (such as Taruni).

But these individual acts of kindness or respect, however reflexively thought through, do not provide the service-user with participatory parity, particularly when accompanied by the sense of guilt (in the UK) and benevolence (in India). In all, in both cultural settings, the service-users were rationalising their engagement with outsourced domestic work within wider class-bounded 'institutionalised thinking styles' (Douglas, 1986/1987) that often re-embedded wider social constructions of housework as low-value 'women's work'. The service-providers' cultural experiences in their work provided further evidence.

Cleaning service-providers' struggles against cultural injustices

The UK service-users whose service-providers came across as bright thought that each of those women was an 'exception' (see Chapter 2). Indeed, many service-providers displayed reflexivity in their struggle to do cleaning as *work*:

> 'I don't [find it embarrassing] but I must admit one of my daughters didn't, didn't like it: "Umm, that's embarrassing mum, you're a cleaner." I said it's not embarrassing, I have my own business and I work hard, and it's the same, same type of importance as my other job. It's just that I don't go to work in a suit.' (*Martha*)

Corinne, the retired teacher who did cleaning to supplement her pension, explained how she resisted the stigma she had been subjected to by academics in her social circle:

> 'At first I felt a little bit … I didn't mind it for myself but when I was talking to people because I, I mix with a lot of academics, I felt a little bit, when people asked me what I did, I tended to say I was an artist, rather than saying I was a cleaner. And same with the child-minding, I tended to say I was a teacher and not – but now, I quite enjoy confronting them with it, because they don't know what to say when I say I do cleaning and child-minding. That's the end then, and I like, I sort of enjoy watching them feel uncomfortable. I am more confident with what I do and what I am I guess.' (*Corinne*)

The stigma faced by cleaning service-providers is twofold. Cleaning itself is stigmatised as dirty, 'brainless' labour, with children, particularly middle-class children, being "threatened with having to get a job as a cleaner or a bin man for poor exam grades" (Mumsnet, 2013a). Someone who cleans for a living must be 'thick and stupid':

> '[M]y mum [an occupational therapist] knows that I'm a clever girl and she'd prefer me to do something more academic I think. … [later] I think I'm conscious anyway … I don't want people to look down on me, because there is … like a bit of a stigma attached to being a cleaner and people think, "Oh, you know, you're a cleaner, you're thick, you're stupid." Umm, and I know I'm not any of those things and I don't want people to think that of me. So sometimes I'll even get embarrassed, if like I go to a work thing with [my partner's] work and people'll say "What do you do *Sheila*?". And I just feel really, yeah! embarrassed saying … Even though it's my own business and I know I probably earn better money than they do. And I've got better hours, more flexibility and stuff, I just … don't like saying it all the time, yes. And I shouldn't be ashamed of it, that's the thing. I should be able to say "cleaner" and I've got my own cleaning business and feel *proud* of it.' (*Sheila*)

Then there is embodied stigma rooted in the historical pathologisation and demonisation of the working-classes by the middle-classes, in which bodies themselves still remain classed; for example, 'they' are smelly. None of my respondents talked in terms of this stigma, but there is ample other research (for example Skeggs, 1997/2002) and anecdotal evidence. Such stigma is also directed at other 'dirty' low-status workers, such as refuse collectors (Hughes et al, 2017) and careworkers (for example see Hyland, 2017) as well as low-wage retail workers (Smith and Elliot, 2012), and so on.

In India again, stigma is widely attached to 'manual' labour per se as well as being embodied, regardless of gender (Coelho, 2016). Cleaning is culturally considered a 'polluting' task, and embodied stigma was historically constructed in terms of caste and untouchability (Ambedkar, 1936/2016; Ilaiah, 1995/2004, 2005/2017). Although these discriminatory practices were constitutionally banned following the creation of the modern Indian state in 1947, the centuries-old understandings of caste formation and polluting labour continue to pervade contemporary 'secular' society; for example, favouring of service-providers who appear 'clean' regardless of their quality of work (see Chapter 5).

Similar to the UK, a few Indian service-users who said their service-providers came across as intelligent people implied that this was not the norm. Under such structural conditions, the Indian service-providers' detachment from their work is unsurprising. But, as the following comment illustrates, there may be considerable mental conflict as a worker reflexively wrestles to live with ressentiment (Rollins, 1985; or self-repression: Elson and Pearson, 1981):

'It is hard work but we have to do it for sustenance ... to bring up our children. So that's why we have to do it [because] what else will uneducated people get? They will only get the work of jhaddhu-pochha.[8] They aren't going to get anything better than that. But, at least we're doing our own work, earning our own bread. If we were educated, we would also be sitting on a chair in some office, doing some "good" work, but since we remained uneducated this is the work for us. But there is no shame in doing this work, it is stealing that is shameful. No, there is no shame in work, whatever work we do. And we will do what we are capable of doing. Yes, now see this, we think, "Oh! those high-status people have come and here I am doing this mopping, doing sweeping", but when this is the work that is assigned to us – you think about this, what is everyone's work? Now you [Lotika] are doing this reading and writing work, some other person is doing jhaddhu-pochha. Someone else is doing something else. ... In that educated world, there are many high-status jobs, but there are lower-status ones too. And there are some high-status ones as well in which some people feel shame, but that also has to be done. Everyone has been assigned some work [in society] – this does not mean that jhaddhu-pochha was inscribed in our fate. No. Okay, I am uneducated, but my daughters have studied, the younger one to class 10. She doesn't think she is going to do this work …' (*Shilpa*)

Some, then, deliberately try to gain some material advantage from the notion of 'mutual dependency'. As *Urvashi* noted, the Indian state did not have time for the likes of *her*. The only people *she* could depend on for support were the people *she* worked for.

Another cultural injustice here is social invisibility. On the macro level, since a large part of housework is carried out in the informal economy, numbers of domestic workers are notoriously underestimated (Ehrenreich, 2002/2010:57; ILO, 2013; Neetha, 2009:490). On the micro level, domestic workers might go about their work 'unseen' and treated as non-persons. This came across in my Indian interviews in particular. However, there are nuances here that require broadening of the lens of analysis. As Hatton (2017) argues, social power structures require invisibilisation of several kinds of work, and this happens through interlinking mechanisms that can be broadly categorised as spatial (site of work), cultural ('naturalising' discourses about aspects of work or the required skills or linking it to particular social groups) and legal (no legal protection or regulatory framework). For instance, wearing of uniforms is said to invisibilise the individual domestic worker (De Casanova, 2013). My Indian respondents did not wear uniforms. Rather, the visible (shabby) condition of their clothes was implicated in their embodied stigma. Among the UK service-providers working in partnerships and running quasi-agencies, some had chosen to have uniforms. *Nora* and her partner deliberately wore their uniforms and drove their branded van to public places such as supermarkets: it made them visible – people often made enquiries.

The notion of invisibility can also be turned on its head to challenge top-down meanings. Many service-providers visited a potential client's house before committing themselves, when an unspoken mutual assessment took place. The act of pre-tidying is indicative of the service-provider's presence in the mind of the customer. Many UK service-users also left 'thank-you' notes or sent appreciative text messages after the weekly clean. 'Guilty' service-users often make themselves scarce when the service-provider doing cleaning as *work* comes, by 'hiding' in the study or going out. This arrangement suits some service-providers, as they prefer to work in the absence of the service-user. The self-employed cleaner in the UK is also commonly a key-holder for at least some clients; although none of my Indian respondents were key-holders, anecdotal evidence indicates that similar practices are also possible in India. Giving access to one's home to another person is not an action taken lightly: "it's quite a big thing having someone in your house and who can go through all your private belongings ..." (Peggy).[9]

Lutz argues that trust in outsourced domestic work is an 'astonishing phenomenon in a society characterized by high functional differentiation in which working relationships are defined by written contracts and contractual compliance is governed by an extensive regulatory system' (2011:81–82). Her argument is based on comparing domestic work with a particular form of modern work relationship that supposedly exists in contemporary large organisations. Small to medium-sized enterprises (SMEs), however, often function differently at many levels, such that there is a continuum of 'functional differentiation' in work relationships even in the UK.[10] Moreover, my respondents said there was a human cost to 'high functional differentiation' (see Chapter 6; also Meagher et al, 2016). I disagree, therefore, that a foundation of trust is antithetical to modern work relationships, in which the various points noted here, including key-holding, make the service-provider highly visible.

Two thirds of my UK service-provider respondents were ambivalent about feminism. Doing cleaning in their own house, in the setting of an unequal division of labour (see Chapter 6) or as paid work, did not diminish their sense of seeing their paid cleaning work as proper work:

> 'I'd like to do whatever I'd like, when I'm young now, go where ever I want to go, ... and get it all out of my system. Then I would like to meet someone and have kids and settle down and have marriage and everything. ... I'd like to have my own business or something and be a housewife to be honest. Do both, still be independent ... I won't like to rely on somebody else, like ... my husband's wage and things. I'd like to want to do stuff on my own and have my own business, but then obviously, still, have my husband and my kids and house and everything and still be, like cooking, cleaning things. ... I don't think it's women's role, I think men or women can do it [her father shared the housework with her since her mother had left]. I think it's just a men thing that women ... are supposed do it and they're not. ... I mean obviously some women like to look after family and things like that. I don't think that's anything – there's nothing wrong with that.' (*Ruby*)

One reason for this may be because most of these women inhabited the same social spaces as other women working in other domestic work, namely childcare workers and carers. They did not see their position as unique, simply because they worked in the client's private space. Eight service-providers identified as feminists and two had an academic feminist background. They argued that even if they were doing traditional 'women's work', it was to ensure their financial independence, and hence, it did not conflict with their feminist ideals:

> 'Not at all ... If anything ... it's good because I'm probably going to be able to support myself. It could be a bit of a scrimp and save ... yeah! but *I* did it, you know, and I've got good clients who want me because I'm *me*, I'm not just 'the cleaner' ... I *do* have self-respect, although I'm not keen on walking down the street with my bucket. So there's a ... dichotomy ... Yeah! ... it's a tricky one ... I feel sad that my son can't tell his girlfriend that I'm a cleaner, because that's how I earn my money ... [The café manageress here] was saying "Lucky you, you know, you earn £10 an hour, [which is] more than a *lot* of people earn, doing a lot more hours", and I'm my own boss, and my own person.' (*Evie*)

> '... Why is it more demeaning to push a mop around someone's floor than it is to organise a spreadsheet for someone's business? Why is it? And that's the crux of my argument. It is work. It is paid work. So it has value in itself because it is paid work. It enabled me to feed my children, so honestly I am not being deliberately obtuse here, but I do not understand why certain – to me that's feminism kind of going backwards, because patriarchy said – oh! there we are – patriarchy said that women's work somehow has less value than men's work. Right? So housework is women's work. How is that a feminist statement? How? Housework is work and has intrinsic value, er, just as ... umm, teaching university undergraduates, ... just as being a CEO of a major company, whatever your gender, just as running a coffee shop ... So that makes me quite angry that feminists say housework is demeaning because the patriarchy says it is women's work. No, it's not. You take that out of the equation, it's not demeaning any more. You're providing a service.' (*Nicola*)

Some UK service-providers offered suggestions for better work conditions. These were primarily based on their singular experiences, as none of them said they were part of a larger domestic worker activist organisation. Those whose experiences were closer to *work* than to *labour* did not put holiday or sick pay at the top of their list of suggestions. As *Sheila* and *Evie* noted, they wanted to be able to do cleaning free from the cultural injustices that labelled their work as *labour* rather than *work*.

Conclusion

Some individual acts by service-users in both cultures, such as pre-tidying and leaving the toilet clean, challenge higher-level ideologies, as they show respect for the person doing cleaning, but their significance is diminished by the moral angst around outsourcing. The 'spreading-the-wealth' justification also does not always challenge the wider social construction of housework as low-value 'women's work' (see also Kordasiewicz, 2015). That is, individual attempts to redress injustices – both when cleaning was done as *work* and as *labour* in my research – were largely affirmative strategies (Fraser, 1996, 2013), as the work remained stigmatised, despite the service-providers' attempts to raise its profile. In this situation, even the 'friendly work relationship' described in the UK fell short of its promise, as it did not allow full participatory parity for the service-providers.

In the final chapter, I bring together the analyses presented in Chapters 3–7 and discuss the implications of my argument.

Concluding the Book, Continuing the Journey

The sociology of gender is always developing, testing its own conceptions (Ahlander and Bahr, 1995; Fraser, 2013). Still, there are times in the process when it is encouraging to remember that others have already made a similar journey: 'The constant discussions [about cleaning as skilled work] at Choices … changed my vision of housework as necessarily demeaning. I began to question my underlying assumptions. …' (Salzinger, 1991:159; see also Bujra, 2000:191)

My argument is a product of the outsourcing of contemporary urban housecleaning in two cultural contexts and my own social location. My findings and my position, as developed through these findings, thus may not be generalisable. The meanings of the work for my respondents in both research contexts, however, add to the broader established understandings of paid domestic work. Before I summarise this contribution, I consider some limitations of my research.

Few studies include male domestic workers (for example Bartolomei, 2010; Bujra, 2000; Lau, 2011; Ray and Qayum, 2009/2010), even though worldwide men continue to do domestic work (ILO, 2013, 2016). Rather, the work is often perceived as 'a matter between women' and theorised accordingly (which is ironic, since feminism and gender studies aim to render the marginalised visible). Although this book is also primarily based on research into the experiences of women, a few service-users had male service-providers, and it challenges the gendered conception of paid domestic work – it shows that the work does not come naturally to women (and men).

The primary data informing the argument were one-off, qualitative, semi-structured interviews, conversations that are not deemed 'natural'. Such interviews, still, often provide rich descriptive data, through which researchers can glean a sense of the context of people's lives and experiences, and the meanings people ascribe to them (Miller and Glassner, 1998; Taylor and Bogdan, 1998). I also drew on secondary data, from media reports to internet discussions to conversations with chance acquaintances ranging from disproval of outsourced cleaning, and notions of cleanliness and cleaning, to knowing an 'interesting' woman who cleaned. As time has gone by, the repetition of themes in these real-life accounts strengthened the primary data analysis – and continues to do so. For locating the work in the wider world of work, I drew on the wider research on work and employment in both the UK and India, as well as other regions when the context was pertinent.

Although the White British service-providers were privileged compared with the Indian service-providers in terms of race and socioeconomic status, they were clearly less privileged than the UK academic service-users. However, while they were dealing with dirt in a classed society, it is a society in which 'class' itself has become a 'dirty' word (see, for example, Hebson, 2009). This situation, in which people at least overtly try to behave in an egalitarian way, revealed meanings of work that might have been difficult to discern in situations complicated by racial and caste exploitation and vast socioeconomic disparities.

Would a more humane society, then, have paid domestic work or not? My analysis does not offer a yes/no answer that can be signed, sealed and put away, but it highlights two important points that require consideration in answering the question. First, as part of the 'civilising process', for various reasons people continue to outsource and provide domestic services. These reasons include an age- or health-related reduction in capacity to do the work and, beyond a point, desiring some order and cleanliness in built private (and public) spaces. In this, the outcomes of housework appear to be valued, even by those who considered its processes mundane, although notions of 'personal' work or of what can and cannot be outsourced – and why – vary. These aspects require further research, including among men, to understand better the social meanings of personal and domestic service work, including housecleaning. Second, there are possibilities in the work, as summarised in this chapter.

Live-out work in the form of formal self-employment appears to be a way of transforming domestic work from *labour* into *work* (Table 8.1). Bailly and colleagues, who, similar to Bowman and Cole (2014) and Meagher (2003), favour the organisational fragmentation-for-efficiency approach, note that the 'complexity and specificity of individual

Table 8.1: What makes outsourced domestic cleaning *work* instead of *labour*

When outsourced domestic cleaning is acknowledged as *work*	When outsourced domestic cleaning is acknowledged as *labour*
Regarding structure of the work (Chapter 5) • Housecleaning should not disturb the aesthetics of the home within a house. This requires developing responsivity between the service-provider and service-user, because people's tolerance for dirt, cleanliness, orderliness or homemaking varies. This will mean working to the same, higher or lower standards in relation to what service-providers do in their own living space. • There will be recognition that the work requires: – a tangible amount of time that is affected by several aspects of the house: size, how dirty, other people living there today, and so on; – mental skills, such as 'crafting an economy of movement', and broader business skills, such as timetabling, negotiation skills, communication skills; – additional mental work to maintain standards of work over time, in different climatic conditions, and to override the worker's own frame of mind (people have good days and bad days, depending on what else is going on in their lives). • The service-provider would have considerable autonomy and do a variety of tasks, including negotiating with clients and deciding which products to use, all of which are commensurate with their own values. (This would require access to modern products that reduce hard graft, and assurance of a constant source of electricity.)	• The work is considered simply an extension of unpaid work with no differentiation between the work required in different houses. What the service-provider does in the unpaid context is taken as the baseline and they work towards that – if service-users ask for more, they may be considered unreasonable. • The work done in each house may be fragmented, with different service-providers for different household tasks. • There is little regard for the time of the worker as compared with the time of the service-user. Work might be added and expected to be done in the same time as prior work. • Mental skills are recast as 'natural' affective labour, with the 'mental' work either assumed by a third party or the client themselves. • Mental work required to maintain a consistent standard of work is subsumed into a generalised mental grit, required simply to sustain the worker as they do work that 'nobody wants to do'.

(continued)

Table 8.1: What makes outsourced domestic cleaning *work* instead of *labour* (continued)

When outsourced domestic cleaning is acknowledged as *work*	When outsourced domestic cleaning is acknowledged as *labour*
Regarding who does the work (Chapters 6 and 7)	
• People would make an active decision to do cleaning as work, selecting it from a range of options.	• Anyone belonging to a *particular* group (classed, racialised, caste or gendered) is considered capable of doing cleaning, because of 'innate' abilities. People are 'pushed' into doing the work.
• Such a person has to have an interest in cleaning, the ability to 'see' what needs doing and 'how' it should be done, which would vary from house to house.	• Literacy is not considered a necessary condition of work; rather, the work is considered appropriate for the illiterate person.
• The work as described also requires the service-provider to be literate and generally in good health. Some formal education and an understanding of how a business works will ensure that both service-providers' and service-users' rights and responsibilities are respected.	• The work is done out of majboori,[1] primarily for the family rather than oneself, when nothing else is possible, and a living is needed.
• The service-provider would be invested in their work, and it would provide a sense of satisfaction.	• They have little investment in the work (or the wrong kind of investment, for instance when a migrant worker pays a third person fees for training and getting them a job in another country). The idea of gaining satisfaction from the work would be hard to describe here.
• The work may be done for part of one's working life, depending on the service-provider's work orientation at different stages of life. The service-provider's progeny may or may not do the same work.	• There is little possibility of the service-provider or their progeny doing other work, except equally alienating work.

(continued)

194

Table 8.1: What makes outsourced domestic cleaning *work* instead of *labour* (continued)

When outsourced domestic cleaning is acknowledged as *work*	When outsourced domestic cleaning is acknowledged as *labour*
Regarding the work relationship and the wider socio-legal framework for the work (Chapters 6 and 7)	
• All of the previous points would be more likely to happen when the service-provider is a live-out, independent, self-employed worker (or part of a collective of self-employed workers). • There will be participatory parity between the service-user and the service-provider, a friendly *work* relationship that can be located within wider work relationships. For this: – the service-provider has to be treated as a fully developed worker rather than being conceived of as a 'helper', and given feedback within a responsive relationship; – the worker's safety at work should be ensured; – they have to receive adequate remuneration (from a range of clients) to be able to live with dignity (take holidays, and so on) and plan for the future (set up a secure pension). • An implicit or explicit contract *for* services[2] may be delivered. • There would be some internationally recognised good practice guidelines and regulatory frameworks for both service-providers and service-users, including sexual safeguarding. These may follow the frameworks that guide the employer–employee relationship, but this needs clarification.	• Both live-in and live-out cleaning can be reduced to *labour*. • The relationship is substantially unequal, because of race, class or gender or because the work done is considered low status. That is, both the work and worker are stigmatised. • The service-provider harbours ressentiment. • Feedback may become a site of tension, experienced as khichh–khichh.[3] • Work is done under an implicit or explicit contract *of* service that resembles conditions of servitude. The service-provider has little autonomy in the method of working or products used or job description. • The service-provider feels like an atomised being. • Guidelines and regulations still consider domestic work to be work like no other in some regards, and this prevents participatory parity between the service-providers and service-users.

195

households are likely to be obstacles to [Taylorised] industrialisation' (Bailly et al, 2013:316). Indeed, as this book shows, good-quality, paid-for housecleaning incorporates responsivity, and will have better chances of being realised when cleaning is done as *work* by an independent worker, rather than as 'professionalised and industrialised' fragmented or caste-segregated *labour*.

Paid work is inherently exploitative, argues Weeks (2011). Still, Table 8.1 shows that cleaning can be done as *work* rather than *labour*, provided that the difference in the social distance (both material and cultural) between the service-providers and service-users allows full participatory parity for both. Fraser had said this distance would 'not be so great as to constitute "two nations" ...' (1996:54). My research shows that not just 'race', but the material and cultural dimensions of class and class–caste, too, can create 'two nations'.

In 2017, Jokela comprehensively reviewed the domestic work policies in several nations, including:

• tax and social contribution exemptions, for example in the Netherlands, Finland and Sweden;
• tax-deductible voucher schemes, for example in Belgium and France;
• regulation of domestic work, by structuring the work as a low-paid, flexibilised 'mini-job', for example in Germany and Austria;
• issuing of legal work permits for migrant workers, for example in Canada, South Korea and Taiwan.

According to Jokela's findings, it appears that all macro-level policies so far are:

> strongly consumer driven ... the regularization of domestic work per se does not always benefit workers. Precarious work is preserved particularly through regulations regarding the employment relationship ... [and] persisting undervaluation of paid domestic labour. Until these issues are addressed when developing the domestic services sector, it is unlikely to see any significant changes in the employment conditions of domestic workers. (Jokela, 2017:298–299[4]; also Bailly et al, 2013; Pérez and Stallaert, 2016; Shire, 2015)

In other words, these models encourage states' abrogation of welfare responsibilities; they legitimise the work as part-time, low-wage, low-value work (for example a 'bit' of cleaning that anyone can do), as the primary aim is to make outsourcing of domestic work more 'affordable' for the knowledge-economy worker, rather than encouraging them to recognise domestic work as proper work and pay a reasonable fee for quality. As Pape (2016) noted earlier, in the context of the setting of labour standards by the ILO, most employer representatives resist attempts to improve working conditions.

Similarly, in India, there is legislation regarding improving the conditions of domestic work, both at the national and state levels. But it has been much watered down, and the general lack of its enforcement is in part due to the lack of commitment by those involved in drafting the legislation and organising it, because they themselves employ domestic workers and so stand to lose out (Sen and Sengupta, 2016:271). In addition, some workers themselves try to capitalise on the gendered myth of 'women's work'. For example, The Si Se Puede! domestic workers' collective in New York 'was founded … to bring together immigrant *women* to create a *women*-run, *women*-owned, eco-friendly housecleaning business' (Cooperative Programme, 2011:7, my emphasis).[5]

The alternative paradigm of paid domestic work, outlined in this book, offers a way to break through the resistance of service-users through its delineation of specific issues in the undervaluation of domestic work, as evidenced in the work of outsourced cleaning:

• not everyone can do quality domestic work for a living – this is an important corollary of the established feminist position that this work is not embodied in particular racialised, caste or class or gendered groups;
• paid domestic work is not a simple extension of unpaid housework that is largely performed by women in many cultures (already noted by Bujra, 2000);
• paid domestic work requires both mental and manual skills;
• just as customers in other situations are not 'always right', and have to agree to certain terms and conditions, those outsourcing housework need to expend some energies in establishing a responsive relationship with their service-provider.

As mentioned in Chapter 6, payment for domestic (and care) work depletes capital. Making paid-for housecleaning *work* rather than *labour* (which includes appropriate fees) requires paying simultaneous attention to this relationship between service work and capital as well the cultural injustices listed here. Moreover, exploitation in paid domestic work cannot be resolved in isolation. Ray and Qayum (2009/2010) observed how domestic workers described remaining dependent on their employers (paradhin lives) in contrast to workers in other occupations, for whom work was associated with 'independence' (swadhin lives). But wider research shows the condition of being paradhin extends far beyond it to other low-wage work, because exploitation does not occur along a single axis of discrimination (Fraser, 1996, 2013). It is rooted not only in legacies of caste practices, colonialism and contemporary imperialism (Anderson, 2000:196; Sagar, 2017[6]), but also in wider top-down understandings of the value of work and (spurious) divisions of mental and manual labour (Ilaiah, 2005/2017; Torlina, 2011).

On the discursive level, in an account of two case studies of American child-carers' advocacy projects, Macdonald and Merrill (2002) noted that if the workers had used a combined vocabulary of skill (to address redistribution) and virtue (to address recognition), rather than either/or, they would have been more successful. However, skill itself is a socially constructed concept, whose boundaries and meanings keep shifting to maintain certain selves in a privileged position vis-à-vis disadvantaged Others; it is a concept of division, rather than cohesion, between people (Cockburn, 1991):

> Many of our depictions of physical and service work – popular accounts but more than a few scholarly treatments as well – tend toward the one-dimensional. Work is seen as ennobling or dehumanizing; it is occasion for opportunity or exploitation; it functions as an arena for identity development or class consciousness … [making it difficult] to capture the complex meaning work has in the lives of people like [my mother, the waitress]. (Rose, 2004/2014:25)

The elaboration of the structure of paid-for cleaning in the UK and India in this book suggests that both recognition and distribution can be addressed with one vocabulary, the unifying vocabulary of *work* as opposed to the divisive vocabulary of *labour*. When the unit of analysis is *work* instead of labour, its 'invisible' component, mental labour, such as responsiveness of the live-out cleaning service-provider, becomes visible and more valuable. Moreover, the link between paid and unpaid housework can be broken as responsiveness becomes a property of the space between the service-user and service-provider, rather than 'just an extension' of nurturing feminine capabilities.

My suggestion is lent support by Boris's (2017) analysis of the approach taken by representatives of domestic workers working with the ILO in the run-up to the writing of ILO Convention 189. Her findings indicated that the workers' appeal to 'affect', the emotional side, that this work is essential for societies to function, underpinned its eventual ambivalent description as 'work like no other' as well as 'work like any other' in the

ILO convention. That is, while this strapline recognises the workplace as just another workplace and the employment relationship as a legitimate one, it also deems it as a peculiar personal service relationship, which again obstructs achieving participatory parity. Boris (2017) argued that highlighting the interdependent nature of society is more likely to result in a breakthrough as regards cultural injustices in domestic work, which locates affect in the relationship rather than embodying it in the domestic worker (or a 'good' employer), just like in any other work.

Here, one point to note is that housecleaning, like many other kinds of work, will remain a job that can be done in a variety of ways: unpaid, paid, or as a favour for a friend or for family. So, complete eradication of the injustices of recognition would require appreciation of both the unpaid and paid versions of the work as well as the differences between them, including thinking about whether paid versions of such work can be done by anyone seeking to earn a living. Related questions might be:

- What kind of regulated self-employment would be attractive for people such as *Charlotte* (see Chapter 6, 'Cleaning on the side in the UK') to work above board?
- Are contracts enabling or disabling?
- What happens when a declared service-provider working alone has ambitions to grow her business?
- What about the prospects of her subcontractors?
- How can a cleaning service-provider grow their own *work*, for example as a quasi-agency, but without introducing conditions of *labour* for the subcontractors (in my research three of the four quasi-agency owners were using zero-hour contracts)?
- Is it possible for cleaning to be done as *work* in more than one way?

Some people may not have the nerve or the ambition to 'go it alone'. Here, the worker-managed collective form of self-employment appears to offer an alternative to an exploitative employee–employer contract (Estey, 2011), provided that its mission is to aim for conditions of *work* rather than *labour*, as Salzinger's (1991) comparison of two cooperatives showed. The ILO (Cooperative Programme, 2013) is mapping how, in these spaces, domestic workers worldwide are gaining much from each other's experiences and knowledge about how to do cleaning as *work* rather than *labour* (see also Smith, 2011; Tandon, 2012). All these areas merit further research.

Here I conclude that the unease around paid domestic work and the gaps in the research prevent recognition of the fact that the exploitation in this work is not fixed and stable, but is contingent on certain societal assumptions of ourselves, others and work. Thus, across cultural contexts intersectional theories of paid domestic work need to include the classed and casteised evolution of the very meanings of work.

For the Mumsnetters (see Chapter 1) who thought that housecleaning was a stupid research topic, this book provides the response: No it isn't, not until the meanings of cleaning work and the conditions under which it is done are duly transformed from conditions of *labour* to conditions of *work*.

Appendices

Appendix A: Sample demographics

See Tables A.1, A.2, A.3 and A.4.

Table A.1: Demographic details of the UK service-providers (n=27)

(a) Age, ethnicity, living arrangements, children, site of work, number of current domestic customers, approximate length of time in the work and mode of travel

Pseudonym	Age in years	Ethnicity	Living arrangements	No. of dependent (or adult) children
Undeclared workers				
Gloria★	33	White British	Civil partnership (M)	2
Olivia	38	White British	Cohabiting (M)	1
Charlotte	38	White British	Married	2
Carrie	52	White British	Cohabiting (F)	–
Nicola	52	White British	Cohabiting (F)	1 (2)
Corinne	61	White British	Single (divorced)	(2)
Davina	75	White Irish	Single (divorced)	(3)
Rebecca	74	White British	Married	(3)
Declared workers				
Self-employed and working alone				
Ruby	20	White British	Single (lives with father)	–
Grace	23	White British	Single (lives with parents)	–
Kate	25	White British	Single parent	2
Sheila	27	White British	Cohabiting (M)	–
Jessica	33	White British	Cohabiting (M)	6
Amelia	39	White British	Cohabiting (M)	(1)
Martha	47	White British	Single (divorced)	2
Evie	48	White British	Cohabiting (M)	2
Abigail	55	White British	Married	(2)
Sophie	55	White British	Single (divorced)	(1)
Self-employed with one business partner				
Celia★	32	White British	Married	4
Helena★	40	White British	Married	4
Zoe	41	White British	Married	2
Nora	54	White British	Married	1 (2)
Quasi-agency owners				
Vera	28	White British	Cohabiting (F)	1
Yvonne	28	White British	Single parent	1
Tamsin	47	White British	Single (divorced)	2
Valerie	47	White British	Single (separated)	(1)
Ex-agency worker, no longer doing cleaning				
Georgia	45	White British	Single parent	1 (1)

AW, agency worker; D, domestic; DC, domestic and commercial; M, male partner; F, female partner; ZHC, zero-hour contracts.

★*Gloria* answered questions by email. *Celia* and *Helena* were interviewed together.

Site of work/ Comments	No. of current domestic customers	Approximate length of time in this work	Mode of travel to work
D	2	6 months	Did not ask
D/AW (1 client)	4	2 years	Did not ask
D	3	6 months	Car
D	1	2 years (+3 years)	Car
D	1 (8 at a time)	10 years (+6 years)	Car
D	2	5 years	Car
D	1	>20 years	Walking
D	1	>40 years	Car
D	3	2 months	Car
DC/Previously AW	12	1 year	Car
D	2	2 months	Public transport
DC	12	1 year	Walking
D	6	1 month	Car
D	2	1.5 years	Public transport
D	4	5 years	Car
D	6	7 years	Car/walking
D/Previously AW	3	8 years	Car
DC/Previously AW	9	2 years	Car
D/Partner is friend	3	1 month	Car
D/Partner is friend	3	1 month	Do not know
DC/Partner is husband	~10	8 years	Husband's car/ public transport
D/Partner is friend	~40	1.3 years	Company van
DC/ZHC	>30	6 months	Car
DC/ZHC	Between 30 and 40	1.5 years	Car
DC/Employees	~25	2 years	Car
DC/ZHC	~40	5 years	Car
D	–	5 years	Do not know

Table A.1: Demographic details of the UK service-providers (n=27) (continued)

(b) Age band when started cleaning work, education level, dependent children when starting work, and job history

Age group when started the work	Pseudonym	Education level
20–29 years	Ruby	A Level (Health and Social Care)
	Grace	FE (Diploma, Hair and Beauty)
	Sheila	FE (Diploma, Beauty Therapies)
	Kate	GCSE
	Yvonne	FE (Art and Design)
	Vera	FE (Diploma, Cleaning Management student)
	Rebecca★	Left school at 15 years
	Davina★	Left school at 15 years
	Georgia†	FE; currently BEd student
30–39 years	Zoe	GCSE
	Jessica	FE (NVQ2, Hairdressing)
	Celia	HE (BA)
	Gloria★	GCSE
	Charlotte★	AS Level
	Valerie	FE (Diploma, Hair and Beauty)
	Olivia★	GCSE
	Amelia	FE (Diploma in Care)

Children's approximate age status at the time of starting work	Job history
No children	Care worker
No children	Call-centre worker; cleaning agency worker; brewery cleaner
No children	Beauty therapist; waitressing
Yes, <16 years	Shop assistant (paid and voluntary)
Yes, <16 years	Call centre worker; sales and targets assistant; food outlet operative; shop assistant
Yes, <16 years	Food outlet operative; call centre worker; door supervisor; care officer; bar work; painter/decorator
Yes, <16 years	Factory work (bottling; spring making; wood cutting); also commercial properties cleaner
Yes, <16 years	Hospital cleaner, factory work, live-out housekeeper cum childminder
Twenties	Secretarial work (before cleaning work); retail and primary education (after cleaning work)
Yes, <16 years	Shop assistant; usherette; commercial property cleaner
Yes, <16 years	Domestic assistant; customer services advisor; barbering; mobile hairdressing; other odd jobs
Yes, <16 years	Mobile phone industry; waitressing; home shopping (supermarket); customer contact centre; selling advertising space; assessment team advisor in a solicitor's practice; legal services department
Yes, <16 years	Nanny; school club supervisor; quality inspector; accounts clerk; lettings manager; purchase ledger clerk; data entry clerk; optical assistant
Yes, <16 and >16 years	Selling insurances; daycare assistant; selling mobile phones; farm admin and maintenance work; bar work
Yes, <16 years	Receptionist; shipping clerk; secretarial work; riding school groom and receptionist
Yes, <16 years	Supermarket job; bar work; shop assistant; factory work
Yes, >16 years	Shop assistant (butcher; fast-food outlet); care worker; cashier; cleaning subcontractor; school kitchen assistant; T-shirt printing

(continued)

Table A.1: Demographic details of the UK service-providers (n=27) (continued)

(b) Age band when started cleaning work, education level, dependent children when starting work, and job history (continued)

Age group when started the work	Pseudonym	Education level
40–49 years	Carrie*§	HE (MA, doctoral student)
	Nicola*§	HE (BA, BEd, MA)
	Evie	A level
	Helena	GCSE
	Martha	A level (Business Studies)
	Tamsin	FE (NVQ3 Childcare)
50–59 years	Nora	FE (Diploma, Health and Social Care)
	Abigail	FE (NVQ, Childcare, incomplete)
	Sophie	HE (Diploma, Nursing)
	Corinne★	HE (BEd hons)

Notes:

FE, further education; GCSE, General Certificate of Secondary Education; HE, higher education.

Further education (16+) in the UK comprises vocational work-related courses that lead to competence-based qualifications. Vocational work does not require a degree qualification (for example hairdressing or beauty therapy). Some A level courses also lead to vocational qualifications (for example health and social care).

★This respondent did not declare the work.

†Georgia had worked for a cleaning agency in her twenties. Since then she had moved on to other work.

§Carrie, who had a same-sex partner, first did cleaning work in her twenties, while pursuing an undergraduate degree. She was single at that time. She went back to higher education in her late forties, after teaching for many years. She was also doing some cleaning work again. Nicola first did cleaning work in her thirties, after leaving her partner because of domestic violence and becoming a single mother with three children. Her second experience in cleaning work occurred in her fifties.

Children's approximate age status at the time of starting work	Job history
No children	Retail assistant; bar work; childminding; sixth form teacher
Yes, <16 and >16 years	School teacher; summer schools; childminder; nanny-housekeeper; currently personal tutor; environmental charity worker; knitting and sewing projects on commission
Yes, <16 years	Theatre/television costumer designer; T-shirt designer in family mail-order business
Yes, <16 and >16 years	Waitressing, shop assistant, supermarket jobs
Yes, <16 years	Secretarial work; bank teller
Yes, <16 years	Customer services; receptionist; head of service department; office administration; nursery nurse
Yes, <16 and >16 years	Care worker
Yes, >16 years	Various jobs (including shift work) at local businesses; school catering manager; voluntary teaching assistant
Yes, >16 years	Nursing; cleaning work (local pub, brewery); waitressing; assistant pub chef; door-to-door selling; shop assistant; brewery tour guide; bar work; assistant manager in retail; sales; cleaning agency worker
Yes, >16 years	Teacher; social services home-help organiser; various 'odd jobs' such as working in a theatre box office

Table A.2: Demographic details of Indian service-providers (n=24)

(a) Age, regional background, living arrangements, children, education level, site of work, length of time in work, number of current customers, mode of travel and husband's paid work status and level of responsibility towards family

Pseudonym	Age in years*	Region of origin	Living arrangements	No. of children	No. of dependent children	Education level
Live-out providers						
Anjali	28	NW	Nuclear family +‡	2	2	None
Urvashi	37	NW	Nuclear family	3	2	None
Priya	35	NW	LAT + children	5	4	None
Brinda	43	NW	Nuclear family	5	3	None
Chetna	28	Same	Nuclear family +§	3	3	Class 8‡‡
Asha	35	NW	Widow + children	5	5	None
Gauri	32	NW	Nuclear family	4	4	None
Indu	35	NW	Nuclear family	4	4	None
Bela	57	Same†	Nuclear family	4	1	None
Kavita	30	NW	LAT + children	4	4	None
Jyotika	30	Same	Nuclear family	2	2	Class 7
Kalpana	37	Same	Nuclear family¶	2	2	None
Divya	30	NW	Nuclear family +**	1	1	None
Madhu	30	NW	Nuclear family	3	3	None
Neena	40	NW	Nuclear family	4	3	None
Sanvi	25	NW	Nuclear family	2	2	None
Shilpa	40	Same	Nuclear family	4	3	None

Site of work	Approximate length of time in this work	No. of current domestic customers	Mode of travel to work	Husband's paid work status§§	Husband's responsibility towards family***
D C	14+	5–6	Walking	1	3
D	12	3	Cycling	2	1
D	5	3	Cycling	2/3	1
D	17+	2	Walking	1	3
D	DNA	2–3	Walking	2	1
D	4+	1	Walking	2 (when alive)	1 (when alive)
D	<1	3	Walking	4	4
D	3+	3	Walking	1	3
D	MD	1	Walking	2	1
D	1	3	Walking	1	2
D	5+	4–5	Cycling	2	1
DC	30+	2	Cycling	2	1†††
D	2.5	2	Walking	2	1
D	DNA	1	Walking	1	1
D	20	4–5	Cycling	1¶¶	4
D	6	1	Cycling	2	1
D	20+	DNA	Do not know	1	3

(continued)

Table A.2: Demographic details of Indian service-providers (n=24)

(a) Age, regional background, living arrangements, children, education level, site of work, length of time in work, number of current customers, mode of travel and husband's paid work status and level of responsibility towards family (continued)

Pseudonym	Age in years*	Region of origin	Living arrangements	No. of children	No. of dependent children	Education level
Part live-out providers						
Mohini	40	NW	Nuclear family	3	1††	None
Anika	24	NW	Nuclear family	2	2	None
Loveleen	40	NW	Nuclear family	4	4	None
Neelam	29	NW	Nuclear family	3	3	Class 5
Sonali	47	NW	Widow + child	3	1	None
Pallavi	35+	Nepal	Widow + child	2	1	None
Rashmi	30	NW	Nuclear family	3	3	None

Notes: Domestic work is generally part of the informal economy in India, and cash-in-hand is the most common form of payment. Hence, the demographic details of the Indian sample are shown differently from the UK sample in Table C.3, that is, on the basis of where the provider lived, rather than on the basis of the working practice.

C, commercial; D, domestic; DNA, did not ask question; LAT, living apart-together; MD, missing data (corrupted audio file); NW, north-western regions of India.

*Approximate age. Most women did not know their date of birth but had a rough idea of their age at marriage and the number of years they had been married.

†Parents were migrants from north-western regions of India.

‡Brother-in-law and another man from her village also live with them.

§ Her husband's brothers and their families live in the same compound.

¶Second husband.

**Brother-in-law also lives with them.

††Older son earns but not enough to live independently.

‡‡ Indian 'class' = UK 'year' – 1.

§§: 1, (irregular) daily manual labourer (for example stitching up gunny bags for transport, rickshaw puller, construction site worker; 2, regular low-waged (manual/non-manual) work (sweeper; peon; labourer in fruit and vegetable market, dhobi; tea shop owner, gardener; factory worker; painter); 3, farm labourer; 4, unemployed or unable to work to full capacity due to ill health.

¶¶Husband not working at present due to illness.

Site of work	Approximate length of time in this work	No. of current domestic customers	Mode of travel to work	Husband's paid work status§§	Husband's responsibility towards family***
D	25+	1		2	1
D	10	1		2	1
D	11	1		2	2
D	6	1		2	1
D	18+	3	Walking ‡‡‡	2	2
D	18+	3	Walking ‡‡‡	2	3
D	2+	1		1	1

***1, husband regular worker or regularly looks for work; wife says decent man (although this does not preclude a degree of domestic violence, such as shouting at or hitting wife); 2, husband is regular worker but alcoholic and inflicts domestic violence; 3, husband is irregular worker, alcoholic and inflicts domestic violence; 4, husband unemployed or working less due to physical ill-health but wife says 'decent' man (although this does not preclude a degree of domestic violence, such as shouting at or hitting wife).

††† First husband was a farm labourer.

‡‡‡To other service-users' houses.

Table A.2: Demographic details of Indian service-providers (n=24) (continued)

(b) Living spaces of the Indian cleaning service-providers: size, rental agreement, access to basic utilities and mobile phones

Pseudonym	Location of living space	No. of rooms	Ownership status	Access to water
Live-out providers				
Anjali	Apartment building	One, with kitchen in a recess	Rented	Private tap
Urvashi	Apartment building	One + kitchen	Rented	Private tap
Priya	Landlord's yard containing several built single-room apartments	One	Rented	Communal tap
Brinda	Jhuggi* in slum	One + covered verandah	Rented	Communal tap
Chetna	Separate room in a joint family accommodation built by father-in-law in a slum	One	Owned by husband's family	Communal tap
Asha	Jhuggi in slum	One + covered verandah	Owned by self	Communal tap
Gauri	Jhuggi in slum	One + covered verandah	Do not know	Communal tap
Indu	Jhuggi in slum	One	Do not know	Communal tap
Bela	Alleyway	One (converted to ironing shack in the day)	Not applicable	Tap in customer's yard
Kavita	Jhuggi in slum	One	Do not know	Communal tap
Jyotika	Jhuggi built on disputed land	One	Owned by self	Communal tap
Kalpana	Apartment building	One	Rented	
Divya	Common green space in a middle-class area	One (converted to ironing shack in the day)	Not applicable	Tap in customer's driveway

212

Access to electricity	Bathing arrangement	Access to toilet	Mobile phone
Yes, legal	Communal bathroom	Communal toilet	Yes
Yes, legal	Private bathroom	Private toilet	Yes
Yes, legal status not known	Communal bathroom	Communal toilet	Yes
No access	In room	Communal toilet	No
Yes, legal status not known	Private bathroom shared with joint family	Toilet built in shared family space (also used by other people from the slum)	No
Yes, possibly illegal	In room	Communal toilet	No
Yes, possibly illegal	In room	Communal toilet	No
Yes, possibly illegal	In room	Communal toilet	No
No access	Communal bathrooms in marketplaces or customer's facility	Toilets in marketplaces/open sheltered spaces	No
Yes, possibly illegal	In room	Communal toilet	No
Yes, possibly illegal	Private bathroom	Private (but not plumbed in)	Yes
Yes, legal	Private bathroom	Private toilet	Yes
Illegal access from customer's supply (paid for by customer)	Communal bathrooms in marketplaces	Communal toilets in marketplaces	No

(continued)

Table A.2: Demographic details of Indian service-providers (n=24) (continued)

(b) Living spaces of the Indian cleaning service-providers: size, rental agreement, access to basic utilities and mobile phones (continued)

Pseudonym	Location of living space	No. of rooms	Ownership status	Access to water
Live-out providers (continued)				
Madhu	Yard with apartments	One	Rented	Communal tap
Neena	Apartment building	One	Rented	Communal tap
Sanvi	Jhuggi in slum	One	Rented	Communal tap
Shilpa	Questions not asked			
Part live-out providers				
Mohini	Outhouse in landlord's backyard	Two	Work done in lieu of rent and also paid a fee	Private tap (water bill paid by landlord)
Anika	Outhouse in landlord's backyard	One	Work done in lieu of rent	Private tap (water bill paid by landlord)
Loveleen	Outhouse in landlord's backyard	One + kitchen	Work done in lieu of rent	Private tap (water bill paid by landlord)
Neelam	Outhouse in landlord's backyard	One	Work done in lieu of rent and also paid a fee	Private tap (water bill paid by landlord)
Sonali	Outhouse in landlord's backyard	One + recess for kitchen	Work done in lieu of rent and also paid a fee	Private tap (water bill paid by landlord)
Pallavi	Rooms attached to landlord's house	One + kitchen	Work done in lieu of rent and also paid a fee	Private tap (water bill paid by landlord)
Rashmi	Outhouse in landlord's backyard	One	Work done in lieu of rent	Private tap (water bill paid by landlord)

*Jhuggi = shack (often built illegally).

Access to electricity	Bathing arrangement	Access to toilet	Mobile phone
Yes, legal status not known	Communal bathroom	Communal toilet	No
Yes, legal status not known	Communal bathroom	Communal toilet (and fields)	Yes but no credit
No access	In room	Open field (and customer's toilet)	Yes but can dial only two numbers
Yes, legal, paid for by landlord	Private bathroom/toilet owned by landlord		No
Yes, legal, paid for by landlord	Private bathroom/toilet owned by landlord		No
Yes, legal, paid for by landlord	Private bathroom/toilet owned by landlord		No
Yes, legal, paid for by landlord	Private bathroom/toilet owned by landlord		No
Yes, legal, paid for by landlord	Private bathroom/toilet owned by landlord		Yes
Yes, legal, paid for by landlord	Private bathroom/toilet owned by landlord		Yes
Yes, legal, paid for by landlord	Private bathroom/toilet owned by landlord		No

Table A.3: Demographic details of the UK service-users (n=21)

Household composition	Pseudonym	Age in years	No. of children
Lone woman household	Iris	66	–
	Harriet★	57	–
Single parent with dependent children	Libby	39	2
	Peggy	53	2
Single parent with adult children sharing home	Pauline	63	1
Dual-earner couple (married/co-habiting) with dependent children§	Tanya	38	2
	Beverley	42	2
	Renee★	42	1
	Samantha★	44	3
	Janet	47	3‡
	Imogen	51	2
Dual-earner couple (married/co-habiting) with no dependent children (younger couples with no children or older couples with children aged 18+ years)	Clare	37	1
	Felicity	37	–
	Una★	51	–
	Lily	62	3
	Naomi★	64	2
Dual-earner couple (married/co-habiting), with or with no dependent children, and jobs in different cities involving significant travelling for one partner	Caitlin	53	2
	Gayle	53	2
	Patricia	65	2
	Maggie†	59	1
	Orla	61	–

★Currently not using cleaning services.

†Also used cleaning services when she was a single parent with a dependent child.

§One partner was temporarily a househusband.

Table A.4: Demographic details of the Indian service-users (n=19)

Household composition	Pseudonym	Age in years	No. of children
Single woman household	Bindu★	38	0
	Nandita	47	0
	Navita	54	0
Single woman living with parent(s)	Vibha	46	0
	Ritika	56	0
Single (divorced/separated) parent with dependent or adult children	Rekha	44	1
	Seema	63	2
Wife, living with parents and dependent children or alone (spouses working and living in a different city)	Meenakshi	47	1
	Lata	53	3
Dual-earner couple (married) with dependent children†	Sarika	34	1
	Pratibha★	43	2
	Urmila	44	1
	Ananya	47	1
	Pooja	51	1
	Kajal	51	2
	Taruni	52	2
Dual-earner couple (married) living in a joint family (and with or without dependent children)	Shobha	47	2
	Geetanjali	52	2
	Ritu	53	1

★Currently not using cleaning services.

†Some of these couples also had the husband's parents living with them, prior to their death.

Appendix B: Selection of webpages consulted on Mumsnet and Netmums

All these webpages were accessed over a period of time in 2013–2015.

Mumsnet (2012a) Mumsnet discussion thread (started 10 October 2012). Am I being unreasonable to get a cleaner? (www.mumsnet.com/Talk/ am_i_being_unreasonable/1584321-to-get-a-cleaner).

Mumsnet (2012b) Mumsnet discussion thread (started 24 November 2012). AIBU To think about getting a cleaner? (www.mumsnet.com/ Talk/am_i_being_unreasonable/1619688-To-think-about-getting-a-cleaner).

Mumsnet (2013a) Mumsnet discussion thread (started 29 April 2013). AIBU To (privately) disapprove of my friend having a cleaner (www. mumsnet.com/Talk/am_i_being_unreasonable/1744098-To-privately-disapprove-of-my-friend-having-a-cleaner).

Mumsnet (2013b) Mumsnet discussion thread (started 14 August 2013). AIBU to ask what jobs you do that fit in well with school hours? (www. mumsnet.com/Talk/am_i_being_unreasonable/1827105-to-ask-what-jobs-you-do-that-fit-in-well-with-school-hours).

Mumsnet (2014a) Mumsnet discussion thread (started 26 February 2014). AIBU Am I the only one who doesn't have a cleaner?? (www.mumsnet. com/Talk/am_i_being_unreasonable/2009337-Am-I-the-only-one-who-doesnt-have-a-cleaner).

Mumsnet (2014b) Mumsnet discussion thread (started 3 May 2014). AIBU To not sack my cleaner? (www.mumsnet.com/Talk/am_i_being_ unreasonable/2069957-To-not-sack-my-cleaner).

Mumsnet (2014c) Mumsnet discussion thread (started 16 May 2014). AIBU To feel a bit weird and embarrassed now we've got a cleaner? (www.mumsnet.com/Talk/am_i_being_unreasonable/2081523-to-feel-a-bit-weird-and-embarrassed-now-weve-got-a-cleaner).

Mumsnet (2014d) Mumsnet discussion thread (started 24 May 2014). Cleaners – advice please. (www.mumsnet.com/Talk/good_ housekeeping/2088485-Cleaners-advice-please).

Mumsnet (2014e) Mumsnet discussion thread (started 10 June 2014). Anyone worked as a cleaner? (www.mumsnet.com/Talk/going_back_ to_work/2102836-Anyone-worked-as-a-cleaner).

Mumsnet (2014f) Mumsnet discussion thread (started 12 June 2014). AIBU To tell DH that we ARE getting a cleaner – no excuses anymore (www. mumsnet.com/Talk/am_i_being_unreasonable/2104739-To-tell-DH-that-we-ARE-getting-a-cleaner-no-excuses-anymore).

Mumsnet (2014g) Mumsnet discussion thread (started 18 June 2014). AIBU Cleaners, anyone who has one come and advise me please (www.mumsnet.com/Talk/good_housekeeping/2110706-Cleaners-anyone-who-has-one-come-and-advise-me-please).

Mumsnet (2014h) Mumsnet discussion thread (started 17 August 2014). AIBU TO be reluctant to hire MIL as a cleaner? (www.mumsnet.com/Talk/am_i_being_unreasonable/2161523-To-be-reluctant-to-hire-MIL-as-a-cleaner).

Mumsnet (2014i) Mumsnet discussion thread (started 19 September 2014). Is £15 p.h. a lot for a cleaner? (www.mumsnet.com/Talk/good_housekeeping/2188704-Is-15-p-h-a-lot-for-a-cleaner).

Mumsnet (2014j) Mumsnet discussion thread (started 24 September 2014). What does your cleaner do? (www.mumsnet.com/Talk/good_housekeeping/2192777-What-does-your-cleaner-do).

Mumsnet (2014k) Mumsnet discussion thread (started 25 September 2014). AIBU To not clean up for the (potential) cleaner? (www.mumsnet.com/Talk/am_i_being_unreasonable/2194146-To-not-clean-up-for-the-potential-cleaner).

Mumsnet (2014l) Mumsnet discussion thread (started 26 September 2014). AIBU That part of me feels like a failure for wanting a cleaner? (www.mumsnet.com/Talk/am_i_being_unreasonable/2194927-That-part-of-me-feels-like-a-failure-for-wanting-a-cleaner).

Mumsnet (2014m) Mumsnet discussion thread (started 22 October 2014). Cleaner problem (www.mumsnet.com/Talk/good_housekeeping/2215792-Cleaner-problem).

Mumsnet (2014n) Mumsnet discussion thread (started 1 November 2014). AIBU To wonder about Mumsnetters and their cleaners? (www.mumsnet.com/Talk/am_i_being_unreasonable/2224055-To-wonder-about-Mumsnetters-and-their-cleaners).

Mumsnet (2014o) Mumsnet discussion thread (started 15 December 2014). AIBU To think cleaners should do the hours they're paid to do (www.mumsnet.com/Talk/am_i_being_unreasonable/2260060-To-think-cleaners-should-do-the-hours-theyre-paid-to-do).

Netmums (2009–2014) Netmums discussion thread (started 8 December 2009, last post 14 November 2014). Cleaning business owners general discussion. (www.netmums.com/coffeehouse/working-childcare-692/working-yourself-self-employed-76/wfy-self-employed-chat-clubs-501/358425-cleaning-business-owners-general-discussion.html).

Netmums (2011) Netmums discussion thread (started 25 October 2011). Do YOU have a cleaner?? (www.netmums.com/coffeehouse/general-coffeehouse-chat-514/coffee-lounge-18/658095-do-you-have-cleaner-all.html).

Netmums (2012) Netmums discussion thread (started 28 November 2012). Is having a cleaner when you're an SAHM jolly lazy? (www. netmums.com/coffeehouse/general-coffeehouse-chat-514/wine-bar-494/855047-having-cleaner-when-you-re-sahm-jolly-lazy.html).

Notes

Introduction

[1]   Ressentiment refers to the negative feelings of hatred, vengeance or envy and so on, brought about by the 'cumulative repression' experienced by domestic workers and which often must remain suppressed (Rollins, 1985: 225).

Chapter 1

[1]   Mumsnet, topics ≫ Media/non-member requests. 31 March 2014. Does having a cleaner conflict with feminism? (46 posts).

[2]   *The Civilising Process* is the title of Elias's 1939 work tracing the historical development, meanings and understandings of everyday social behaviours, manners and etiquette in the European context. In this, Elias emphasises the role of wider institutional changes, particularly the shift of 'acceptable' violent behaviours from the individual to the macro level. (See Elias, 1994/2003.)

[3]   A few Indian states have introduced regulations, but their implementation has been irregular (Neetha and Palriwala, 2011; Sen and Sengupta, 2016).

[4]   The debate has been revisited more recently in related contexts, for instance the 'problem' with work (Weeks, 2011).

[5]   A British Broadcasting Corporation (BBC) Radio 4 programme that discusses topical issues for and about women.

[6]   Also in other northern and central European countries (Sarti, 2005; see also Bujra, 2000, for a Tanzanian context).

[7]   Census Customer Services (2014) Email to Lotika Singha. With extracts from census tables from 1951, 1961, 1971 and 1981, 14 October 2014. See Mayer-Ahuja (2004) and van Walsum (2011) for the German and Dutch context, respectively.

[8]   See Chaney and Garcia Castro (1989) for the Latin American context.

[9]   See Bharati and Tandon Mehrotra (2008), Chaney and Garcia Castro (1989), de Santana Pinho and Silva (2010), Driscoll (2011), Estévez-Abe and Hobson (2015), Ray and Qayum (2009/2010) and Singh (2007).

[10] See de Santana Pinho and Silva (2010) for Brazil.

[11] For example, Anderson (2000), Chin (1998), Constable (2007), Lutz (2011), Momsen (1999), Triandafyllidou (2013) and Yilmaz and Ledwith (2017).

[12] For example, see Calleman (2011), Cox (2006), Ehrenreich and Hochschild (2003), Estévez-Abe (2015), Flanagan (2004), Gutiérrez-Rodríguez (2014), Lahiri (2017) and Windebank (2007).

[13] For example, see Chaney and Garcia Castro (1989), Hondagneu-Sotelo (2001), Molinier (2009/2012) and Romero (2002).

[14] See Anderson (2000, 2001), Chaney and Garcia Castro (1989), Chin (1998), de Santana Pinho and Silva (2010), Ehrenreich and Hochschild (2003), Glenn (1981, 1992), Lutz (2002, 2008, 2011), Pérez and Stallaert (2016), Scrinzi (2010) and Triandafyllidou (2013).

[15] In association with the London-based charity Kalayaan (see also Lalani, 2011).

[16] *The Lady* is a British magazine that carries adverts (wanted/seeking position) for domestic help in upper-middle/upper-class households. Its modern incarnation retains its 'genteel' Victorian English character (Wheen, 2012).

[17] Bharati and Tandon Mehrotra (2008), Bujra (2000), Chin (1998), Constable (2007), De Casanova (2013), King (2007), Lan (2006), Mattila (2011), Ray and Qayum (2009/2010).

[18] ESS Round 7: European Social Survey Round 7 Data (2014). Data file edition 2.1. doi:10.21338/NSD-ESS7-2014; ESS Round 6: European Social Survey Round 6 Data (2012). Data file edition 2.3.doi:10.21338/NSD-ESS6-2012; ESS Round 5: European Social Survey Round 5 Data (2010). Data file edition 3.3. doi:10.21338/ NSD-ESS5-2010; ESS Round 4: European Social Survey Round 4 Data (2008). Data file edition 4.4. doi:10.21338/NSD-ESS4-2008; ESS Round 3: European Social Survey Round 3 Data (2006). Data file edition 3.6. doi:10.21338/NSD-ESS3-2006; ESS Round 2: European Social Survey Round 2 Data (2004). Data file edition 3.5. doi:10.21338/NSD-ESS2-2004; and ESS Round 1: European Social Survey Round 1 Data (2002). Data file edition 6.5. doi:10.21338/NSD-ESS1-2002. NSD – Norwegian Centre for Research Data, Norway – Data Archive and distributor of ESS data for ESS ERIC.

[19] For example, Calleman (2011), Cox (2006), Lyonette and Crompton (2015), Lutz (2011), Seierstad and Kirton (2015), Swan (2012) and van Walsum (2011).

[20] Suggested in Anderson (2000), de Santana Pinho and Silva (2010), Ehrenreich (2002/2010), Groves and Lui (2012) and Näre (2016).

[21] For other struggles and successes, see Bapat (2014), Bernardino-Costa (2014), Blackett (2011), Bujra (2000), Chaney and Garcia Castro (1989), Magnus (1934b), Lai (2007), Lalani (2011), Neetha and Palriwala (2011) and Schwartz (2014).

[22] Although alliances with parallel feminist struggles were not always successful, because many feminisms view domestic work as inherently oppressive (Bernardino-Costa, 2014).

[23] Malaysian employers in Chin (1998) gave sweeping descriptions of Indonesians as dirty, lazy and untrustworthy and Filipinas as better educated, better behaved and hygienic.

[24] An extreme version of this ideology was part of the domestic service delivered through slavery (King, 2007).

[25] The areas where the ILO convention for domestic work falls short, because it tries to follow the Fordist model of regulation, is mostly in areas that concern live-in workers, such as being on call 24 hours, and immunity from prosecution of diplomats who abuse their employees (Albin, 2012).

[26] The Dalits form a significant proportion of the caste groups that continue to be ostracised and perform manual work in demeaning and some dehumanising ways (for example manual scavenging) (Chagar, 2011; Human Rights Watch, 2014; Ilaiah, 1995/2004; Irudayam et al, 2011).

[27] Other jobs such as factory work, residential care work, hospital housekeeping, hairdressing and agricultural work (for example see Gregson and Lowe, 1994a; Hondagneu-Sotelo, 2001; Jones, 2004; Meagher, 1997, 2003; Rollins, 1985; Romero, 2002).

Chapter 2

[1]   Two service-providers lived in southern England.

[2]   Detailed geographical locations of the research sites are not provided, due to risk of disclosure for some participants.

[3]   A dyad is a service-user and a service-provider who works for that service-user.

[4]   The label 'feminist' is contentious in India, often because of 'its unavoidable association' with 'Western' feminism(s) (Chaudhuri, 2004/2011:xi). So another term commonly used is 'gender sensitisation'.

[5]   One service-user also shared an unpublished piece she had written about her experiences of outsourcing as a follow-up to the interview, and gave me permission to quote from it.

[6]   Pseudonym.

[7]   A bed comprising a wooden frame strung with hemp rope or cotton tape.

[8]   One respondent's father was Italian.

[9]   Levels of education as defined in the UK Qualifications and Credit Framework (www.accreditedqualifications.org.ukqualifications-and-credit-framework-qcf. html).

[10] Marriage remains a mainstay of life in many Indian communities (Desai et al, 2010; Uberoi, 1993/2011).

[11] Most younger women were aware of birth control and many had undergone sterilisation or had an intrauterine device, but its timing was complicated by societal pressures to produce male children.

[12] The outhouse may also be rented in exchange for the husband's work, either inside the main house or in the garden. The wife then may not work, or may work for the landlord or elsewhere.

[13] Full-time equivalent.

[14] This question is not asked of singletons, which means the survey underestimates outsourcing.

[15] Appendix B lists a selection of the webpages consulted on these two websites.

[16] See also online comment by O'Neill in response to Foreman (2014).

[17] One was currently working for a quasi-governmental agency in a higher education setting.

[18] Lata's parents-in-law had lived on the ground floor, while her nuclear family occupied the first floor of a two-storey house.

[19] For example: Brazil: de Santana Pinho and Silva (2010); Honk Kong: Constable (2007); India: Dickey (2000a,b), Mattila (2011), Ray and Qayum (2009/2010), Verma and Larson (2001); Malaysia: Chin (1998); South Africa: King (2007); Taiwan: Lan (2006); Tanzania: Bujra (2000).

Chapter 3

[1]   In terms of absolute incomes, due to differences in currency valuations, the Indian respondents' estimated incomes in pound sterling were markedly less than the UK respondents' (data not shown).

[2]   See Chin (1998) for a comparable situation in Malaysia.

[3]   Such attitudes are also not confined to the domestic space. Cleaning the office is not part of many 'higher-status' job descriptions. People may appreciate the cleaners, but do they think the cleaners are doing *their* work?

[4]   Sullivan and Gershuny's analysis of ONS time-use data showed that outsourcing

had 'little overall impact ... on the total domestic/caring workload of either part-ner in dual-earner households' (2012:2; see also Windebank, 2007). Also, couples in intact relationships reporting 'sharing' housework may in fact be describing a mutually agreed division of housework (Singha, 2012; see also examples of 'shared' housework in Blaisure and Allen, 1995; Risman and Johnson-Sumerford, 1998; VanEvery, 1995).

5   De Casanova (2013) describes a similar situation in Ecuador.

6   See also de Santana Pinho and Silva (2010) for similar findings regarding Brazil; and De Casanova regarding Ecuador, where lower-middle-class families employ at least a cleaner because that might be their 'only claim to middle-class status' (2013:562–566).

7   For example, Ahmed (2016), Belliappa (2013), Fernando and Cohen (2014), Hinze (2004), Ledwith and Manfredi (2000), Mavin and Grandy (2016), Meyers (2013), Radhakrishnan (2009), Sang et al (2014), Shrivastava (2015) and Williams et al (1999).

Chapter 4

1   www.merriam-webster.com/dictionary/menial

2   Because that is what 'civilised' humans' work is about, 'impos[ing] system' on the 'inherently untidy' disorder that is life on earth (Douglas, 1966/2002:5), whether it is through housecleaning or higher-level social control.

3   Squatting is not demeaning in itself, for instance when this position is adopted as part of paid-for 'exercise' or 'yoga'. But when a person is paid to squat, it becomes associated with low status. I thank the acquaintance who pointed this out as we con-versed about my research, while cooking for volunteers in Calais in February 2016.

4   Is wearing gloves simply about modern 'hygienic' practices, or is it also a way of distancing oneself from symbolic meanings of dirt? This question requires more research.

5   Hindi term for sweeping and mopping.

6   Taylorisation refers to the step-wise fragmentation of work into tasks that are performed by separate workers in a repetitive manner (Edgell, 2012).

7   Cow-dung mixed with mud is applied to floors and walls of non-brick dwellings for insulation. Cow-dung is also an efficient cooking fuel, because it burns slowly (for example production of biogas).

Chapter 5

1   The Chicana women in Romero's (2002) sample were of Mexican American heritage, but they had been born in and had grown up in the US.

2   The 20th-century British workers' struggles led to widespread awareness of work-ers' rights, which likely encourage greater respect in social interactions. Feedback also needs to be understood in terms of wider cultural norms around politeness and courtesy, which vary between world regions and are also classed and gendered (Mills, 2004).

3   As previously reported, while many Indian service-users considered domestic workers unquestionably necessary, a clean appearance and honesty are more important criteria than the quality of work (Dickey, 2000b; Mattila, 2011; Ray and Qayum, 2009/2010).

4   I didn't ask this question to the Indian service-providers, because of the extreme low status accorded to their work.

5   No-one in my research used independent ironing services, a growing occupation, often offered alongside alteration and/or dry-cleaning services.

6   For examples of contemporary versions of Victorian household cleaning manuals, see Mackenzie (2009) and *Reader's Digest* (2011).

7   Although Cox claimed *The Lady* was the 'single most important source of advertisements for domestic workers in Britain', her Hampstead employers' sample used various methods, of which word-of-mouth recommendations were 'very important in the recruitment of cleaners' (1999:134, 142). My service-user sample also mostly did the same, but the service-providers were also using the internet – I found most of them through their online presence.

8   See also Sen and Sengupta (2016), whose detailed account of domestic work in Kolkata, India, is helpful for understanding the structure of the work when done as *labour*.

9   Such logics of 'rationalisation' also lay behind the fragmentation of paid domestic work in Victorian Britain (Davidoff, 1995).

10 That is, the fraught relationship is attributed to modern capitalist-style employment relations and service-providers' increasing awareness of their (non)rights (Mattila, 2011; Ray and Qayum, 2009/2010).

11 Vimla was helping with her live-in male servant's children's education.

12 Many Indian service-providers used this English word to explain their lived experience.

13 There is anecdotal and research evidence (Lahiri, 2017; Sen and Sengupta, 2016; personal communications) that other Indian domestic workers are key-holders and savvy with mobile and social media, but this was not the case in my sample.

14 Paraphrasing Salzinger (1991:158).

Chapter 6

1   As do age, race, and so on.

2   Jackson drew on Mead's early 20th-century work to highlight the fallacies of late-modern Western-centric theories of reflexivity in relation to East Asian sexuality and intimacy practices. The essence of Jackson's argument, however, is generally relevant to everyday life.

3   At Feminism in London 2015, I was telling a woman that my interest in the session on domestic slavery was related to my research. She said her boyfriend came from a middle-class family that routinely employed cleaners. But his mother had worked as a cleaner herself during the 1980s recession, when money had been tight.

4   Bright and Beautiful: 'A flexible domestic cleaning franchise opportunity' (www. brightandbeautifulhome.com/domestic-cleaning-franchise-opportunities/)

5   A Mumsnetter, now a cleaner, also used to work as a bank manager (Mumsnet, 2013a).

6   See, for instance, the *Canadian Journal of Women and the Law* special issue 'Regulating Decent Work for Domestic Workers' (2011:23(1)).

7   Employment Status Indicator (https://esi2calculator.hmrc.gov.uk/esi/app/ investigate.action?entity=%2F&factid=complete). The website and tool were redesigned in April 2015 (see http://tools.hmrc.gov.uk/esi/screen/ESI/en-GB/ summary?user=guest). The self-employed status of providers of other outsourced home-maintenance services is not similarly contested.

[8] See also Mayer-Ahuja (2004) for Germany; and Meagher (2003) for exclusion of non-English speakers in Australia.

[9] £26 per person for a standard check and £44 for an enhanced check at the time of writing (January 2017 to January 2019) (https://www.gov.uk/disclosure-barring-service-check/overview).

[10] For example, not wearing uniforms, inadequate note-taking, doing acts for service-users 'forbidden' by organisational policies.

[11] A state of haplessness or having to do something out of compulsion.

[12] Sweeping and mopping.

[13] Although patriarchy generally accords women lower status than men, women's unfreedoms are a chief mechanism through which higher castes maintained their social position. Over time, features of brahminical patriarchy have filtered down and been adopted by other castes too, because they remain a marker of status (Ambedkar, 1916/1979/2004).

[14] Temporary tenement.

[15] Singh (2001) found that 20% and 22.7% of husbands were problem drinkers and gamblers, respectively, and Duggal (2010) reported that half of slum-dwelling men were alcoholic.

[16] This may happen anywhere, but in communities where divorce is less stigmatised, male alcoholism may present as part of an impoverished single woman's history.

[17] Waste-picking is another economically better low-status occupation, because it includes sorting regular domestic waste (Gill, 2009/2012).

[18] Domestic worker organisations such as the Self-Employed Women's Association (SEWA) are developing an empowerment-as-process model of self-employment within India's informal economy, by encouraging workers to adopt practices that develop their self-worth as a first step (Bali, 2016).

[19] Perhaps the Western working-class people who say 'It isn't for the likes of me' are also subconsciously rejecting uninspiring 'education'.

[20] This has been suggested to be an attribute of kin-based societies, as opposed to individualist societies, but such sweeping generalisations are problematic. As noted in Chapter 3, Western working-class women's lives also include a strong narrative of 'for the family' (Damaske, 2011; Metcalfe, 2013).

[21] Libby had paid her previous service-provider travel costs, when Libby moved homes.

[22] This is not unique to domestic work. For instance, wages of construction workers in Kerala, India, depend on various factors, including regional citizenship status (local or in-country migrant), caste, union membership status, employee/casual labourer status and gender (Prasad-Aleyamma, 2017).

[23] The Indian working week often includes half or full Saturdays. Thus domestic workers probably cannot expect more than four days off a month, but many are permitted only two days.

Chapter 7

[1] See also the 'maternalists' in Romero's (2002) typology of feminist employers.

[2] cf. Romero's 'contractors'.

[3] I have not reproduced website text, to preserve anonymity of my respondents.

[4] Very few respondents in either country talked about the worker as 'part of the family', possibly because they were not live-in workers.

[5] Also Groves and Lui (2012); N. Mitra, Tata Institute of Social Sciences, personal communication, 2012.

[6]   These accounts were validated by some service-provider accounts.

[7]   Compare the notion of noblesse oblige in Victorian/Edwardian Britain: the upper classes had a 'moral' duty to be philanthropic, to take paternalistic interest in the welfare of their servants and other 'dependants', while retaining their privilege (Gunn and Bell, 2002; Todd, 2009). More contemporaneously, this cultural injustice has been described variously, and in depth, as maternalism, paternalism, (p) maternalism and pseudo-maternalism (see Chapter 1).

[8]   Sweeping and mopping.

[9]   When cleaning agencies hold the keys, though, their employees are not visible in the same way as the independent service-provider, because the responsibility for the key lies with the organisation rather than individual employees.

[10] See *Work, Employment and Society* (2017). E-special issue: Small business revivalism: employment relations in small and medium-sized enterprises (http://journals. sagepub.com/page/wes/collections/e-special-issues/small-business-revivalism).

Chapter 8

[1]   A state of haplessness or having to do something out of compulsion.

[2]   See contract for service versus contract of service in Meagher (2002).

[3]   The constant quibbling around work apparently half done or not done.

[4]   For example, the post-war employment conditions of domestic work in Germany and Austria have been shaped by an underlying assumption that this work – the 'mini-job' (part-time work with many legal restrictions and fewer regulations) – will attract a particular type of woman: the housewife who works for pin money rather than a livelihood and social protections, or an older woman supplementing her (meagre) pension (Lutz, 2011:33; Shire, 2015:196).

[5]   See also Bradshaw (2015), Chigateri (2007), Cooperative Programme (2011), and Soni-Sinha and Yates (2013), for similar issues in the commercial cleaning sector.

[6]   This report reveals how caste remains contentious in the efforts to ensure adequate toilet facilities for all Indians: problems range from siting of communal toilets to their funding, use and maintenance in caste-ridden social environments (Sagar, 2017).

References

Aalto, K. and Varjonen, J. (2007) Balancing time and money for family wellbeing in families with children and in younger couples' households. Unpublished paper presented at the International Association for Time Use Research (IATUR), XXIX Conference. 17–19 October 2007. Washington, DC, US (www.atususers.umd.edu/wip2/papers_i2007/Aalto.pdf).

Abrantes, M. (2014a) 'I know it sounds nasty and stereotyped': searching for the competent domestic worker. *Gender, Work & Organization*, 21(5), 427–442.

Abrantes, M. (2014b) What about the numbers? A quantitative contribution to the study of domestic services in Europe. *International Labour Review*, 153(2), 223–243.

Adams, B. (1995) *Timewatch. The Social Analysis of Time*. Cambridge: Polity Press.

Ahlander, N.R. and Bahr, K.S. (1995) Beyond drudgery, power, and equity: toward an expanded discourse on the moral dimensions of housework in families. *Journal of Marriage and Family*, 57(1), 54–68.

Ahmed, S. (2016) Resignation. 30 May 2016. feministkilljoys (https://feministkilljoys.com/2016/05/30/resignation/).

Albin, E. (2012) From 'domestic servant' to 'domestic worker'. In J. Fudge, S. McCrystal and K. Sankaran (eds) *Challenging the Legal Boundaries of Work Regulation*. Oxford: Hart, pp. 231–250.

Albin, E. and Mantouvalou, V. (2012) The ILO convention on domestic workers: from the shadows to the light. *Industrial Law Journal*, 41, 67–78.

Alisa (2008) My cleaning lady saved my marriage! 28 October 2008. *Project Happily Ever After* (www.projecthappilyeverafter.com/2008/10/my-cleaning-lady-saved-my-marriage).

Ambedkar, B.R. (1916/1979/2004) Castes in India: their mechanism, genesis and development. In M. Mohanty (ed.) *Class, Caste and Gender*. New Delhi: Sage, pp. 131–153.

Ambedkar, B.R. (1936/2016) *Annihilation of Caste: The Annotated Critical Edition*. S. Anand (ed.). London: Verso.

Anderson, B. (1993) *Britain's Secret Slaves: An Investigation into the Plight of Overseas Domestic Workers*. London: Anti-Slavery International and Kalayaan.

Anderson, B. (1999) Overseas domestic workers in the European Union: invisible women. In J.H. Momsen (ed.) *Gender, Migration and Domestic Service*. London: Routledge, pp. 117–133.

Anderson, B. (2000) *Doing the Dirty Work? The Global Politics of Domestic Labour*. London: Zed Books.

Anderson, B. (2001) Just another job? Paying for domestic work. *Gender and Development*, 9(1), 25–33.

Anderson, B. (2003) Just another job? The commodification of domestic labor. In B. Ehrenreich and A.R. Hochschild (eds) *Global Women. Nannies, Maids and Sex Workers in the New Economy*. London: Granta Books, pp. 104–114.

Anderson, B. (2007) A very private business: exploring the demand for migrant domestic workers. *European Journal of Women's Studies*, 14(3), 247–264.

Anderson, B. and Ruhs, M. (2012) Reliance on migrant labour: inevitability or choice? *Journal of Poverty and Social Justice*, 20(1), 23–30.

Anzaldúa, G. (1987) How to tame a wild tongue. In G. Anzaldúa (ed.) *Borderland/La Frontera: the New Mestiza*. San Francisco: Aunt Lute Books, pp. 53–64.

Archarya, S.S. and Reddy, S. (2017) Migrant women workers in construction and domestic work: issues and challenges. In S.S. Acharya, S. Sen, M. Punia and S. Reddy (eds) *Marginalization in Globalizing Delhi: Issues of Land, Livelihoods and Health*. New Delhi: Springer India, pp. 207–226.

Archive on 4 (2016). *A Guide to the Modern Snob*. 4 June 2016 (www.bbc. co.uk/programmes/b07djnzb).

Ashforth, B.E. and Kreiner, G.E. (1999) 'How can you do it?': dirty work and the challenge of constructing a positive identity. *Academy of Management Review*, 24(3), 413–434.

Atkinson, W. (2010) The myth of the reflexive worker: class and work histories in neo-liberal times. *Work, Employment and Society*, 24(3), 413–429.

Baby Center (2013) 'Going home to a CLEAN house tonight!!'. 27 February 2013 (http://community.babycenter.com/post/a40296826/going_home_to_a_clean_house_tonight).

Bailey, C. and Madden, A. (2017) Time reclaimed: temporality and the experience of meaningful work. *Work, Employment and Society*, 31(1), 3–18.

Bailly, F., Devetter, F.-X. and Horn, F. (2013) Can working and employment conditions in the personal services sector be improved? *Cambridge Journal of Economics*, 37, 299–321.

Bali, N. (2016) *Naam, kaam, gaam*: educating women for self-employment, cooperation and struggle. *International Labor and Working-Class History*, 90, 164–175.

Banerjee, S.M. (2015) Baby Halder's *A Life Less Ordinary*: a transition from India's colonial past? In V.K. Haskins and C. Lowrie (eds) *Colonization and Domestic Service: Historical and Contemporary Perspectives*. New York, NY: Routledge, pp. 239–255.

Bapat, S. (2014) *Part of the Family? Nannies, Housekeepers, Caregivers and the Battle for Domestic Workers' Rights*. New York: Ig Publishing.

Barnes, H. (2013) Work advisers 'pushing jobless into self-employment'. BBC News. 3 February 2013 (www.bbc.co.uk/news/uk-politics-21260331).

Barstad, A. (2014) Equality is bliss? Relationship quality and the gender division of household labor. *Journal of Family Issues*, 35(7), 972–992.

Bartolomei, M.R. (2010) Migrant male domestic workers in comparative perspective: four case studies from Italy, India, Ivory Coast, and Congo. *Men and Masculinities*, 13, 87–110.

Bates, K.G. (2013) History makes hiring household help a complex choice. Code Switch (www.npr.org/sections/codeswitch/2013/05/24/185508615/going-to-meet-the-ma-am).

Baxter, J., Hewitt, B. and Western, M. (2009) Who uses paid domestic labor in Australia? Choice and constraint in hiring household help. *Feminist Economics*, 15(1), 1–26.

BBC News (2013) Charles Saatchi 'made threat to destroy' Nigella Lawson. BBC News. 4 December 2013 (www.bbc.co.uk/news/uk-england-25216157).

BBC One (2013) *Panorama*. Amazon: the truth behind the click. BBC One television. 25 November 2013 (www.bbc.co.uk/programmes/b03k5kzp).

BBC Radio 4 (2010) *Woman's Hour*. History and science archive. The first Women's Liberation Movement conference. 25 February 2010 (www.bbc.co.uk/radio4/womanshour/03/2010_08_thu.shtml).

BBC Radio 4 (2012) *Woman's Hour*. Housework week. 9 July 2012 (www.bbc.co.uk/programmes/p00vwhcr).

BBC Radio 4 (2015) *Analysis*. Caring in the new old age. 16 March 2015 (www.bbc.co.uk/programmes/b055g1jv).

BBC Two (2012) *Servants: The True Story of Life Below Stairs*. BBC Two television. 28 September–12 October 2012 (www.bbc.co.uk/programmes/b01n5wjx).

BBB Two (2014) *Watermen: a Dirty Business*. BBC Two television. 15 April–20 May 2014 (www.bbc.co.uk/programmes/b041j9l7).

BBB Two (2015a) *Wastemen*. BBC Two television. 28 April–12 May 2015 (www.bbc.co.uk/programmes/p02npms8).

BBC Two (2015b) *Modern Times. The Secret Life of Cleaners*. BBC Two television. 18 June 2015 (www.bbc.co.uk/programmes/b05xcwf9).

Behling, F. and Harvey, M. (2015) The evolution of false self-employment in the British construction industry: a neo-Polanyian account of labour market formation. *Work, Employment and Society*, 29(6), 969–988.

Belliappa, J.L. (2013) *Gender, Class and Reflexive Modernity in India*. Basingstoke, Hants: Palgrave Macmillan.

Benegal, V., Nayak, M., Murthy, P., Chandra, P. and Gururaj, G. (2005) Women and alcohol in India. In I.S. Obot and R. Room (eds) *Alcohol, Gender and Drinking Problems: Perspectives from Low and Middle Income Countries*. Geneva: World Health Organization, pp. 89–124 (www.who.int/substance_abuse/publications/alcohol_gender_drinking_problems.pdf).

Benston, M. (1969/1980) The political economy of women's liberation. In E. Malos (ed.) *The Politics of Housework*. London: Allison and Busby, pp. 119–129.

Bergmann, B. (1998) The only ticket to equality: total androgyny, male style. *Journal of Contemporary Legal Issues*, 9 (Spring), 75–86.

Bernardino-Costa, J. (2014) Intersectionality and female domestic workers' unions in Brazil. *Women's Studies International Forum*, 46, 72–80.

Bharati, M. and Tandon Mehrotra, S. (2008) *Rights and Dignity: Women Domestic Workers in Jaipur*. New Delhi: Jagori.

Bhasin, K. and Khan, N.S. (1986/2005) Some questions on feminism and its relevance to South Asia. In M. Chaudhuri (ed.) *Feminism in India*. London: Zed Books, pp. 3–7.

Bhavnani, K.-K. (1993) Tracing the contours: feminist research and feminist objectivity. *Women's Studies International Forum*, 16(2), 95–104.

Bianchi, S.M., Milkie, M.A., Sayer, L.C. and Robinson, J.P. (2000) Is anyone doing the housework? Trends in the gender division of household labor. *Social Forces*, 79, 191–228.

Bianchi, S.M., Sayer, L.C., Milkie, M.A. and Robinson, J.P. (2012) Housework: who did, does or will do it, and how much does it matter? *Social Forces*, 91(1), 55–63.

Birbili, M. (2000) Translating from one language to another. *Social Research Update*, Issue 31, Winter 2000 (http://sru.soc.surrey.ac.uk/SRU31.html).

Birch, E.R., Le, A.T. and Miller, P.W. (2009) *Household Division of Labour*. Basingstoke, Hants: Palgrave Macmillan.

Bittman, M., Matheson, G. and Meagher, G. (1999) The changing boundary between home and market: Australian trends in outsourcing domestic labour. *Work, Employment and Society*, 13, 249–273.

Blackett, A. (2011). Introduction: regulating decent work for domestic workers. *Canadian Journal of Women and the Law*, 23(1), 1–97.

Blaisure, K.R. and Allen, K.R. (1995) Feminism and the ideology and practice of marital equality. *Journal of Marriage and Family*, 57, 5–19.

Blake, D. (2016) *We Need a National Narrative: Building a Consensus Around Retirement Income. Summary.* Independent Review of Retirement Income (www.pensions-institute.org/IRRIReport.pdf).

Boris, E. (2017) Decent work in the home: affect and rights talk. *Santa Clara Journal of International Law*, 79, 80–102.

Bose, C. (1979) Technology and the changes in the division of labour in the American home. *Women's Studies International Quarterly*, 2, 295–300.

Bose, M.L. (1998) *Social and Cultural History of Ancient India* (2nd edn). New Delhi: Concept Publishing Company.

Bowman, J.R. and Cole, A.M. (2009) Do working mothers oppress other women? The Swedish 'maid debate' and the welfare state politics of gender equality. *Signs: Journal of Women in Culture and Society*, 35(1), 157–184.

Bowman, J.R. and Cole, A.M. (2014) Cleaning the 'People's Home': the politics of the domestic service market in Sweden. *Gender, Work & Organization*, 21(2), 187–201.

Bradshaw, A. (2015) Home economics: the labor struggle of domestic workers. *Leo Weekly*. 8 July 2015 (www.leoweekly.com/2015/07/home-economics-the-labor-struggle-of-domestic-workers/).

Branca, P. (1975) A new perspective on women's work: a comparative typology. *Journal of Social History*, 9(2), 129–153.

Bremen, J. (2013) *Work in the Informal Economy in India. A Perspective from the Bottom Up.* New Delhi: Oxford University Press.

Breslin, D. and Wood, G. (2016) Rule breaking in social care: hierarchy, contentiousness and informal rules. *Work, Employment and Society*, 30(5), 750–765.

Bryman, A. (2008) *Social Research Methods* (3rd edn). Oxford: Oxford University Press.

Bujra, J. (2000) *Serving Class: Masculinity and Feminisation of Domestic Service in Tanzania.* Edinburgh: Edinburgh University Press.

Calleman, C. (2011) Domestic services in a 'land of equality': the case of Sweden. *Canadian Journal of Women and the Law*, 23(1), 121–140.

Campkin, B. and Cox, R. (2007/2012) Introduction: materialities and metaphors of dirt and cleanliness. In B. Campkin and R. Cox (eds) *Dirt: New Geographies of Cleanliness and Contamination*. London: I.B. Taurus, pp. 1–8.

Carey, M. (2007) White-collar proletariat? Braverman, the deskilling/upskilling of social work and the paradoxical life of the agency care manager. *Journal of Social Work*, 7(1), 93–114.

Carter, B., Danford, A., Howcroft, D., Richardson, H., Smith, A. and Taylor, P. (2011) 'All they lack is a chain': lean and the new performance management in the British civil service. *New Technology, Work and Employment*, 26(2), 83–97.

Chagar, R. (2011) The Dalit women of India. In D.W. Pike (ed.) *Crimes Against Women*. New York, NY: Nova Science Publishers, pp. 235–239.

Chakrabortty, A. (2016) Being self-employed means freedom. Freedom to be abused and underpaid. *The Guardian*. 5 April 2016 (www.theguardian.com/commentisfree/2016/apr/05/self-employed-freedom-underpaid-contractors?).

Chan, T.W. and Halpin, B. (2002) Union dissolution in the United Kingdom. *International Journal of Sociology*, 32(4), 76–93.

Chandra Mohan, N. (2015) The spectre of jobless growth in India. Inter Press Service News Agency. 2 October 2015 (www.ipsnews.net/2015/10/the-spectre-of-jobless-growth-in-india/).

Chaney, E.M. and Garcia Castro, M. (eds) (1989) *Muchachas No More. Household Workers in Latin America and the Caribbean*. Philadelphia: Temple University Press.

Channel 4 (2016) *Obsessive Compulsive Cleaners*. Last updated 2016 (www.channel4.com/programmes/obsessive-compulsive-cleaners/episode-guide).

Chatterjee, M. (1990) *Indian Women, Health, and Productivity*. Policy, Research, and External Affairs working paper no. WPS 442. Washington, DC: World Bank (http://documents.worldbank.org/curated/en/1990/10/700170/indian-women-health-productivity).

Chaudhuri, M. (ed.) (2004/2011) *Feminism in India*. Delhi: Kali for Women & Women Unlimited.

Chigateri, S. (2007) Articulations of injustice and the recognition–redistribution debate: locating caste, class and gender in paid domestic work in India. *Law, Social Justice and Global Development Journal (LGD)*, 1, n.p. (http://go.warwick.ac.uk/lgd/2007_1/chigateri).

Chin, C.B.N. (1998) *In Service and Servitude: Foreign Female Domestic Workers and the Malaysian 'Modernity' Project*. New York: Columbia University Press.

Christy, M. (2005) Urine: your own perfect medicine. *All Natural* (http://all-natural.com/natural-remedies/urine/).

Chun, L. (1997) Feminism and women's movements in contemporary China. In W.J. Scott, C. Kaplan and D. Keates (eds) *Transitions, Environments, Translations: Feminisms in International Politics*. London: Taylor and Francis, pp. 11–20.

Cockburn, C. (1991) *Brothers. Male Dominance and Technological Change*. London: Pluto Press.

Cockburn, C. (1997) Domestic technologies: Cinderella and the engineers. *Women's Studies International Forum*, 20(3), 361–371.

Coelho, K. (2016) Occupational domestication in a post-resettlement context: an analysis of women's work in Kannagi Nagar, Chennai. In S. Raju and S. Jatrana (eds) *Women Workers in Urban India*. New Delhi: Cambridge University Press, pp. 97–120.

Collins, G. (2007) Cleaning and the work–life balance. *International Journal of Human Resource Management*, 18(3), 416–429.

Colombo, A. (2007) 'They call me a housekeeper, but I do everything.' Who are domestic workers today in Italy and what do they do? *Journal of Modern Italian Studies*, 12(2), 207–237.

Constable, N. (2007) *Maid to Order in Hong Kong: Stories of Migrant Workers*. Ithaca, NY: Cornell University Press.

Cooke, L.P. (2004) The gendered division of labor and family outcomes in Germany. *Journal of Marriage and Family*, 66, 1246–1259.

Cooper, C. and Taylor, P. (2000) From Taylorism to Ms Taylor: the transformation of the accounting craft. *Accounting, Organizations and Society*, 25(6), 555–578.

Cooper, S.M. (2005) Service to servitude? The decline and demise of life-cycle service in England. *History of the Family*, 10, 367–386.

Cooperative Programme (EMP/COOP), International Labour Office (ILO) (2011) Domestic workers organize. *EMP/COOP – COOP NEWS*, No. 1, 7–8 (www.ilo.org/wcmsp5/groups/public/---ed_emp/---emp_ent/---coop/documents/publication/wcms_157995.pdf).

Cooperative Programme (EMP/COOP), International Labour Office (ILO) (2013) Domestic workers cooperatives. *EMP/COOP – COOP NEWS*, No. 1, 8 (www.ilo.org/wcmsp5/groups/public/---ed_emp/---emp_ent/---coop/documents/publication/wcms_213244.pdf).

Corden, A. and Sainsbury, R. (2006) Aspects of presentation. In *Using Verbatim Quotations in Reporting Qualitative Social Research: the Views of Research Users*. York: Social Policy Research Unit, University of York, pp. 17–23.

Cornelisse-Vermaat J.R., van Ophem, J.C., Antonides, G. and van den Brink, H.M. (2013) Outsourcing child care, home cleaning and meal preparation. *International Journal of Consumer Studies*, 37, 530–537.

Costas, J. and Kärreman, D. (2016) The bored self in knowledge work. *Human Relations*, 69(1), 61–83.

Cotterill, P. (1992) Interviewing women. Issues of friendship, vulnerability and power. *Women's Studies International Forum*, 15(5–6), 593–606.

Cox, P. and Hobley, A. (2014) *Shopgirls: The True Story of Life Behind the Counter*. London: Hutchinson.

Cox, R. (1997) Invisible labour: perceptions of paid domestic work in London. *Journal of Occupational Science Australia*, 4(2), 62–68.

Cox, R. (1999) The role of ethnicity in shaping the domestic employment sector in Britain. In J.H. Momsen (ed.) *Gender, Migration and Domestic Service*. London: Routledge, pp. 134–147.

Cox, R. (2000) Exploring the growth of paid domestic labour: a case study of London. *Geography*, 85(3), 241–251.

Cox, R. (2006) *The Servant Problem. Domestic Employment in a Global Economy*. London: I.B. Tauris.

Cox, R. (2007/2012a) Introduction to Section 1. Home: domestic dirt and cleaning. In B. Campkin and R. Cox (eds) *Dirt: New Geographies of Cleanliness and Contamination*. London: I.B. Taurus, pp. 11–14.

Cox, R. (2007/2012b) Introduction to Section 3. Country: constructing rural dirt. In B. Campkin and R. Cox (eds) *Dirt: New Geographies of Cleanliness and Contamination*. London: I.B. Taurus, pp. 153–155.

Cox, R. (2011) Dishing the dirt: dirt in the home. In R. Cox, R. George, R.H. Horne, R. Nagle, E. Pisani, B. Ralph and V. Smith (eds) *The Filthy Reality of Everyday Life. DIRT*. London: Profile Books, pp. 37–73.

Cox, R. (2016) Cleaning up: gender, race and dirty work at home. In C. Lewe, T. Othold and N. Oxen (eds) *Müll. Interdisziplinäre Perspektiven auf das Übrig-Gebliebene*. Bielefeld: transcript, pp. 97–116.

Cox, R. (ed.) (2015a) *Au Pairs' Lives in Global Context: Sisters or Servants?* Basingstoke, Hants: Palgrave Macmillan.

Cox, R. (2015b) From our own backyard? Understanding UK au pair policy as colonial legacy and neocolonial dream. In V.K. Haskins and C. Lowrie (eds) *Colonization and Domestic Service: Historical and Contemporary Perspectives*. New York, NY: Routledge, pp. 256–272.

Cox, R. and Watt, P. (2002) Globalization, polarization and the informal sector: the case of paid domestic workers in London. *Area*, 34(1), 39–47.

Craig, L., Powell, A. and Brown, J.E. (2016) Gender patterns in domestic labour among young adults in different living arrangements in Australia. *Journal of Sociology*, 52(4), 772–788.

Crompton, R. (2006) *Employment and the Family: the Reconfiguration of Work and Family Life in Contemporary Societies*. Cambridge: Cambridge University Press.

Crompton, R. and Scott, J. (2005) Class analysis: beyond the cultural turn. In F. Devine and M. Savage, J. Scott and R. Crompton (eds) *Rethinking Class. Culture, Identities, Lifestyles*. Basingstoke, Hants: Palgrave Macmillan, pp. 186–203.

Crompton, R. and Lyonette, C. (2008) Who does the housework? The division of labour within the home. In A. Park, J. Curtice, K. Thomson, M. Phillips, M. Johnson and E. Clery (eds) *British Social Attitudes, the 24th Report*. National Centre for Social Research. London: Sage, pp. 53–80.

Crompton, R. and Lyonette, C. (2011) Women's career success and work–life adaptations in the accountancy and medical professions in Britain. *Gender, Work & Organization*, 18(2), 231–254.

Cross, J. (2009) From dreams to discontent: educated young men and the politics of work at a Special Economic Zone in Andhra Pradesh. *Contributions to Indian Sociology*, 43(3), 351–379.

Cruz, K., Hardy, K. and Sanders, T. (2017) False self-employment, autonomy and regulating for decent work: improving working conditions in the UK stripping industry. *British Journal of Industrial Relations*, 55(2), 274–294.

Curthoys, A. (1988) *For and Against Feminism. A Personal Journey into Feminist Theory and History*. Sydney: Allen and Unwin.

Curtis, V.A. (2007) Dirt, disgust and disease: a natural history of hygiene. *Journal of Epidemiology and Community Health*, 61(8), 660–664.

D'Arcy, C. and Gardiner, L. (2014) *Just the Job – or a Working Compromise? The Changing Nature of Self-Employment in the UK*. London: Resolution Foundation.

Daily Mail (2015) How hiring a cleaner is a dirty secret: Two thirds of Britons who pay someone to clean their home don't tell their friends. *Daily Mail*, 11 November (www.dailymail.co.uk/news/article-3314544/How-hiring-cleaner-dirty-secret-Two-thirds-Britons-pay-clean-home-don-t-tell-friends.html).

Dalla Costa, M. and James, S. (1973) *The Power of Women and the Subversion of the Community* (3rd edn). Bristol: Falling Wall Press.

Damaske, S. (2011) *For the Family? How Class and Gender Shape Women's Work*. New York: Oxford University Press.

Davidoff, L. (1995) The rationalization of housework. In *Worlds Between. Historical Perspectives on Gender and Class*. Cambridge: Polity Press, pp. 73–102.

Davis, A. (1981/1983) The approaching obsolescence of housework: a working-class perspective. In *Women, Race and Class*. New York: Vintage Books, pp. 222–244.

Davis, S.N. and Greenstein, T.N. (2013) Why study housework? Cleaning as a window into power in couples. *Journal of Family Theory & Review*, 5(2), 63–71.

De Casanova, E.M. (2013) Embodied inequality: the experience of domestic work in urban Ecuador. *Gender & Society*, 27(4), 561–585.

de Ruijter, E. and van der Lippe, T. (2007) Effects of job features on domestic outsourcing as a strategy for combining paid and domestic work. *Work and Occupations*, 34(2), 205–230.

de Ruijter, E., van der Lippe, T. and Raub, W. (2003) Trust problems in household outsourcing. *Rationality and Society*, 15(4), 473–507.

de Ruijter, E., Treas, J. and Cohen, P.N. (2005) Outsourcing the gender factory: living arrangements and service expenditures on female and male tasks. *Social Forces*, 94, 305–322.

de Santana Pinho, P. and Silva, E.B. (2010) Domestic relations in Brazil: legacies and horizons. *Latin American Research Review*, 45(2), 90–113.

Delap, L. (2007) 'Campaigns of curiosity': class crossing and role reversal in British domestic service, 1890–1950. *Left History*, 12(2), 33–63.

Delap, L. (2011a) *Knowing Their Place. Domestic Service in the Twentieth Century*. Oxford: Oxford University Press.

Delap, L. (2011b) Housework, housewives, and domestic workers. *Home Cultures*, 8(2), 189–209.

Delphy, C. and Leonard, D. (1992). *Familiar Exploitation. A New Analysis of Marriage in Contemporary Western Societies*. Cambridge: Polity Press.

Department for Education (2011) *Childcare and Early Years Providers Survey 2010*. Crown Copyright (www.gov.uk/government/statistics/childcare-and-early-years-providers-survey-2010).

Department for Education (2012) *Childcare and Early Years Providers Survey 2011*. Crown Copyright (www.gov.uk/government/statistics/childcare-and-early-years-providers-survey-2011).

Department for Education (2014) *Childcare and Early Years Providers Survey 2013*. TNS BMRB Report JN 117328. Crown Copyright (https://www.gov.uk/government/statistics/childcare-and-early-years-providers-survey-2013).

Department of Employment and Workplace Relations (2006) *Recruitment in the Cleaning Services Industry*. Canberra: Department of Employment and Workplace Relations (http://webarchive.nla.gov.au/gov/20110604035943/http://www.deewr.gov.au/Employment/LMI/RegionalReports/Industry/Pages/2006.aspx).

Desai, S.B., Dubey, A., Joshi, B.J., Sen, M., Sharif, A. and Vanneman, R. (2010) *Human Development in India. Challenges for a Society in Transition.* New Delhi: Oxford University Press.

Devetter, F.-X. (2016) Can public policies bring about the democratization of the outsourcing of household tasks? *Review of Radical Political Economics*, 48, 365–393.

Devetter, F.-X. and Rousseau, S. (2009) The impact of industrialization on paid domestic work: the case of France. *European Journal of Industrial Relations*, 15, 297–316.

Devine, F. and Savage, M. (2005) The cultural turn, sociology and class analysis. In F. Devine, M. Savage, J. Scott and R. Crompton (eds) *Rethinking Class. Culture, Identities, Lifestyles.* Basingstoke, Hants: Palgrave Macmillan, pp. 1–23.

Dickey, S. (2000a) Mutual exclusions. Domestic workers and employers on labor, class, and character in South India. In K.M. Adams and S. Dickey (eds) *Home and Hegemony. Domestic Service and Identity Politics in South and Southeast Asia.* Ann Arbor: University of Michigan Press, pp. 31–62.

Dickey, S. (2000b) Permeable homes: domestic service, household space, and the vulnerability of class boundaries in urban India. *American Ethnologist*, 27(2), 462–489.

Dill, B.T. (1988) 'Making your job good yourself': domestic service and the construction of personal dignity. In A. Bookman and S. Morgen (eds) *Women and the Politics of Empowerment.* Philadelphia, PA: Temple University Press, pp. 33–52.

Dill, B.T. (1994) *Across the Boundaries of Race and Class: an Exploration of Work and Family Among Black Female Domestic Servants.* New York: Garland Publishing.

Dodson, L. and Zincavage, R.M. (2007) 'It's like a family'. Caring labor, exploitation, and race in nursing homes. *Gender & Society*, 21(6), 905–928.

Douglas, M. (1966/2002) *Purity and Danger: an Analysis of Concept of Pollution and Taboo.* With a new preface. London: Routledge.

Douglas, M. (1986/1987) *How Institutions Think.* London: Routledge/ Kegan Paul.

Douglas, M. (2002) *Risk and Blame: Essays in Cultural Theory.* London: Routledge.

Douglas, M. and Wildavsky, A. (1983) *Risk and Culture: an Essay on the Selection of Technological and Environmental Dangers.* Berkeley, CA: University of California Press.

Dowling, T. (2014) Our cleaner is going home. *The Guardian.* 26 October 2014 (www.theguardian.com/lifeandstyle/2013/oct/26/tim-dowling-cleaner-leaving#comments).

Draycott Nursing (n.d.) Carers job description (www.draycottnursing. co.uk/pdfs/Job-Description-Carer.pdf).

Driscoll, E.T. (2011) *Class and Gender in the Philippines: Ethnographic Interviews with Female Employer-Female Domestic Dyads.* Sociology – Dissertations and Theses. Paper 68 (http://surface.syr.edu/soc_etd/68).

du Preez, J., Beswick, C., Whittaker, L. and Dickinson, D. (2010) The employment relationship in the domestic workspace in South Africa: beyond the apartheid legacy. *Social Dynamics*, 36(2), 395–409.

Duggal, B. (2010) *Chandigarh Slums. Issues of Poverty and Human Rights.* Chandigarh: Centre for Research in Rural and Industrial Development.

Edgell, S. (2012) *The Sociology of Work: Continuity and Change in Paid and Unpaid Work* (2nd edn). London: Sage.

Ehrenreich, B. (1976) What is socialist feminism? *WIN Magazine* (6/3/76) (https://www.marxists.org/subject/women/authors/ehrenreich-barbara/socialist-feminism.htm).

Ehrenreich, B. (2000) Maid to order. *The Guardian.* 20 August 2000 (https://www.theguardian.com/profile/barbaraehrenreich).

Ehrenreich, B. (2002/2010) *Nickel and Dimed.* London: Granta.

Ehrenreich, B. (2003) Maid to order. In B. Ehrenreich and A.R. Hochschild (eds) *Global Women. Nannies, Maids and Sex Workers in the New Economy.* London: Granta Books, pp. 85–103.

Ehrenreich, B. and English, D. (1978/1988) *For Her Own Good: 150 Years of the Experts' Advice to Women.* London: Pluto Press.

Ehrenreich, B. and Hochschild, A.R. (eds) (2003) *Global Women. Nannies, Maids and Sex Workers in the New Economy.* London: Granta Books.

Eichler, M. and Albanese, P. (2007) What is household work? A critique of assumptions underlying empirical studies of housework and an alternative approach. *Canadian Journal of Sociology*, 32(2), 227–258.

Elias, N. (1994/2003) *The Civilising Process: Sociogenetic and Pyschogenetic Investigations.* Translated by E. Jephcott and edited by E. Dunning, J. Goudsblom and S. Mennell (revised edn). Oxford: Blackwell Publishing.

Elson, D. and Pearson, R. (1981) 'Nimble fingers make cheap workers': an analysis of women's employment in Third World export manufacturing. *Feminist Review*, 7, 87–107.

Estévez-Abe, M. (2015) The outsourcing of house cleaning and low skill immigrant workers. *Social Politics*, 22(2), 147–169.

Estévez-Abe, M. and Hobson, B. (2015) Outsourcing domestic (care) work: the politics, policies, and political economy. *Social Politics*, 22(2), 133–146.

Estey, K. (2011) Domestic workers and cooperatives: BeyondCare goes beyond capitalism, a case study in Brooklyn, New York. *Working USA, The Journal of Labor and Society*, 14, 347–365.

Eurofound (2006) *Employment Developments in Childcare Services for School-Age Children: Sweden* (www.eurofound.europa.eu/sites/default/files/ef_publication/field_ef_document/ef0623enc5.pdf).

European Federation for Services to Individuals (2013) *White Book on Personal and Household Services in Ten EU Member States* (www.efsi-europe.eu/fileadmin/MEDIA/Event/5th_European_Conference/White_book_final_december_2013.pdf).

Fauve-Chamoux, A. (ed.) (2004) *Formation of European Identity. Understanding the Globalization of Domestic Work, 16th–21st Century*. Bern: Peter Lang AG.

Fernando, W.D.A. and Cohen, L. (2014) Respectable femininity and career agency: exploring paradoxical imperatives. *Gender, Work & Organization*, 21, 149–164.

Flanagan, C. (2004) How serfdom saved the women's movement. *Atlantic Monthly*, 293(2), 109–128 (www.theatlantic.com/past/docs/issues/2004/03/flanagan.htm).

Flather, A.J. (2013) Space, place, and gender: the sexual and spatial division of labor in the early modern household. *History and Theory*, 52(3), 344–360.

Foreman, J. (2014) The servant problem. *red pepper blog*. 9 June 2014 (www.redpepper.org.uk/the-servant-problem/#comment-248195).

Fraser, N. (1996) Social justice in the age of identity politics: redistribution, recognition, and participation. The Tanner Lectures on Human Values. Delivered at Stanford University, 30 April–2 May 1996 (http://tannerlectures.utah.edu/_documents/a-to-z/f/Fraser98.pdf).

Fraser, N. (2013) *The Fortunes of Feminism: From State-Managed Capitalism to Neoliberal Crisis*. London: Verso.

Friedan, B. (1963/1983) *The Feminine Mystique*. New York, NY: Laurel.

Frøystad, K. (2003) Master-servant relations and the domestic reproduction of caste in Northern India. *Ethnos*, 68(1), 73–94.

Gabb, J. and Fink, J. (2015) *Couple Relationships in the 21st Century*. Basingstoke, Hants: Palgrave MacMillan.

Gamburd, M. (2003) Breadwinners no more. In B. Ehrenreich and A.R. Hochschild (eds) *Global Women. Nannies, Maids and Sex Workers in the New Economy*. London: Granta Books, pp. 190–206.

Game, A. and Pringle, R. (1983) *Gender at Work*. Sydney: George Allen and Unwin.

Gatrell, C. (2004) *Hard Labour: the Sociology of Parenthood, Family Life and Career*. Berkshire: McGraw-Hill Professional Publishing.

Gatrell, C. (2008) *Embodying Women's Work*. Maidenhead, Berkshire: Open University Press.

Gavanas, A. (2010) *Who Cleans the Welfare State? Migration, Informalization, Social Exclusion and Domestic Services in Stockholm.* Research Report 2010/3. Stockholm: Institute for Future Studies.

Geary, J.F. (1992) Employment flexibility and human resource management: the case of three American electronics plants. *Work, Employment and Society,* 6(2), 251–270.

Gershuny, J. (2005) Busyness as the badge of honour for the new superordinate working class. *Social Research: An International Quarterly,* 72(2), 287–314.

Gill, K. (2009/2012) *Of Poverty and Plastic: Scavenging and Scrap Trading Entrepreneurs in India's Urban Informal Economy.* Oxford Scholarship Online (www.oxfordscholarship.com/view/10.1093/acprof:o so/9780198060864.001.0001/acprof-9780198060864).

Gill, R. (2010) Breaking the silence: the hidden injuries of the neoliberal university. In R. Ryan-Flood and R. Gill (eds) *Secrecy and Silence in the Research Process. Feminist Reflections.* London: Routledge, pp. 228–224.

Gittins, D. (1993) *The Family in Question. Changing Households & Familiar Ideologies.* Basingstoke, Hants: MacMillan.

Glenn, E.N. (1981) Occupational ghettoization: Japanese American women and domestic service, 1905–1970. *Ethnicity,* 8, 352–386.

Glenn, E.N. (1986) *Issei, Nisei, War Bride: Three Generations of Japanese American Women in Domestic Service.* Philadelphia, PA: Temple.

Glenn, E.N. (1992) From servitude to service work: historical continuities in the racial division of paid reproductive labor. *Signs: Journal of Women in Culture and Society,* 18(1), 1–43.

Glenn, E.N. (2000) Creating a caring society. *Contemporary Sociology,* 29(1), 84–94.

Goerdeler, K.J., Wegge, J., Schrod, N., Bilinska, P. and Rudolf, M. (2015) 'Yuck that's disgusting!' – 'No not to me': antecedents of disgust in geriatric care and its relation to emotional exhaustion and intention to leave. *Motivation and Emotion,* 39, 247–259.

Gopal, M. (1999) Disempowered despite wage work: women workers in beedi industry. *Economic and Political Weekly,* 34(16/17), WS12–WS20.

Goyan Kittler, P. and Sucher, K. (2008) *Food and Culture* (5th edn). Belmont, CA: Thompson Wadsworth.

Gregson, N. and Lowe, M. (1994a) *Servicing the Middle Classes: Class, Gender and Waged Domestic Work in Contemporary Britain.* London: Routledge.

Gregson, N. and Lowe, M. (1994b) Waged domestic labour and the renegotiation of the domestic division of labour within dual career households. *Sociology,* 28, 55–78.

Gregson, N. and Lowe, M. (1995) 'Too much work?' Class, gender and the reconstitution of middle-class domestic labour. In T. Butler and M. Savage (eds) *Social Change and the Middle Classes*. London: UCL Press Limited, pp. 148–165.

Grose, J. (2013) Cleaning: the final feminist frontier. *New Republic*. 19 March 2013 (https://newrepublic.com/article/112693/112693).

Grover, S. (2017) Revisiting the Devyani Khobragade controversy: The value of domestic labor in the global south. *Asian Journal of Women's Studies*, 23(1), 121–128.

Groves, J.M. and Lui, L. (2012) The 'gift' of help: domestic helpers and the maintenance of hierarchy in the household division of labour. *Sociology*, 46, 57–73.

Gullikstad, B., Kristensen, G.K. and Ringrose, P. (2016) Paid migrant domestic labour, gender equality, and citizenship in a changing Europe: an introduction. In B. Gullikstad, G.K. Kristensen and P. Ringrose (eds) *Paid Migrant Domestic Labour in a Changing Europe. Questions of Gender Equality and Citizenship*. London: Palgrave Macmillan, pp. 1–30.

Gunn, S. and Bell, R. (2002) *Middle Classes: Their Rise and Sprawl*. London: Orion.

Gutiérrez-Rodríguez, E. (2014) Domestic work–affective labor: on feminization and the coloniality of labor. *Women's Studies International Forum*, 46, 45–53.

Hall, C. (1973/1980) The history of the housewife (extract 1973). In E. Malos (ed.) *The Politics of Housework*. London: Allison and Busby, pp. 44–71.

Hand, E. (1992) *Sociological Aspects of Women's Beliefs about the Family; Staffordshire Housewives' Awareness of Alternatives within Family Life*. Unpublished: University of Keele. PhD.

Hansen, K.T. (1990) Domestic trials: power and autonomy in domestic service in Zambia. *American Ethnologist*, 17(2), 360–375.

Hardyment, C. (1988) *From Mangle to Microwave: The Mechanization of Household Work*. Cambridge: Polity Press.

Harris, J. (2012) Self-employed business opportunity? No thanks. *The Guardian*. 22 January 2012 (www.theguardian.com/commentisfree/2012/jan/22/self-employment-proper-jobs-cameron).

Harvey, G., Rhodes, C., Vachhani, S.J. and Willams, K. (2017) Neo-villeiny and the service sector: the case of hyper flexible and precarious work in fitness centres. *Work, Employment and Society*, 31(1), 19–35.

Hatton, E. (2017) Mechanisms of invisibility: rethinking the concept of invisible work. *Work, Employment and Society*, 32(3), 336–351.

Hawksley, H. (2014) Why India's brick kiln workers 'live like slaves'. BBC News, 2 January 2014 (www.bbc.co.uk/news/world-asia-india-25556965).

Hebson, G. (2009) Renewing class analysis in studies of the workplace: a comparison of working-class and middle-class women's aspirations and identities. *Sociology*, 43(1), 27–44.

Hebson, G., Rubery, J. and Grimshaw, D. (2015) Rethinking job satisfaction in care work: looking beyond the care debates. *Work, Employment and Society*, 29(2), 314–330.

Henry, M. (2007) If the shoe fits: authenticity, authority and agency feminist diasporic research. *Women's Studies International Forum*, 30, 70–80.

Hettige, S. and Paranagama, D. (2005) Gender and alcohol in Sri Lanka. In I.S. Obot and R. Room (eds) *Alcohol, Gender and Drinking Problems: Perspectives from Low and Middle Income Countries*. Geneva: World Health Organization, pp. 167–188 (www.who.int/substance_abuse/publications/alcohol_gender_drinking_problems.pdf).

Hill, B. (1996) *Servants: English Domestics in the Eighteenth Century*. Oxford: Clarendon Press.

Hinsliff, G. (2014) The forelock-tugging's gone, but most of us still depend on servants. *The Guardian*. 24 October 2014 (https://www.theguardian.com/commentisfree/2014/oct/24/still-depend-servants-amazon-toffs-bygone-age).

Hinze, S.W. (2004) 'Am I being oversensitive?' Women's experience of sexual harassment during medical training. *Health: An Interdisciplinary Journal for the Social Study of Health, Illness and Medicine*, 8(1), 101–127.

Hochschild, A.R. (2001) *The Time Bind. When Work Becomes Home and Home Becomes Work*. With a new introduction. New York: Henry Holt.

Hochschild, A.R. (2012) *The Outsourced Self: Intimate Life in Market Times*. New York: Metropolitan Books.

Hodkinson, P. (2009) Grounded theory and inductive research. In N. Gilbert (ed.) *Researching Social Life* (3rd edn). London: Sage, pp. 80–100.

Hoerder, D., van Nedereveen Meerkerk, E. and Neunsinger, S. (eds) (2015) *Towards a Global History of Domestic and Caregiving Workers*. Leiden, the Netherlands: Koninklijke Brill.

Holtz, P., Kronberger, N. and Wagner, W. (2012) Analyzing internet forums: a practical guide. *Journal of Media Psychology: Theories, Methods, & Applications*, 24(2), 55–66.

Hom, S. (2008/2010) Housekeepers and nannies in the homework economy: on the morality and politics of paid housework. In R. Whisnant and P. Des Autels (eds) *Global Feminist Ethics*. Lanham, MD: Rowman & Littlefield, pp. 23–42.

Hondagneu-Sotelo, P. (2001) *Doméstica: Immigrant Workers Cleaning and Caring in the Shadows of Affluence*. Berkeley, CA: University of California Press.

Hondagneu-Sotelo, P. (2007) Preface to the 2007 edn. In *Doméstica: Immigrant Workers Cleaning and Caring in the Shadows of Affluence*. With a new preface. Berkeley, CA: University of California Press, pp. ix–xvi.

Horn, P. (2012) *Life Below Stairs: The Real Lives of Servants, the Edwardian Era to 1939*. Stroud: Amberley Publishing.

Hu, Y. and Stewart, F. (2009) *Pension coverage and informal sector workers: international experiences*. OECD working papers on insurance and private pensions, No. 31. Paris: Financial Affairs Division, Directorate for Financial and Enterprise Affairs, Organisation for Economic Co-operation and Development.

Hughes, J., Simpson, R., Slutskaya, N., Simpson, A. and Hughes, K. (2017) Beyond the symbolic: a relational approach to dirty work through a study of refuse collectors and street cleaners. *Work, Employment and Society*, 31(1), 106–122.

Human Rights Watch (2014) *Cleaning Human Waste: 'Manual Scavenging', Caste, and Discrimination in India* (www.hrw.org/sites/default/files/reports/india0814_ForUpload.pdf).

Hyland, B. (2017) From factory workers to care workers … Women's Views on the News, 21 April 2017 (www.womensviewsonnews.org/2017/04/from-factory-workers-to-care-workers/?utm_source=feedburner&utm_medium=email&utm_campaign=Feed%3A+WomensViewsOnNews+%28Women%27s+Views+on+News%29).

IDWN (International Domestic Workers' Network) (2011) *Myths and realities about domestic workers. What THEY say and what WE say* (www.idwfed.org/en/resources/myths-and-realities-about-domestic-workers/@@display-file/attachment_1).

Ilaiah, K. (1995/2004) Caste or class or caste–class: a study in Dalitbahujan consciousness and struggles in Andhra Pradesh in 1980s. In M. Mohanty (ed.) *Class, Caste and Gender*. New Delhi: Sage, pp. 227–255.

Ilaiah, K. (2005/2017) *Why I am not a Hindu. A Sudra Critique of Hindutva Philosophy, Culture and Political Economy* (2nd edn). Kolkata: Samya.

ILO (n.d.) Ratifications of C189 – Domestic Workers Convention, 2011 (No. 189) (www.ilo.org/dyn/normlex/en/f?p=NORMLEXPUB:11300:0::NO::P11300_INSTRUMENT_ID:2551460).

ILO (2010) *Decent Work for Domestic Workers*. Report IV(1). International Labour Conference, 99th Session, 2010. Geneva: International Labour Office.

ILO (2011) *Convention No. 189. Decent Work for Domestic Workers*. Geneva: International Labour Office.

ILO (2013) *Domestic Workers Across the World: Global and Regional Statistics and the Extent of Legal Protection*. Geneva: International Labour Office.

ILO (2016) *Formalization of Domestic Work*. Geneva: International Labour Office.

indiatoday.in (2014) Indian Administrative Service salary and perks. 13 June 2014 (http://indiatoday.intoday.in/education/story/ias-salary-and-perks/1/366752.html).

Irudayam, A., Mangubhai, J.P. and Lee, J.G. (2011) *Dalit Women Speak Out. Caste, Class and Gender Violence in India*. New Delhi: Zubaan.

Jackson, C. and Griffiths, P. (2014) Dirt and disgust as key drivers in nurses' infection control behaviours: an interpretative, qualitative study. *Journal of Hospital Infection*, 87(2), 71–76.

Jackson, S. (1992) Towards a historical sociology of housework. A material feminist analysis. *Women's Studies International Forum*, 15(2), 153–172.

Jackson, S. (2011) Materialist feminism, the self and global late modernity: some consequences for sexuality and intimacy. In A. Jónasdóttir, V. Bryson and K.B. Jones (eds) *Sexuality, Gender and Power: Intersectional and Transnational Perspectives*. Abingdon, Oxon: Routledge, pp. 15–29.

Jacobs, A.W. and Padavic, I. (2015) Hours, scheduling and flexibility for women in the US low-wage labour force. *Gender, Work & Organization*, 22, 67–86.

James, L. (2008) United by gender or divided by class? Women's work orientations and labour market behaviour. *Gender, Work & Organization*, 15(4), 394–412.

Jayawarna, D., Rouse, J. and Macpherson, A. (2014) Life course pathways to business start-up. *Entrepreneurship & Regional Development: an International Journal*, 26(3–4), 282–312.

Jeffrey, C., Jeffrey, R. and Jeffrey, P. (2004) Degrees without freedom: the impact of formal education on Dalit young men in North India. *Development and Change*, 35(5), 963–986.

Jeffrey, C., Jeffrey, P. and Jeffrey, R. (2005) When schooling fails: young men, education and low-caste politics in rural north India. *Contributions to Indian Sociology*, 39(1), 1–38.

Johnson, J. (2002) *Getting By on the Minimum. The Lives of Working-Class Women*. New York: Routledge.

Johnson, L. and Lloyd, J. (2004) *Sentenced to Everyday Life: Feminism and the Housewife*. Oxford: Berg.

Joinson, A. (1999) Social desirability, anonymity, and Internet-based questionnaires. *Behavior Research Methods, Instruments, & Computers*, 31(3), 433–438.

Jokela, M. (2017) The role of domestic employment policies in shaping precarious work. *Social Policy & Administration*, 51(2), 286–307.

Jones, A. (2004) *Domestics: UK Domestic Workers and Their Reluctant Employers*. London: The Work Foundation.

Jones, H. (1997) Introduction. In H. Jones (ed.) *Towards a Classless Society?* London: Routledge, pp. 1–12.

Joshi, A. (2012) Fact sheet: the pension bill. *Wall Street Journal*, WSJ Blogs, 22 November 2012 (http://blogs.wsj.com/indiarealtime/2012/11/22/fact-sheet-the-pension-bill/).

Kabeer, N. (2001) Reflections on the measurement of women's empowerment. In A. Sisask (ed.) *Discussing Women's Empowerment. Theory and Practice*. Sida Studies no. 3. Stockholm: Sida (www.sida.se/contentassets/5e45d330e16743179cefc93de34e71ac/15611.pdf).

Kaluzynska, E. (1980) Wiping the floor with theory: a survey of writings on housework. *Feminist Review*, 6, 27–54.

Kennedy, M. (2001) One woman's reflections on the Ruskin conference, 'Celebrating the Women's liberation movement thirty years on', Ruskin College, Oxford, 18 March 2000. *Women's History Review*, 10(2), 349–352.

Kent, D.A. (1989) Ubiquitous but invisible: female domestic servants in mid-eighteenth century London. *History Workshop Journal*, 28, 111–128.

Kessler, I., Heron, P. and Dopson, S. (2015) Managing patient emotions as skilled work and being 'one of us'. *Work, Employment and Society*, 29(5), 775–791.

Khare, R. (2001) 'Do rats have rights?'. In *People Unlike Us: the India that is Invisible*. Contemporary Essays series. New Delhi: Harper Collins, pp. 159–211.

Kilkey, M., Perrons, D. and Plomein, A. (2013) *Gender, Migration and Domestic Work. Masculinities, Male Labour and Fathering in the UK and USA*. Basingstoke, Hants: Palgrave Macmillan.

Kindler, M. (2008) Risk and risk strategies in migration: Ukrainian domestic workers in Poland. In H. Lutz (ed.) *Migration and Domestic Work: a European Perspective on a Global Theme*. Aldershot, Hants: Ashgate Publishing, pp. 145–159.

King, A.J. (2007) *Domestic Service in Post-Apartheid South Africa: Deference and Disdain*. Aldershot, Hants: Ashgate Publishing.

Kishwar, M. (1991/2005) A horror of 'isms': why I do not call myself a feminist. In M. Chaudhuri (ed.) *Feminism in India*. London: Zed Books, pp. 26–51.

Kitzinger, C. and Wilkinson, S. (1996) Theories representing the Other. In C. Kitzinger and S. Wilkinson (eds) *Representing the Other. A Feminism and Psychology Reader*. London: Sage, pp. 1–32.

Kordasiewicz, A. (2015) Class guilt? Employers and their relationships with domestic workers in Poland. In A. Triandafyllidou and S. Marchetti (eds) *Employers, Agencies and Immigration: Paying for Care*. Surrey: Ashgate, pp. 53–72.

Lachance-Grzela, M. and Bouchard, G. (2010) Why do women do the lion's share of housework? A decade of research. *Sex Roles*, 63, 767–780.

Lader, D., Short, S. and Gershuny, J. (2006) *The Time Use Survey, 2005. How We Spend Our Time*. London: Office for National Statistics (www. timeuse.org/sites/ctur/files/public/ctur_report/1905/lader_short_and_ gershuny_2005_kight_diary.pdf).

Lahiri, T. (2017) *Maid in India. Stories of Opportunities and Inequalities in Our Homes*. New Delhi: Aleph.

Lai, M.-Y. (2007) Field note: in your face – Indonesian domestic workers' activism at the World Trade Organization ministerial in Hong Kong. *Women's Studies Quarterly*, 35(3/4), 123–127.

Lalani, M. (2011) *Ending the Abuse. Policies that Work to Protect Migrant Domestic Workers*. London: Kalayaan (www.kalayaan.org.uk).

Lalani, M. and Metcalf, H. (2012) *Forced Labour in the UK: the Business Angle*. JRF programme paper, forced labour. York: Joseph Rowntree Foundation (https://www.jrf.org.uk/report/forced-labour-uk-business-angle).

Lan, P.-C. (2006) *Global Cinderellas*. Durham, NC: Duke University Press.

Landry, J.T. (2011) The coming age of corporate paternalism. *HBR Blog Network*. 11 April 2011 (http://blogs.hbr.org/hbr/hbreditors/2011/04/ in_hbr_and_elsewhere_a_1.html).

Lau, L. (2011) The male South Asian domestic servant: master-servant relationships, class chasms, and systematic emasculation. *The Sri Lanka Journal of the Humanities*, XXXVII (1&2), 35–54.

Laub, J.A. (2013) APS model. OLA group (www.olagroup.com/Display. asp?Page=aps_model).

Lawler, S. (2005) Introduction: class, culture and identity. *Sociology*, 39, 797–806.

Ledwith, S. and Manfredi, S. (2000) Balancing gender in higher education: a study of the experience of senior women in a 'new' UK university. *European Journal of Women's Studies*, 7, 7–33.

Lee, Y.-S. and Waite, L.J. (2005) Husbands' and wives' time spent on housework: a comparison of measures. *Journal of Marriage and Family*, 67(2), 328–336.

Letherby, G. (2003) *Feminist Research in Theory and Practice*. Maidenhead, Berks: Open University Press.

Leung, W., Gill, R. and Randle, K. (2015) Getting in, getting on, getting out? Women as career scramblers in the UK film and television industries. *The Sociological Review*, 63 (Suppl. 1), 50–65.

Linder, M. and Houghton, J. (1990) Self-employment and the petty bourgeoisie: comment on Steinmetz and Wright. *American Journal of Sociology*, 93(3), 727–735.

Lloyd, C. and Payne, J. (2009) 'Full of sound and fury, signifying nothing': interrogating new skill concepts in service work – the view from two UK call centres. *Work, Employment and Society*, 23(4), 617–634.

Longhurst, R. (2000) Men's bodies and bathrooms. In *Bodies: Exploring Fluid Boundaries*. London: Routledge, pp. 66–90.

Lucas, K. (2011) Blue-collar discourses of workplace dignity: using outgroup comparisons to construct positive identities. *Papers in Communication Studies*, paper 13 (http://digitalcommons.unl.edu/commstudiespapers/13).

Lucas, K. and Buzzanell, P.M. (2004) Blue-collar work, career, and success: occupational narratives of *Sisu. Journal of Applied Communication Research*, 2(4), 273–292.

Lutz, H. (2002) At your service madam! The globalization of domestic service. *Feminist Review*, 70, 90–101.

Lutz, H. (2008) When home becomes a workplace: domestic work as an ordinary job in Germany? In H. Lutz (ed.) *Migration and Domestic Work: a European Perspective on a Global Theme*. Aldershot, Hants: Ashgate Publishing, pp. 43–60.

Lutz, H. (2011) *The New Maids: Transnational Women and the Care Economy*. Translated by Deborah Shannon. London: Zed Books.

Lyonette, C. and Crompton, R. (2015) Sharing the load? Partners' relative earnings and the division of domestic labour. *Work, Employment and Society*, 29(1), 23–40.

Macdonald, C.L. and Merrill, D.A. (2002) 'It shouldn't have to be a trade': recognition and redistribution in care work advocacy. *Hypatia*, 17, 67–83.

Mackenzie, A. (2009) *Ask Aggie: For All Your Cleaning Solutions*. London: Penguin Books.

Magnus, E. (1934a) The social, economic and legal conditions of domestic servants: I. *International Labor Review*, 30, 190–207.

Magnus, E. (1934b) The social, economic and legal conditions of domestic servants: II. *International Labor Review*, 30, 336–364.

Mainiero, L.A. and Sullivan, S.E. (2005) Kaleidoscope careers: an alternate explanation for the 'opt-out' revolution. *Academy of Management Executive*, 19(1), 106–123.

Marriage Savers Calgary Cleaning Services (2016) About Marriage Savers (http://themarriagesavers.ca/).

Marshall, J. (1995) *Women Managers Moving On: Exploring Career and Life Choices*. London: Routledge.

Martens, L. (2007/2012) The visible and invisible: (de)regulation in contemporary cleaning practices. In B. Campkin and R. Cox (eds) *Dirt: New Geographies of Cleanliness and Contamination*. London: I.B. Taurus, pp. 34–48.

Mattila, K. (2016) Gendered vulnerabilities: work–life trajectories of female domestic workers in Jaipur. In S. Raju and S. Jatrana (eds) *Women Workers in Urban India*. New Delhi: Cambridge University Press, pp. 67–96.

Mattila, P. (2011) *Domestic Labour Relations in India. Vulnerability and Gendered Life Courses in Jaipur*. Unpublished: University of Helsinki. PhD. Helsinki: Interkont Books 19.

Maushart, S. (2003) *Wifework: What Marriage Really Means for Women*. London: Bloomsbury.

Mavin, S. and Grandy, G. (2016) Women elite leaders doing respectable business femininity: how privilege is conferred, contested and defended through the body. *Gender, Work & Organization*, 23, 379–396.

Mayer-Ahuja, N. (2004) Three worlds of cleaning: women's experiences of precarious labor in the public sector, cleaning companies and private households of West Germany, 1973–1998. *Journal of Women's History*, 16(2), 116–141.

Mayyasi, A. (2013) The IIT entrance exam. Pricenomics (http://priceonomics.com/the-iit-entrance-exam/).

McGuire, D. and Lozada, M. (2017) 'I'll do it step by step': care, cover and quiet campaigning. *Work, Employment and Society*, 31(1), 175–184.

Meagher, G. (1997) *Just Another Lousy Job? Evaluation of the Construction of Paid Household Work*. Unpublished: University of Sydney. PhD (http://ses.library.usyd.edu.au/bitstream/2123/1881/1/The%20Ultimate%20Lousy%20Job%20Evaluating%20the%20Construction%20of%20Paid%20Household%20Work.pdf).

Meagher, G. (2002) Is it wrong to pay for housework? *Hypatia*, 17(2), 52–66.

Meagher, G. (2003) *Friend or Flunkey. Paid Domestic Work in the New Economy*. Sydney: UNSW Press.

Meagher, G., Szebehely, M. and Mears, J. (2016) How institutions matter for job characteristics, quality and experiences: a comparison of home care work for older people in Australia and Sweden. *Work, Employment and Society*, 30(5), 731–749.

Mendez, J.B. (1998) Of mops and maids: contradictions and continuities in bureaucratized domestic work. *Social Problems*, 45(1), 114–135.

Metcalfe, G. (2013) *Young Women's Everyday Lives: Home and Work in the North East of England*. Unpublished: Newcastle University School of Geography, Politics and Sociology. PhD.

Meyers, M. (2013) The war on academic women: reflections on postfeminism in the neoliberal academy. *Journal of Communication Inquiry*, 37(4), 274–283.

Milkman, R., Reese, E. and Roth, B. (1998) The macrosociology of paid domestic labor. *Work and Occupations*, 25(4), 483–510.

Miller, J. and Glassner, B. (1998) The 'inside' and the 'outside'. Finding realities in interviews. In D. Silverman (ed.) *Qualitative Research. Theory, Method and Practice*. London: Sage, pp. 125–139.

Mills, S. (2004) Class, gender and politeness. *Multilingua*, 23, 171–190.

Mirchandani, K., Mukherjee, S. and Tambe, S. (2016) Old jobs in new forms: women's experiences in the housekeeping sector in Pune. In S. Raju and S. Jatrana (eds) *Women Workers in Urban India*. New Delhi: Cambridge University Press, pp. 121–138.

Molinier, P. (2009/2012) Of feminists and their cleaning ladies: caught between the reciprocity of care & [sic] the desire for depersonalisation. *The Commoner*, 15, 287–306. Originally published in *Multitudes* (2009), 37–38, 113–121.

Momsen, J.H. (ed.) (1999) *Gender, Migration and Domestic Service*. London: Routledge.

Moosvi, S. (2004) Domestic service in pre-colonial India: bondage, caste and market. In A. Fauve-Chamoux (ed.) *Formation of European Identity. Understanding the Globalization of Domestic Work, 16th–21st century*. Bern: Peter Lang AG, pp. 543–576.

Morel, N. (2015) Servants for the knowledge-based economy? The political economy of domestic services in Europe. *Social Politics*, 22(2), 170–192.

Morgan, D.H.J. (2011) *Rethinking Family Practices*. Basingstoke, Hants: Palgrave Macmillan.

Morgan, S. (2009) Review of theorising feminist history: a thirty-year perspective. *Woman's History Review*, 18(3), 381–407.

Moya, J.C. (2007) Domestic service in a global perspective: gender, migration, and ethnic niches. *Journal of Ethnic and Migration Studies*, 33(4), 559–579.

Mumsnet Census (2009) (www.mumsnet.com/info/media/census-2009).

Mundlak, G. and Shamir, H. (2011) Bringing together or drifting apart – targeting care work as work like no other. *Canadian Journal of Women and the Law*, 23(1), 289–308.

Narayan, U. (1998) Essence of culture and a sense of history: a feminist critique of cultural essentialism. *Hypatia*, 13(2), 86–106.

Näre, L. (2011) The moral economy of domestic and care labour: migrant workers in Naples, Italy. *Sociology*, 45, 396–412.

Näre, L. (2016) Neoliberal citizenship and domestic service in Finland: A return to a servant society? In B. Gullikstad, G.K. Kristensen and P. Ringrose (eds) *Paid Migrant Domestic Labour in a Changing Europe. Questions of Gender Equality and Citizenship*. London: Palgrave Macmillan, pp. 31–53.

Narula, R. (1999) Cinderellas need not apply. A study of paid domestic work in Paris. In J.H. Momsen (ed.) *Gender, Migration and Domestic Service*. London: Routledge, pp. 148–163.

NCEUS (2008) *Report on Definitional and Statistical Issues Relating to the Informal Economy*. New Delhi: National Commission for Enterprises in the Unorganised Sector.

NCEUS (2009) *The Challenge of Employment in India: an Informal Economy Perspective. Volume I – Main Report*. New Delhi: National Commission for Enterprises in the Unorganised Sector.

Neetha, N. (2004) Making of female breadwinners. Migration and social networking of women domestics in Delhi. *Economic and Political Weekly*, 24, 1681–1688.

Neetha, N. (2008) Regulating domestic work. *Economic and Political Weekly*, 13 September, 26–28.

Neetha, N. (2009) Contours of domestic service: characteristics, work relations and regulation. *Indian Journal of Labour Economics*, 52(3), 489–506.

Neetha, N. (2016) Persistent inequalities and deepened burden of work? An analysis of women's employment in Delhi. In S. Raju and S. Jatrana (eds) *Women Workers in Urban India*. New Delhi: Cambridge University Press, pp. 36–66.

Neetha, N. and Palriwala, R. (2011) Absence of state law: domestic workers in India. *Canadian Journal of Women and the Law*, 23(1), 97–120.

Nelson, M.K. (2004) How men matter: housework and self-provisioning among rural single-mother and married-couple families in Vermont, US. *Feminist Economics*, 10(2), 9–36.

Nicholson, V. (2015) *Perfect Wives in Ideal Homes: the Story of Women in the 1950s*. London: Penguin UK.

O'Dwyer, B. (2007) Qualitative data analysis: illuminating the process for transforming a 'messy' but 'attractive' 'nuisance'. In C. Humphrey and B. Lee (eds) *The Real Life Guide to Accounting Research. A Behind-the-Scenes View of Using Qualitative Research Methods*. Oxford: Elsevier, pp. 391–408.

Oakley, A. (1974/1977) *Housewife*. Harmondsworth: Penguin.

Oakley, A. (1974/1985) *The Sociology of Housework*. London: Martin Robinson.

ONS (2010) *Standard Occupational Classification 2010. Volume 1 Structure and Descriptions of Unit Groups.* Basingstoke, Hants: Palgrave Macmillan.

ONS (2011) *Labour Force Survey. User Guide. Volume 1 – LFS Background and Methodology 2011* (www.esds.ac.uk/doc/6782%5Cmrdoc%5Cpdf%5Clfs_user_guide_vol1_background2011.pdf).

ONS (2013) *Families and Households in England and Wales: 2011* (https://www.ons.gov.uk/peoplepopulationandcommunity/birthsdeathsandmarriages/families/articles/familiesandhouseholdsinenglandandwales/2013-01-30).

ONS (2015a) *Harmonised Concepts and Questions for Social Data Sources. Primary Principles. Ethnic Group* (http://webarchive.nationalarchives.gov.uk/20160105160709/http://www.ons.gov.uk/ons/guide-method/harmonisation/primary-set-of-harmonised-concepts-and-questions/index.html).

ONS (2015b) *Labour Force Survey. User Guide. Volume 3 – Details of LFS Variables 2015* (www.ons.gov.uk/ons/guide-method/method-quality/specific/labour-market/labour-market-statistics/index.html).

Orr, D. (2013) Lawson, Saatchi and Grillo: the messy bond between master and servant. *The Guardian.* 20 December 2013 (www.theguardian.com/commentisfree/2013/dec/20/lawson-saatchi-grillo-messy-bond-master-servant).

Pai, H.-H. (2008) *Chinese Whispers. The True Story Behind Britain's Hidden Army of Labour.* London: Penguin Books.

Palriwala, R. and Uberoi, P. (2008) Exploring the links: gender issues in marriage and migration. In R. Palriwala and P. Uberoi (eds) *Marriage, Migration and Gender.* New Delhi: Sage Publications, pp. 23–62.

Pape, K. (2016) ILO Convention C189 – a good start for the protection of domestic workers: An insider's view. *Progress in Development Studies,* 16(2), 189–202.

Pedersen, S. and Smithson, J.S. (2013) Mothers with attitude – how the Mumsnet parenting forum offers space for new forms of femininity to emerge online. *Women's Studies International Forum,* 38, 97–106.

Pellegrini, E.K., Scandura, T.A. and Jayaram, V. (2010) Cross-cultural generalizability of paternalistic leadership: an expansion of leader-member exchange theory. *Group and Organization Management,* 35(4), 391–420.

Penz, O., Sauer, B., Gaitsch, M., Hofbauer, J. and Glinsner, B. (2017) Post-bureaucratic encounters: affective labour in public employment services. *Critical Social Policy,* 37(4), 540–561.

Pérez, I. and Stallaert, C. (2016) The professionalization of paid domestic work and its limits: experiences of Latin American migrants in Brussels. *European Journal of Women's Studies,* 23(2), 155–168.

Perry, S.E. (1998) *Dirty Work, Clean Jobs, Proud People. Collecting Garbage.* New Brunswick, NJ: Transaction Publishers.

Peschek-Bohmer, F. and Schreiber, G. (n.d.) Healing yourself using urine therapy (www.innerself.com/Health/urine.htm).

Philpott, J. (2012) *The Rise in Self-Employment.* Work Audit series. London: Chartered Institute of Personnel and Development.

Platzer, E. (2006) From private solutions to public responsibility and back again: the new domestic services in Sweden. *Gender & History*, 18(2), 211–221.

Pollert, A. (1981) *Girls, Wives, Factory Lives.* London: Palgrave Macmillan.

Pollert, A. (1996) Gender and class revisited; or, the poverty of 'patriarchy'. *Sociology*, 30(4), 639–659.

Pooley, S. (2009) Domestic servants and their urban employers: a case study of Lancaster, 1880–1914. *Economic History Review*, 62(2), 405–429.

Potter, J. (2015) *Crisis at Work. Identity and the End of Career.* Basingstoke, Hants: Palgrave Macmillan.

Potter, M. and Hamilton, J. (2014) Picking on vulnerable migrants: precarity and the mushroom industry in Northern Ireland. *Work, Employment and Society*, 28(3), 390–406.

Prasad-Aleyamma, M. (2017) The cultural politics of wages: ethnography of construction work in Kochi, India. *Contributions to Indian Sociology*, 51(2), 163–193.

Praxis India/Institute of Participatory Practice (2014) *Down the Drain – Participatory Video Made by Sewage Workers in Delhi.* [Video] (https://www.youtube.com/watch?v=3azx-jUT1sY).

Press, J.E. and Townsley, E. (1998) Wives' and husbands' housework reporting: gender, class, and social desirability. *Gender & Society*, 12(2), 188–218.

Qi, X. (2011) Face. A Chinese concept in a global sociology. *Journal of Sociology*, 47(3), 279–295.

Radhakrishnan, S. (2009) Professional women, good families: respectable femininity and the cultural politics of a 'new' India. *Qualitative Sociology*, 32, 195–212.

Rafkin, L. (1998) *Other People's Dirt: A Housecleaner's Curious Adventures.* Chapel Hill, NC: Algonquin Books of Chapel Hill.

Raghuram, P. (1999) Interlinking trajectories. Migration and domestic work in India. In J.H. Momsen (ed.) *Gender, Migration and Domestic Service.* London: Routledge, pp. 215–228.

Raghuram, P. (2001). Caste and gender in the organisation of paid domestic work in India. *Work, Employment and Society*, 15, 607–617.

Raju, S. and Bose, D. (2016) Women workers in urban India and the cities. In S. Raju and S. Jatrana (eds) *Women Workers in Urban India*. New Delhi: Cambridge University Press, pp. 36–66.

Raju, S. and Jatrana, S. (eds) (2016a) *Women Workers in Urban India*. New Delhi: Cambridge University Press.

Raju, S. and Jatrana, S. (2016b) Setting the backdrop. In S. Raju and S. Jatrana (eds) *Women Workers in Urban India*. New Delhi: Cambridge University Press, pp. 1–35.

Rani, P. and Kaul, P. (1986) For two meals a day. A report on Tamil maids. *Manushi*, 35, 2–15.

Rankin, J. and Butler, S. (2015) City Link's army of self-employed workers count cost of business failure. *The Guardian*. 1 January 2015 (www.theguardian.com/business/2015/jan/01/city-link-army-self-employed-count-cost-failure).

Ray, R. and Qayum, S. (2009/2010) *Cultures of Servitude. Modernity, Domesticity, and Class in India*. New Delhi, Oxford University Press.

Reader's Digest (2011) *How to Clean Just About Everything*. London: Vivat Direct.

Reay, D. (2004). 'Mostly roughs and toughs': social class, race and representation in inner city schooling. *Sociology*, 38(5), 999–1017.

Reinharz, S. (1992) *Feminist Methods in Social Research*. New York: Oxford University Press.

Risman, B. and Johnson-Sumerford, D. (1998) Doing it fairly: a study of postgender marriages. *Journal of Marriage and Family*, 60, 23–40.

Rivas, L.M. (2003) Invisible labors: caring for the independent person. In B. Ehrenreich and A.R. Hochschild (eds) *Global Women. Nannies, Maids and Sex Workers in the New Economy*. London: Granta Books, pp. 70–84.

Rivera, L.A. (2015) *Pedigree: How Elite Students Get Elite Jobs*. Princeton, NJ: Princeton University Press.

Roberts, D.E. (1997) Spiritual and menial housework. University of Pennsylvania Law School, paper 1282. *Faculty Scholarship* (http://scholarship.law.upenn.edu/faculty_scholarship/1282).

Robinson, J.P. and Milkie, M.A. (1998) Back to basics: trends in and role determinants of women's attitudes towards housework. *Journal of Marriage and Family*, 60(1), 205–218.

Rolfe, H. (2006) Where are the men? Gender segregation in the childcare and early years sector. *National Institute Economic Review*, 195, 103–117.

Rollins, J. (1985) *Between Women: Domestics and Their Employers*. Philadelphia, PA: Temple University Press.

Romero, M. (2002) *M.A.I.D. in the USA. 10th Anniversary Edition*. London: Routledge.

Rose, D. and Pevalin, D.J. (with O'Reilly, K.) (2005) *The National Statistics Socio-economic Classification: Origins, Development and Use.* London: Palgrave Macmillan.

Rose, M. (2004/2014) *The Mind At Work: Valuing the Intelligence of the American Worker. 10th Anniversary Edition.* New York, NY: Penguin Books.

Roy, A. and Barsiaman, D. (2004) *The Check Book and the Cruise Missile: Conversations with Arundhati Roy.* Interviews with David Barsiaman. Cambridge, MA: South End Press.

Rubery, J., Hebson, G., Grimshaw, D., Carroll, M., Marchington, L., Smith, L., et al. (2011) *The Recruitment and Retention of a Care Workforce for Older People.* London: Department of Health.

Russell, S. (2006) Netmums: online support for parents. *Community Practitioner: the Journal of the Community Practitioners' & Health Visitors' Association*, 2, 44–45.

Sagar (2017) Down the drain. How the Swachh Bharat Mission is heading for failure. *The Caravan*, 9(5), 30–55.

Saldaña-Tejeda, A. (2015) Un/Identifying reflexive subjects: the case of women in paid domestic work in Mexico. *Current Sociology*, 63(7), 943–960.

Salzinger, L. (1991) A maid by any other name: the transformation of 'dirty work' by Central American immigrants. In M. Burawoy (ed.) *Ethnography Unbound: Power and Resistance in the Modern Metropolis.* Berkeley, CA: University of California Press, pp. 139–160.

Sambrook, P. (2005/2009) *Keeping Their Place: Domestic Service in the Country House.* Stroud: The History Press.

Sang, K.J.C., Dainty, A.R.J. and Ison, S.G. (2014) Gender in the UK architectural profession: (re)producing and challenging hegemonic masculinity. *Work, Employment and Society*, 28, 247–264.

Sarti, R. (2005) Conclusion: Domestic service and European identity. In S. Pasleau and I. Schopp (eds, with R. Sarti). *The Modelization of Domestic Service. Proceedings of the Servant Project, Vol. V.* Liège: Les Éditions de l'Université de Liège, pp. 195–284.

Sassen, S. (2009) The other workers in the advanced corporate economy. *S&F Online*, Issue 8.1 (Valuing Domestic Work) (http://sfonline.barnard.edu/work/sassen_01.htm).

Schober, P.S. (2013) Gender equality and outsourcing of domestic work, childbearing, and relationship stability among British couples. *Journal of Family Issues*, 34(1), 25–52.

Schwartz, L. (2014) 'What we think is needed is a union of domestics such as the miners have': the Domestic Workers' Union of Great Britain and Ireland 1908–14. *Twentieth Century British History*, 25(2), 173–198.

Schwartz, L. (2015) A job like any other? Feminist responses and challenges to domestic worker organizing in Edwardian Britain. *International Labour and Working-Class History*, 88, 30–48.

Scrinzi, F. (2010) Gender, migration and the ambiguous enterprise of professionalizing domestic service: the case of vocational training for the unemployed in France. *Feminist Review*, 98, 153–172.

Seale, C., Charteris-Black, J., MacFarlane, A. and McPherson, A. (2010) Interviews and internet forums: a comparison of two sources of qualitative data. *Qualitative Health Research*, 20(5), 595–606.

Seierstad, C. and Kirton, G. (2015) Having it all? Women in high commitment careers and work–life balance in Norway. *Gender, Work & Organization*, 22(4), 390–404.

Sen, S. and Sengupta, N. (2016) *Domestic Days: Women, Work and Politics in Contemporary Kolkata*. New Delhi: Oxford University Press.

Shah, R.A. (2015). Work-life balance and gender: a study of professionals in India. *Review of Management*, 5(1/2), 5–18.

Sherman, K.F. (2000) *A Housekeeper is Cheaper Than a Divorce: Why You Can Afford to Hire Help and How to Get It*. Mountain View, CA: Life Tools Press.

Shildrick, T., MacDonald, R., Webster, C.S. and Garthwaite, K. (2012) *Poverty and Insecurity: Life in Low-Pay, No-Pay Britain*. Bristol: Policy Press.

Shire, K. (2015) Family supports and insecure work: the politics of household service employment in conservative welfare regimes. *Social Politics*, 22(2), 193–219.

Shrivastava, H. (2015) Harassment at the workplace, powerlessness and identity: experiences of women civil servants in India. *Indian Journal of Gender Studies*, 22(3), 437–457.

Simpson, R., Hughes, J., Slutskaya, N. and Balta, M. (2014) Sacrifice and distinction in dirty work: men's construction of meaning in the butcher trade. *Work, Employment and Society*, 28(5), 754–770.

Singh, A.N. (2001) *Women Domestic Workers: Socio-Economic Life*. Delhi: Shipra Publications.

Singh, V. (2007) *Women Domestics: Workers Within Households*. Jaipur: Rawat Publications.

Singha, L. (2012) Negotiating the domestic sphere: dual-career Indian migrant couples. Master's dissertation, University of York, York.

Singha, L. (2015) Housework as 'family practices' in transnational couples: an exploratory study of middle-class Indians in the UK. *Families, Relationships and Societies*, 4(1), 131–147.

Skeggs, B. (1997/2002) *Formations of Class and Gender*. London: Sage.

Skeggs, B. (2004) *Self, Class, Culture*. London: Routledge.

Skrivankova, K. (2014) *Forced Labour in the United Kingdom*. York: Joseph Rowntree Foundation (https://www.jrf.org.uk/report/forced-labour-united-kingdom).

Slutskaya, N., Simpson, R., Hughes, J., Simpson, A. and Uygur, S. (2016) Masculinity and class in the context of dirty work. *Gender, Work & Organization*, 23(2), 165–182.

Smith, A. and Elliot, F. (2012) The demands and challenges of being a retail store manager: 'handcuffed to the front doors'. *Work, Employment and Society*, 26(4), 676–684.

Smith, E. (2009) Social construction of skill viewed through the lens of training for the cleaning industry. Unpublished paper presented at 'Aligning Participants, Policy and Pedagogy: Traction and Tensions in VET Research'. 12th Annual Conference, AVETRA. 16–17 April 2009. Sydney, Australia (https://avetra.org.au/data/Conference_2009_pres./9._Erica_Smith_paper.pdf).

Smith, P.R. (2011) The pitfalls of home: protecting the health and safety of paid domestic workers. *Canadian Journal of Women and the Law*, 23, 309–339.

Soni-Sinha, U. (2006) Where are the women? Gender, labor, and discourse in the Noida Export Processing Zone and Delhi. *Feminist Economics*, 12(3), 335–365.

Soni-Sinha, U. (2008) Dynamics of the 'field': multiple standpoints, narrative and shifting positionality in multisited research. *Qualitative Research*, 8, 515–537.

Soni-Sinha, U. and Yates, C.A.B. (2013) 'Dirty work?' Cleaning, race and the union in industrial cleaning. *Gender, Work & Organization*, 20, 599–758.

Soukup, R. (2012) Why I make my bed: 10 reasons I keep my house clean (www.livingwellspendingless.com/2012/02/15/why-i-make-my-bed-10-reasons-i-keep-my-house-clean/).

Spitze, G. (1999) Getting help with housework. Household resources and social networks. *Journal of Family Issues*, 20(6), 724–745.

Spitze, G. and Loscocco, K.A. (1999) The labor of Sisyphus? Women's and men's reactions to housework. *Social Science Quarterly*, 81(4), 1087–1100.

Spivak, G.C. (2000) The politics of translation. In L. Venuti (ed.) *The Translation Studies Reader*. London: Routledge, pp. 397–416.

Srinivas, L. (1995) Master-servant relationship in a cross-cultural perspective. *Economic and Political Weekly*, 30, 269–278.

Srinivasan, S. (1997) Breaking rural bonds through migration: the failure of development for women in India. *Journal of Comparative Family Studies*, 28, 89–102.

Stacey, C.L. (2005). Finding dignity in dirty work: the constraints and rewards of low-wage home care labour. *Sociology of Health & Illness*, 27, 831–854.

Stancanelli, E.G.F. and Stratton, L.S. (2010) *Her Time, His Time, or the Maid's Time: an Analysis of the Demand for Domestic Work*. IZA DP No. 5253. Discussion paper series, Institute for the Study of Labor (http://ftp.iza.org/dp5253.pdf).

Steinmetz, G. and Wright, E.O. (1989) The fall and rise of the petty bourgeoisie: changing patterns of self-employment in the postwar United States. *American Journal of Sociology*, 94(5), 973–1018.

Sturges, J. (2013) A matter of time: young professionals' experiences of long work hours. *Work, Employment and Society*, 27, 343–359.

Sullivan, O. (1996) Time co-ordination, the domestic division of labour and affective relations: time use and the enjoyment of activities within couples. *Sociology*, 30(1), 79–100.

Sullivan, O. (2006) *Changing Gender Relations, Changing Families: Tracing the Pace of Change Over Time*. Lanham, MD: Rowan and Littlefield.

Sullivan, O. and Gershuny, J. (2012) Domestic outsourcing and multitasking: how much do they really contribute? Sociology working papers, paper number 2012-05, Department of Sociology, University of Oxford (www.sociology.ox.ac.uk/working-papers/domestic-outsourcing-and-multitasking-how-much-do-they-really-contribute.html).

Sultana, F. (2007) Reflexivity, positionality and participatory ethics: negotiating fieldwork dilemmas in international research. *ACME: An International E-Journal for Critical Geographies*, 6(3), 374–385.

Suresh Reddy, B. and Snehalatha, M. (2011) Sanitation and personal hygiene: what does it mean to poor and vulnerable women? *Indian Journal of Gender Studies*, 18(3), 381–404.

Swan, E. (2012) Cleaning up? Transnational corporate femininity and dirty work in magazine culture. In R. Simpson, N. Slutskaya, P. Lewis and H. Höpfl (eds) *Dirty Work: Concepts and Identities*. Basingstoke, Hants: Palgrave Macmillan, pp. 182–202.

Sykes, W., Groom, G., Desai, P. and Kelly, J. (2014) *Coming Clean: The Experience of Cleaning Operatives*. Equality and Human Rights Commission research report 95. Manchester: Equality and Human Rights Commission.

Tandon, A. (2006) Domestic workers continue to be vulnerable to abuse, HIV: survey. *The Tribune*. 17 August 2006 (www.tribuneindia.com/2006/20060817/cth1.htm).

Tandon, P. (2012) Domestic workers: how to give them their due. Researching Reality summer internship working paper. New Delhi: Centre for Civil Society.

Tatano Beck, C. (2005) Benefits of participating in internet interviews: women helping women. *Qualitative Health Research*, 15(3), 411–422.

Taylor, S.J. and Bogdan, R. (1998) *Introduction to Qualitative Research Methods* (3rd edn). New York: John Wiley and Sons.

Tellis-Nayak, V. (1983) Power and solidarity: clientage in domestic service. *Current Anthropology*, 24(1), 67–79.

Thapar-Björkert, S. (1999) Negotiating 'otherness': dilemmas of a non-Western researcher in the Indian sub-continent. *Journal of Gender Studies*, 8(1), 57–69.

Thapar-Björkert, S. and Henry, M. (2004) Reassessing the research relationship: location, position and power in fieldwork accounts. *International Journal of Social Methodology*, 7(5), 363–381.

Tijdens, K., van der Lippe, T. and de Ruijter, E. (2003) Working women's choices for domestic help. The effects of financial and time resources. AIAS working paper 03/17. Amsterdam: Amsterdam Institute for Advanced Labour Studies (https://wageindicator.org/documents/publicationslist/w17).

Todd, S. (2009) Domestic service and class relations in Britain, 1900–1950. *Past and Present*, 203, 181–204.

Tomei, M. (2011) Decent work for domestic workers: reflections on recent approaches to tackle informality. *Canadian Journal of Women and the Law*, 23(1), 185–212.

Torlina, J. (2011) *Working Class: Challenging Myths about Blue-Collar Labor*. Boulder, CO: Lynne Rienner Publishers.

Toynbee, P. (2003) *Hard Work: Life in Low-Pay Britain*. London: Bloomsbury Publishing.

Toynbee, P. (2014) What if Downton Abbey told the truth about Britain? *The Guardian*. 22 December 2014 (https://www.theguardian.com/commentisfree/2014/dec/22/downton-abbey-truth-about-britain).

Treas, J. and Drobnic, S. (eds) (2010) *Dividing the Domestic: Men, Women, and Household Work in Cross-National Perspective*. Palo Alto, CA: Stanford University Press.

Tregenna, F. (2011) What does the 'services sector' mean in Marxian terms? *Review of Political Economy*, 23(2), 281–298.

Triandafyllidou, A. (2013) Irregular migration and domestic work in Europe: who cares? In A. Triandafyllidou (ed.) *Irregular Migrant Domestic Workers in Europe: Who Cares?* Farnham, Surrey: Ashgate Publishing, pp 1–16.

Triandafyllidou, A. and Marchetti, S. (2015) Paying for care: advantages and challenges for employers. In A. Triandafyllidou and S. Marchetti (eds) *Employers, Agencies and Immigration: Paying for Care*. Surrey: Surrey, Ashgate, pp. 227–240.

Truss, C., Alfes, K., Shantz, A. and Rosewarne, A. (2013) Still in the ghetto? Experiences of secretarial work in the 21st century. *Gender, Work & Organization*, 24(4), 349–362.

Two Maids and a Mop (2006) Hire a maid and save your marriage. *Two Maids Blog*. 19 September 2006 (http://blog.ineedamaid.com/2006/09/hire-a-maid-and-save-your-marriage.html).

Uberoi, P. (ed.)(1993/2011) *Family, Kinship and Marriage in India*. New Delhi: Oxford University Press.

Understanding Society (n.d.) About the study (https://www.understandingsociety.ac.uk/about).

University of Essex (2015) Institute for Social and Economic Research, Understanding Society: Waves 1–5, 2009–2014 [computer file]. 7th edn. Colchester, Essex: UK Data Archive [distributor], November 2015. SN: 6614, http://dx.doi.org/10.5255/UKDA-SN-6614-7.

Usdansky, M.L. (2011) The gender-equality paradox: class and incongruity between work-family attitudes and behaviors. *Journal of Family Theory & Review*, 3, 163–178.

Valk, R. and Srinivasan, V. (2011). Work–family balance of Indian women software professionals: a qualitative study. *IIMB Management Review*, 23(1), 39–50.

van Berkel, M. and de Graf, N.D. (1999) By virtue of pleasantness? Housework and the effects of education revisited. *Sociology*, 33(4), 785–808.

van der Geest, S. (2002) The night-soil collector: bucket latrines in Ghana. *Postcolonial Studies*, 5(2), 197–206.

van der Lippe, T., Frey, V. and Tsvetkova, M. (2013) Outsourcing of domestic tasks: a matter of preferences? *Journal of Family Issues*, 34, 1574–1597.

van Dongen, E. (2001) It isn't something to yodel about, but it exists! Faeces, nurses, social relations and status within a mental hospital. *Aging & Mental Health*, 5(3), 205–215.

van Walsum, S. (2011) Regulating migrant domestic work in the Netherlands: opportunities and pitfalls. *Canadian Journal of Women and the Law*, 23(1), 141–166.

VanEvery, J. (1995) *Heterosexual Women Changing the Family: Refusing to Be a Wife!* London: Taylor and Francis.

Varghese, L. (2006) Constructing a worker identity: class, experience, and organizing in Worker's Awaaz. *Cultural Dynamics*, 18(2), 189–211.

Vasanthi, N. (2011) Addressing paid domestic work: a public policy concern. *Economic and Political Weekly*, XLVI(43), 85–93.

Vera-Sanso, P. (2008) 'Who's money is it?': on misconceiving female autonomy and economic empowerment in low-income households. *IDS Bulletin*, 39(6), 51–59.

Verma, S. and Larson, R.W. (2001) Indian women's experience of household labour: oppression or personal fulfillment. *Indian Journal of Social Work*, 62(1), 46–66.

Visram, R. (1986/2015) *Ayahs, Lascars and Princes: the Story of Indians in Britain, 1700–1947*. London: Routledge.

Wall, S. (2015) Dimensions of precariousness in an emerging sector of self-employment: a study of self-employed nurses. *Gender, Work & Organization*, 22, 221–236.

Walters, P. and Whitehouse, G. (2012) A limit to reflexivity: the challenge for working women of negotiating sharing of household labour. *Journal of Family Issues*, 33(8), 1117–1139.

Walters, S. (2005) Making the best of a bad job? Female part-timers' orientations and attitudes to work. *Gender, Work & Organization*, 12(3), 193–216.

Warhurst, C. and Nickson, D. (2009) 'Who's got the look?' Emotional, aesthetic and sexualized labour in interactive services. *Gender, Work & Organization*, 16(3), 385–404.

Warren, T. (2000) Women in low status part-time jobs: a class and gender analysis. *Sociological Research Online*, 4(4), n.p. (www.socresonline.org.uk/4/4/warren.html).

Warren, T., Fox, E. and Pascall, G. (2009) Innovative social policies: implications for work–life balance among low-waged women in England. *Gender, Work & Organization*, 16(1), 126–150.

Weeks, K. (2011) *The Problem with Work: Feminism, Marxism, Antiwork Politics and Postwork Imaginaries*. Durham: Duke University.

Westwood, S. (1984) *All Day, Every Day: Factory and Family in the Making of Women's Lives*. London: Pluto Press.

Wheen, F. (2012) *The Lady* and the vamp. *Vanity Fair* (www.vanityfair.com/culture/2012/10/english-magazine-the-lady-revival).

White, J. (1980) *Rothschild Buildings: Life in an East End Tenement Block 1887–1920*. London: Pimlico.

Wilhoit, E.D. (2014) Opting out (without kids): understanding non-mothers' workplace exit in popular autobiographies. *Gender, Work & Organization*, 21(3), 260–272.

Williams, C.L., Giuffre, P.A. and Dellinger, K. (1999) Sexuality in the workplace: organizational control, sexual harassment, and the pursuit of pleasure. *Annual Review of Sociology*, 25, 73–93.

Williams, Z. (2012) A cleaner conscience: the politics of domestic labour. *The Guardian*. 10 March 2012 (www.guardian.co.uk/world/2012/mar/10/childcare-nanny-cleaner-housework-feminism).

Wills, J., May, J., Datta, K., Evans, Y., Herbert, J. and McIllwaine, C. (2009) London's migrant division of labour. *European Urban and Regional Studies*, 16(3), 257–271.

Windebank, J. (2007) Outsourcing women's domestic labour: the Chèque Emploi-Service Universel in France. *Journal of European Social Policy*, 17(3), 257–270.

Windebank, J. (2010) Barriers to outsourcing domestic chores in dual-earner households. *International Journal of Sociology and Social Policy*, 30(7/8), 387–398.

Wolkowitz, C. (2007/2012) Leakiness or really dirty? Dirt in social theory. In B. Campkin and R. Cox (eds) *Dirt: New Geographies of Cleanliness and Contamination*. London: I.B. Taurus, pp. 15–24.

World Health Organization (2012) *Progress on Drinking Water and Sanitation. 2012 Update*. Geneva: World Health Organization (www.who.int/water_sanitation_health/publications/2012/jmp_report/en/).

Yilmaz, G. and Ledwith, S. (2017) *Migration and Domestic Work. The Collective Organisation of Women and Their Voices from the City*. Basingstoke: Palgrave Macmillan.

Zick, C.D., McCullough, J. and Smith, K.R. (1996) Trade-offs between purchased services and time in single-parent and two-parent families. *Journal of Consumer Affairs*, 30(1), 1–23.

Index

Page numbers in *italics* refer to figures and tables.